★ OUR COUNTRY'S ★

PRESIDENTS

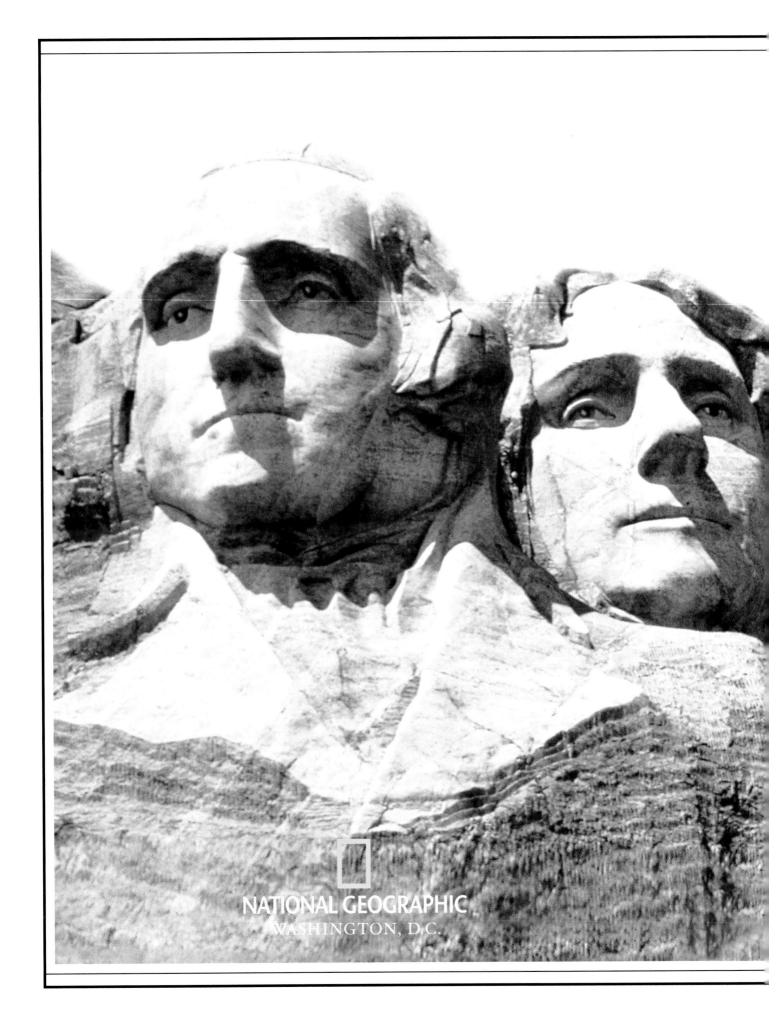

NATIONAL GEOGRAPHIC
WASHINGTON, D.C.

OUR COUNTRY'S
PRESIDENTS

Ann Bausum

WITH A FOREWORD BY
PRESIDENT GEORGE W. BUSH

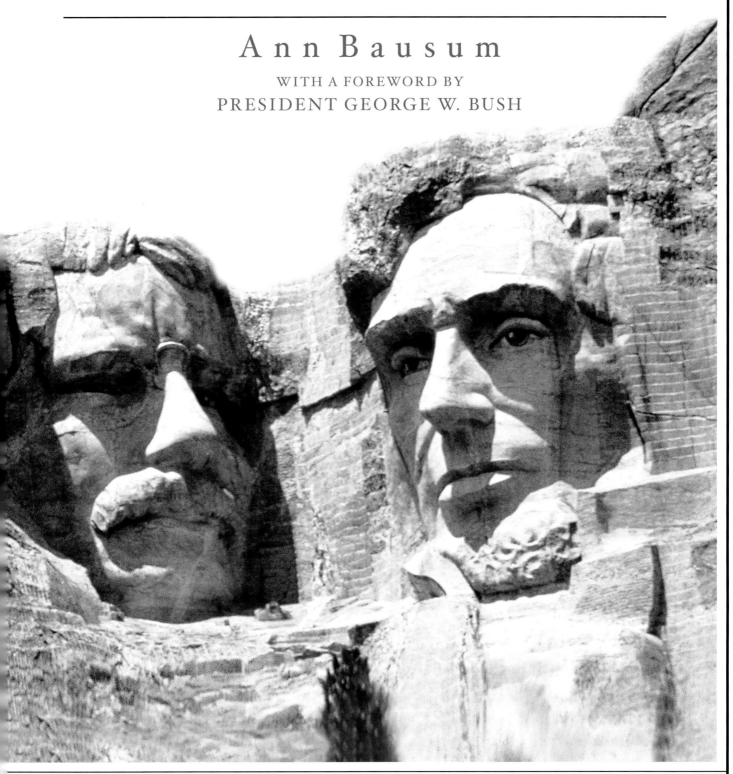

TABLE OF CONTENTS

FOREWORD ★ 6–7

ABOUT THE PRESIDENCY: AN INTRODUCTION ★ 8–11

★ THE PRESIDENCY AND HOW IT GREW ★ 12–13 ★

GEORGE WASHINGTON   14–19

JOHN ADAMS   20–23

★ THE WHITE HOUSE: THE BUILDING AND ITS HISTORY ★ 24–25 ★

THOMAS JEFFERSON   26–31

JAMES MADISON   32–35

★ THE POWERS OF THE PRESIDENT: THE EXECUTIVE BRANCH IN GOVERNMENT ★ 36–37 ★

JAMES MONROE   38–41

JOHN QUINCY ADAMS   42–43

ANDREW JACKSON   44–47

★ FROM SEA TO SHINING SEA ★ 48–49 ★

MARTIN VAN BUREN   50–53

WILLIAM HENRY HARRISON   54–55

JOHN TYLER   56–57

★ THE VICE PRESIDENTS: LEADERS JUST A HEARTBEAT AWAY ★ 58–59 ★

JAMES K. POLK   60–63

★ PRESIDENTIAL CAMPAIGNS: A BLEND OF PARTY POLITICS AND HARD WORK ★ 64–65 ★

ZACHARY TAYLOR   66–67

MILLARD FILLMORE   68–69

FRANKLIN PIERCE   70–71

JAMES BUCHANAN   72–73

★ A NEW BIRTH OF FREEDOM ★ 74–75 ★

ABRAHAM LINCOLN   76–81

ANDREW JOHNSON   82–83

★ U.S. POLITICAL PARTIES: THE TWO-PARTY SYSTEM ★ 84–85 ★

ULYSSES S. GRANT   86–89

RUTHERFORD B. HAYES   90–91

★ PRESIDENTIAL LANDMARKS: FROM LOG CABINS TO LIBRARIES ★ 92–93 ★

JAMES A. GARFIELD   94–95

CHESTER A. ARTHUR   96–97

GROVER CLEVELAND   98–101

★ PRESIDENTIAL FACTS AND COMPARISONS: A LOOK AT THE STATS ★ 102–103 ★

BENJAMIN HARRISON   104–105

★ AMERICA TAKES CENTER STAGE ★ 106–107 ★

WILLIAM MCKINLEY   108–111

THEODORE ROOSEVELT   112–115

★ KIDS IN THE WHITE HOUSE: AT HOME IN THE SPOTLIGHT ★ 116–117 ★

WILLIAM HOWARD TAFT   118–121

WOODROW WILSON   122–125

★ PRESIDENTS AT WAR: SERVING AS THE COMMANDER IN CHIEF ★ 126–127 ★

WARREN G. HARDING   128–129

CALVIN COOLIDGE   130–131

HERBERT HOOVER   132–133

★ SEEKING STABILITY IN THE ATOMIC AGE ★ 134–135 ★

FRANKLIN D. ROOSEVELT   136–141

★ THE FIRST LADIES: PARTNERS, HOSTESSES, AND ADVOCATES ★ 142–143 ★

HARRY S. TRUMAN   144–147

DWIGHT D. EISENHOWER   148–151

JOHN F. KENNEDY   152–155

★ PRESIDENTS WHO DIED IN OFFICE: THE MYSTERIOUS TWENTY-YEAR CURSE ★ 156–157 ★

LYNDON B. JOHNSON   158–161

RICHARD M. NIXON   162–165

GERALD R. FORD   166–167

★ THE ELECTORAL COLLEGE: GATEKEEPERS OF THE PRESIDENCY ★ 168–169 ★

JIMMY CARTER   170–173

★ FOOTPRINTS ON THE GLOBAL FRONTIER ★ 174–175 ★

RONALD REAGAN   176–179

GEORGE BUSH   180–183

★ IN THE PRESIDENT'S SHADOW: SECURITY, THE MEDIA, AND PRESIDENTIAL PERKS ★ 184–185 ★

WILLIAM JEFFERSON CLINTON   186–189

★ ELECTION DAY: LANDSLIDES, UPSETS, AND CONTESTED RESULTS ★ 190–191 ★

GEORGE W. BUSH   192–195

★ FORMER PRESIDENTS: SERVING AS ELDER STATESMEN ★ 196–197 ★

★ CHART OF PRESIDENTIAL ELECTION RESULTS ★ 198–201

INDEX/RESOURCE GUIDE/BIBLIOGRAPHY ★ 202–206

CREDITS ★ 207–208

George W. Bush

GROWING UP in Midland, Texas, American history was my favorite subject. I was fascinated by the stories of the men and women who made America great. I wanted to know about their lives. I wanted to know about their stories.

In the following pages, you will find some of these stories—the stories of America's Presidents. I enjoyed reading about the leadership of George Washington as he became America's first President. I was impressed by the courage of Abraham Lincoln during the Civil War. And I was inspired by the confidence of Franklin Delano Roosevelt throughout the Great Depression and World War II. All three of these stories are here.

What is so interesting about America is that anybody can make a difference. You don't have to be a great leader to do great things. You don't have to be somebody important to do something important. And, no, you don't have to be a President to be a leader. But our Presidents have made an impact. In this book, you can read about men who stood tall, as well as some who came up short. You can read about leaders who served the nation, and some who saved the world.

The American Presidency is the story of 42 Americans who took office at different times with different agendas. Each used his power to try and make America, and the world, a safer, more secure place.

I hope this book will inspire young people. I hope it will remind young Americans that history is shaped by individuals willing to make a difference. For better or for worse, that's what each of these men did. This is their story.

George W. Bush

43RD PRESIDENT OF THE UNITED STATES

About the Presidency

AN INTRODUCTION

ON FEBRUARY 4, 1789, a few dozen men held simultaneous meetings in the various United States. By unanimous vote they selected George Washington to be the nation's first President. These electors hoped Washington would head an unbroken chain of capable national leaders. At that point, though, no one knew for certain whether the American experiment in democracy would last. Only time would tell.

Eleven years later the nation's second President, John Adams, moved into the still unfinished home that is known today as the White House. "May none but Honest and Wise Men ever rule under this Roof," he wrote. Those who followed him to the Presidency have tried to honor his hopes, and so will the men and women who become President in the future.

Each President takes a short oath of office:

"I do solemnly swear that I will faithfully execute the Office of the President of the United States, and will to the best of my Ability, preserve, protect and defend the Constitution of the United States."

Each person meets a simple list of qualifications in order to seek the Presidency: he or she must be born as a U.S. citizen, be at least 35 years old, and have lived in the country for at least 14 years. Each candidate represents the best hopes of fellow countrymen for meeting the nation's needs.

Places change over time. The 1790 census counted not even four million people in the United States, including more than half a million slaves. Women, African Americans, and Native Americans could not vote. Broader rights came later on. Over the years, transportation advanced from horse power to steam

George Washington (center) placed his hand on a Bible to take the first presidential oath of office on Thursday, April 30, 1789, in New York City, one of the nation's early capitals. His Vice President, John Adams, stands to his left. Both men wore clothes made of American-made fabric, not European cloth, to celebrate their confidence in the independence of their new nation. Today January 20 serves as Inauguration Day. Before 1937, March 4 was favored. Since the passage of a 1951 Constitutional amendment, Presidents are limited to two elected terms as Chief Executive.

power to jet power. Inventors, scientists, and explorers changed the landscape with factories, technologies, and discoveries. The United States grew from a tentative experiment in democracy into a world superpower.

U.S. Presidents helped shape this evolution. Some, such as Abraham Lincoln, led the nation through critical periods of national and world history. Others, such as Thomas Jefferson, transformed the country's geography and outlook with their visions for change. Many left a personal stamp on the outcome of the nation. Most served as good stewards; they tried to do their best work. All marked their place in the history of the nation.

U.S. Presidents are a favorite topic of study for young and old alike. Presidents attract attention for different reasons, whether it's for bold policies, as with Franklin D. Roosevelt, for their power to inspire, as with John F. Kennedy, or simply for their adventuresomeness, as with Teddy Roosevelt. Readers are curious about how Presidents coped with the challenges of their eras and how they lived their personal lives.

Presidents come with funny stories (like the one who got stuck in his bathtub), unexpected facts (some were slaveholders), and overlooked insights (how they helped establish national traditions). They give us words that inspire ("Ask not what your country can do for you—ask what you can do for your country.") and words that reassure ("The only thing we have to fear is fear itself.").

We give Presidents nicknames—from Uncle Jumbo to Tricky Dick, from Honest Abe to Old Rough-and-Ready. We remember them for their extremes, their milestones, and their originality. Who was the only unmarried President? Who won the closest election? How many Presidents died on the Fourth of July? How many died in office? Who was our youngest President? Who was the oldest? Which Presidents are regarded as our best leaders? Who might be seen as among the worst?

Our Country's Presidents answers these questions and hundreds more. It introduces the Presidents as individuals, with full disclosure of good traits as well as flaws. By viewing the Presidents in full dimension, it is possible to breathe life into the darkened portraits that survive them. Readers may measure their own dreams, accomplishments, and challenges against those of their national leaders, perhaps gaining personal knowledge along the way.

The Presidents' stories, both personal and professional, are part of the nation's story. By understanding them, they become part of the reader's extended family history. Welcome to the stories of our country's Presidents.

How to Use This Book

You may choose to read *Our Country's Presidents* from cover to cover, just browse through the photos, or investigate one topic of interest. Knowing a bit more about how the book is organized should help you use it with greater success.

TIMELINES

This book presents the U.S. Presidents in chronological order grouped by six historical periods. A brief essay explains the common themes shared by the Presidents within these groupings. An illustrated timeline accompanies the essay. It introduces readers to important events of the period, from wars to inventions, from explorations to protests.

PROFILES

Individual essays present key elements of the history of each President, including family background, childhood, education, prepresidential careers, election highlights, important events during the Presidency, and activities pursued in retirement years. The opening paragraph of each essay summarizes major points about the significance of each leader and his administration. Multiple illustrations provide a visual dimension to the story. Profiles range in length from two to six pages depending on the significance of the individual. Longer essays feature notable quotes by

the Presidents that have been highlighted with large-format type.

PRESIDENTIAL PORTRAITS

Each presidential profile is introduced by a full-page reproduction of the leader's official portrait. These paintings are unveiled after the President leaves office and are displayed throughout the White House. The portraits of the most recent Presidents hang in places of honor near the main entrance to the White House.

FACT BOXES

A fact box appears on the opening spread of each profile. It features the President's signature as well as quick reference facts in categories ranging from the person's nickname to his chief election opponent, from important dates to the number of states in the Union at the start of each Presidency. Each box includes a list of selected landmarks that help readers make geographic connections with the lives of the Presidents.

THEMATIC SPREADS

Fifteen two-page spreads are placed strategically throughout the book to explain particular themes that relate to the Presidency. By reading these topical essays, you will be able to make connections between Presidents. Your

OFFICIAL PRESIDENTIAL PORTRAIT   FACT BOX   INTRODUCTORY SUMMARY PARAGRAPH

understanding of U.S. history and the function of the federal government will grow, too. Some essays cover topics of human interest, such as background about the wives and children of the Presidents. Others explain how the government functions, including the workings of the electoral college and the three branches of government. Additional thematic spreads help readers understand the election process, from the start of campaigns to the exciting conclusion of Election Day.

REFERENCE AIDS

A summary of U.S. election history introduces the reference material in the final pages of *Our Country's Presidents*. This chart shows the results of every election, including victors and major challengers. A resource guide follows with ideas for how to find out more about the Presidents. Information on sources used for the book's text and photos as well as a comprehensive index conclude the book.

THE PRESIDENCY AND HOW IT GREW

★ *1789 – 1837* ★

1789

Delegates wrote a new set of laws for governing the United States at the Constitutional Convention of 1787. By 1789 the Constitution was ratified, and the nation's first President was in place.

1795

The Constitution put the federal government in charge of issuing money. The $10 "eagle" coin was minted from 1795 to 1933. The capped figure of "Liberty" faced the coin.

1803

Thomas Jefferson offered to buy the Mississippi port of New Orleans. France sold it and the rest of its North American lands to the United States as the Louisiana Purchase.

1804–1806

A handful of men and Sacagawea, a Native American woman, helped Meriwether Lewis and William Clark explore the land between the Mississippi River and the Pacific Ocean.

The authors of the U.S. Constitution only sketched a loose outline of the Presidency when they defined the federal government in 1787. They expected the first Presidents to work out the details of the job in cooperation with Congress and the Supreme Court. As a result, the first officeholders helped shape the way Presidents make decisions, fight wars, work with Congress, add territory to the country, entertain, and so on. The Presidency became a position that could be revised and improved as needed by future Presidents.

1810

John Marshall served as the nation's Chief Justice longer than anyone else. His 1810 Supreme Court ruling in Fletcher v. Peck *was the first to declare a state law unconstitutional.*

1814

Francis Scott Key wrote a poetic description of the British bombardment of Baltimore's Fort McHenry near the end of the War of 1812. It became the U.S. national anthem.

circa 1820

Eli Whitney's cotton gin made it possible for cotton to be grown and processed on a large scale. Slaves labored on sizable plantations to raise more of the crop.

1836

Susanna Dickinson and her baby were among the few survivors of the Battle of the Alamo. Texans battled Mexico for two more months before gaining independence.

George Washington

1ST PRESIDENT OF THE UNITED STATES ★ *1789 – 1797*

NICKNAME	Father of His Country
BORN	Feb. 22, 1732, at Pope's Creek, Westmoreland County, Va.
POLITICAL PARTY	Federalist
CHIEF OPPONENTS	none (elected unanimously)
TERM OF OFFICE	April 30, 1789–March 3, 1797
AGE AT INAUGURATION	57 years old
NUMBER OF TERMS	two
VICE PRESIDENT	John Adams (1735–1826)
FIRST LADY	Martha Dandridge Custis Washington (1731–1802), wife (married Jan. 6, 1759)
CHILDREN	none; 2 stepchildren from his wife's first marriage
GEOGRAPHIC SCENE	11 states and 2 former colonies still debating ratification of the Constitution
NEW STATES ADDED	Vermont (1791), Kentucky (1792), Tennessee (1796)
DIED	Dec. 14, 1799, at Mount Vernon, Va.
AGE AT DEATH	67 years old
SELECTED LANDMARKS	Pope's Creek, Va. (birthplace); Valley Forge National Historical Park, Valley Forge, Pa.; Mount Vernon, Va. (homestead and grave); Washington Monument, Washington, D.C.; Mount Rushmore National Memorial, Keystone, S. Dak.

George's legendary cherry tree confession

GEORGE WASHINGTON HELPED TRANSFORM 13 British colonies into a new nation through a lifetime of public service as both a military leader and a statesman. As the first President of the United States, he set precedents, or patterns of behavior, for future Presidents to follow. After his death, he was praised for being "first in war, first in peace, and first in the hearts of his countrymen."

Little is known about the early life of the man who grew up to be called the "Father of His Country." Stories about his virtues—such as his honest confession of chopping down his father's cherry tree—were actually invented by an admiring "biographer" soon after Washington's death. The son of a Virginia landowner and planter, Washington grew up in colonial Virginia. His father died when George was 11, and his older brother, Lawrence, helped raise him. Washington was educated in basic subjects including reading, writing, and mathematics, but he did not attend college.

His skill with mathematics led to early work as a surveyor, or measurer and mapper of land. While still a teenager, Washington surveyed the unsettled wilderness of Virginia's Blue Ridge Mountains. He ventured farther

George Washington survived an icy crossing of the Allegheny River (above) as a British scout in 1753. Later, he made a trustworthy President because citizens knew Washington, being childless, could not place a family heir in power to succeed him. He truly was the "Father of His Country" and no one else.

General George Washington served as commander-in-chief of the Continental Army throughout the Revolutionary War. He led a daring attack across the ice-filled Delaware River in 1776 (below), struggled to keep up morale among troops wintering over at Valley Forge, Pennsylvania, in 1777–1778 (left), and planned battle strategy for the defeat of the British at Yorktown, Virginia, in 1781 (above). Weapons, ammunition, food, shelter, clothing, and even shoes were often in short supply.

west during his 20s—this time as a soldier. Washington fought in the French and Indian War, Great Britain's territorial dispute with France over the lands of the Ohio River Valley. His reputation spread after he published first-hand accounts of his experiences.

Virginians elected Washington to their colonial legislature, the House of Burgesses, when he was 26. Soon after, Washington married Martha Dandridge Custis, a wealthy widow with two young children. They settled at Mount Vernon, a family home Washington had inherited.

As a colonial legislator, Washington spoke out against unfair aspects of British rule. Later he was one of Virginia's representatives at the First and Second Continental Congresses. These meetings led to the organization of a Continental Army, opposed to the British. Washington, who attended the meetings in his military uniform, was chosen to head the Army. He was 43 years old. His selection added an influential Southerner to a Revolutionary War movement that was led mostly by Northerners.

> "Liberty, when it begins to take root, is a plant of rapid growth."
>
> George Washington, letter to James Madison, March 2, 1788

New York residents gave George Washington a hero's welcome (right) when he entered the city in 1783 after the end of the Revolutionary War. Four years later he presided over the Constitutional Convention (below) in Philadelphia. Delegates drafted a plan for a new national government with hopes that Washington would serve as the country's first President.

Washington held the Continental Army together for six years of fighting against British forces. His troops suffered significant defeats, but they won important victories in the fight for independence, too. Aided by the French, Washington finally forced the British to surrender most of their troops on October 19, 1781, at Yorktown, Virginia. He retired from the Army after the 1783 peace treaty and returned to private life.

Six years passed between the signing of a peace treaty with Great Britain and the election of Washington as President. During that time the former colonies operated under the Articles of Confederation, a document that reserved most power for the states. Each state printed its own money, for example. There was no national Chief Executive. States sent representatives to a federal Congress, but this legislature did not even have the authority to collect taxes. Neither the states nor the federal government was able to repay the millions of dollars that had been spent on the Revolutionary War. The states were so poorly linked

George Washington helped lay the cornerstone of the U.S. Capitol (left) during his first year as President. He is shown (right, at far right) with key Cabinet advisers (from left to right): Thomas Jefferson (State), Henry Knox (War), Alexander Hamilton (Treasury), and Edmund Randolph (Attorney General).

that their fate as a nation seemed in jeopardy.

In 1787 state representatives gathered in Philadelphia to try to resolve these problems. George Washington, one of Virginia's delegates at this Constitutional Convention, was selected to preside. By the time the convention ended four months later, the delegates had written the Constitution of the United States. This document outlined the basic design for a strong federal government, with two chambers of legislators, a federal court system, and a President. It continues to serve as the foundation for the United States government today.

Nine state governments were required to ratify, or approve, the document before the new federal government

could form. By the next summer more than enough states had ratified the Constitution for it to take effect. Following the Constitution's directions, states chose representatives to serve as electors for the President. These members of the first electoral college cast two votes apiece. All of them gave one vote—for a total of 69—to George Washington, thus making him President. John Adams received the greatest number of remaining votes and became Vice President. Washington was reelected unanimously four years later, with Adams again voted in as Vice President. No other

After retiring from public office, George Washington welcomed a stream of visitors, including his Revolutionary War ally the Marquis de Lafayette of France, to Mount Vernon. His wife, Martha, is seated at the far right with her family members. Washington's image has been preserved over the years on everything from postage stamps (above) to geographic landmarks. He is the only President to have a state named for him.

President was ever unanimously elected.

After his first election, Washington traveled by horse and boat from Mount Vernon to be inaugurated in New York City, which was then the nation's capital. The next year the capital moved temporarily to Philadelphia. Although Washington helped plan a permanent national capital, his Presidency ended before the federal government moved to the city later named in his honor.

President Washington set many precedents for future Chief Executives to follow. A few, like bowing in greeting, quickly went out of fashion. (Thomas Jefferson introduced the custom of shaking hands.) Many other precedents, such as seeking regular advice from department secretaries in Cabinet meetings, remain essential today. Washington established how the U.S. negotiates treaties, what kinds of legislation should be vetoed, whether the Chief Justice had to be the oldest member of the Supreme Court (no), if the President could decide who would join the Cabinet (yes), and even how many terms he thought a President should serve. He established speechmaking traditions, too, from his Inaugural Addresses to State of the Union messages to a farewell address upon leaving office.

Washington appointed the first federal judges, signed laws that established basic government services like banking and currency, and sought to keep the nation out of wars with Native American and European nations. During his Presidency, political parties began to form despite Washington's objections. He became identified with the Federalist Party.

Martha Washington, who had joined her husband at winter battle camps during the Revolutionary War, left Mount Vernon again to be with him during his Presidency. "Lady Washington," as she was called, helped set presidential social customs.

Washington established one more tradition—attending the Inauguration of his successor—before he and his wife retired to Mount Vernon in 1797. He was not left at peace for long. In 1798 he agreed to take charge of the Army once more, this time to defend the country in case war developed with France. (It did not, and he was able to complete his service from home.)

In December 1799 Washington became ill after spending hours riding around his property in poor weather. What started as a simple sore throat developed into what was probably a strep infection. Doctors tried the usual cures of the day, including draining nearly a third of the blood from his body, but his condition did not improve. His throat became so swollen that he could not swallow or breathe. He died within two days of falling ill. Washington, one of the largest slaveholders in the country, arranged in his will for his own slaves to be freed by the time of his wife's death.

After retiring from the Presidency, George Washington returned to his family estate, Mount Vernon, Virginia. An expert horseman, he loved to review his property on horseback. Washington had perfected his skills in the saddle during his youth. As a teenager, Washington had wanted to join the British navy. His mother, widowed when George was 11, refused to grant his wish.

"Many things which appear of little importance in themselves and at the beginning may have great and durable consequences."

George Washington, letter to John Adams, May 10, 1789

John Adams

2ND PRESIDENT OF THE UNITED STATES ★ *1797 – 1801*

John Adams	
NICKNAME	Father of American Independence
BORN	Oct. 30, 1735, in Braintree (now Quincy), Mass.
POLITICAL PARTY	Federalist
CHIEF OPPONENT	Thomas Jefferson, (1743–1826) Democratic-Republican
TERM OF OFFICE	March 4, 1797–March 3, 1801
AGE AT INAUGURATION	61 years old
NUMBER OF TERMS	one
VICE PRESIDENT	Thomas Jefferson (1743–1826)
FIRST LADY	Abigail Smith Adams (1744–1818), wife (married Oct. 25, 1764)
CHILDREN	Abigail, John Quincy, Charles, Thomas, plus a daughter died young
GEOGRAPHIC SCENE	16 states
NEW STATES ADDED	none
DIED	July 4, 1826, in Quincy, Mass.
AGE AT DEATH	90 years old
SELECTED LANDMARKS	Adams National Historical Site, Quincy, Mass. (birthplace and family home); United First Parish Church, Quincy, Mass. (grave)

JOHN ADAMS DEVOTED HIS ADULT LIFE to the twin causes of creating the United States and securing its long-term survival. Adams—as the President who succeeded, or followed, George Washington—showed that the nation's most important office could survive a change of leadership. He helped his new country avoid war with France during his single term of office.

The man who became known as the "Father of American Independence" was born a British subject in the colony of Massachusetts. The son of an educated farmer and leather craftsman, Adams grew up enjoying toy boats, marbles, kites, hunting, books, and learning. He graduated from Harvard University in 1755 and took up the study of law.

Adams practiced law in Boston for 12 years and served briefly in the Massachusetts Legislature before becoming a delegate to the First and Second Continental Congresses. At these meetings in Philadelphia he encouraged the colonists to seek independence from Great Britain. It was Adams who suggested that George

This pair of farmhouses served as the birthplaces for two U.S. Presidents: John Adams and his son, John Quincy Adams.

John Adams, the nation's second President, went to school in a setting like the one pictured in this illustration. Adams cherished his status as a U.S. citizen, a right he earned thanks to the American Revolution. "I have not one drop of blood in my veins, but what is American," Adams said two years before becoming President.

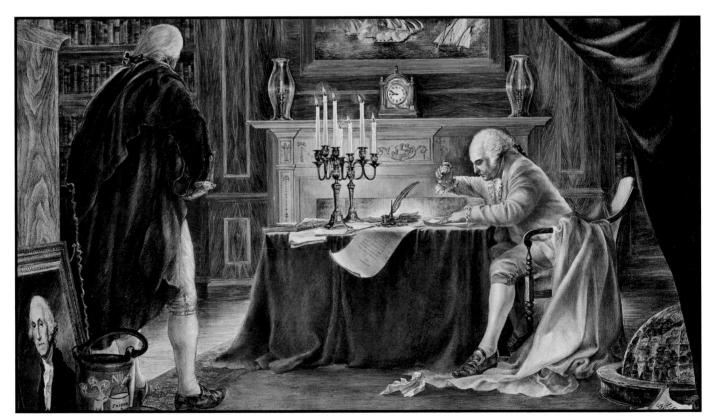

Abigail Adams and her husband wrote hundreds of letters to each other during their marriage because John Adams was frequently away on government business. In 1776, when he was a delegate to the Continental Congress in Philadelphia, she reminded him to "remember the ladies. Be more generous and favorable to them than your ancestors." She went on to suggest that women should "not hold ourselves bound by any laws in which we have no voice or representation." It would be the 20th century before politicians honored her wishes.

Washington command the new Continental Army, and Adams co-ordinated the crafting of the Declaration of Independence.

Adams was overseas during much of the Revolutionary War. He represented his new country to governments in Europe. During his stay in the Netherlands he arranged for important loans to help fund the Revolutionary War effort. Later he helped negotiate the peace treaty that ended the war with Great Britain.

After the war, Adams served as the first U.S. Ambassador, or representative, to Great Britain. He returned to the United States in 1788 just as a federal government was being organized with the new U.S. Constitution. He was elected to serve as Vice President to George Washington. Adams held the post for both of Washington's terms, but he found the job dull. He observed: "My country has in its wisdom contrived for me the most insignificant office that ever the invention of man contrived or his imagination conceived." His efforts while Vice President to establish flattering terms of address for the President (such as "His Highness") only earned him nasty nicknames like "His Rotundity" (Adams was very overweight) and "Bonny Johnny Adams."

Whereas Washington had become President by

John Adams at work in the new White House. Adams at times felt overshadowed by other significant figures of the day. He joked: "The history of our Revolution will be one continued lie from one end to the other. The essence of the whole will be that Dr. Franklin's electrical rod smote the earth and out sprang General Washington. That Franklin electrified him with his rod and thenceforward these two conducted all the policies, negotiations, legislatures, and war."

John Adams is called the "Father of the American Navy" for establishing a permanent U.S. naval fleet. Among the ships constructed during his Presidency was the Philadelphia *(left). The U.S.* Constellation *captured* L'Insurgente *of France in 1799 (right) when the two nations were on the brink of war.*

a unanimous vote of the electoral college, Adams had no such luck. The Constitution originally called for all candidates to be considered for President. It directed that the runner-up, or second-place finisher, become Vice President. This plan failed to anticipate the development of political parties. In 1796 Adams (a Federalist) became President with only a three-vote lead over Thomas Jefferson, a member of the rival Democratic-Republican Party. (A constitutional amendment in 1804 solved this flaw; it called for separate votes for each office.) Tensions developed between Adams and Jefferson during their shared administration. Adams was defeated by Jefferson during his bid for a second presidential term.

Adams devoted much of his Presidency to avoiding war with France. Relations with this former Revolutionary War ally had become tense over the United States war settlement with Great Britain. Adams helped the U.S. establish an uneasy balance of relations with both of these European superpowers. He appointed hundreds of new federal judges, too,

including the influential Chief Justice John Marshall. However, many of his final choices, the so-called midnight judges, were named too late in his term to take their seats.

In 1801 Adams retired to his home in Massachusetts. He had the longest marriage of any President—54 years. Throughout he had a close, respectful relationship with his wife, Abigail.

After their Presidencies were over, John Adams and Thomas Jefferson restored the friendship of their Revolutionary War days through lively letter writing. The two men were the only signers of the Declaration of Independence to become President. Curiously, they both died on the same day—the 50th anniversary of the approval of the Declaration of Independence. That day, Adams observed: "It is the glorious Fourth of July. God bless it." His final words were: "Thomas Jefferson still survives." He did not know his friend had died only a short while earlier. Adams, who had been ill, stopped breathing later that day.

"I am but an ordinary man.
The times alone have destined me to fame."

John Adams, diary entry, April 26, 1779

The White House

★ The Building and Its History ★

BUILDING THE FIRST WHITE HOUSE

WASHINGTON D.C. 1798

SINCE 1800 every U.S. President has lived in the national landmark known today as the White House. George Washington was the only President who never slept there, but he left his mark on the structure by choosing its location and approving its design. The place has been endlessly modified, expanded, and rebuilt ever since John Adams, the nation's second President, moved into the incomplete house near the end of his term of office.

Thomas Jefferson, the home's second resident, directed many early improvements to the structure and its grounds. Subsequent Presidents have added basic conveniences such as running water, toilets, and electricity; others have modernized it with telephones, a bowling alley, and a movie theater. The West Wing evolved from a temporary office building added by Theodore Roosevelt. Its famous Oval Office became the President's center of business. Harry Truman had the original White House structure shored up and rebuilt after one inspector proclaimed that the building "was standing up purely from habit." More recently, workers painstakingly removed all of the building's exterior paint, some 40 layers thick, then repainted it its trademark white. Today the President's home includes 132 rooms on four main floors (plus two basement levels).

Over the years the occupants of the White House have sat for portraits, collected priceless furnishings, and purchased notable works of art. Many of these items remain in use today, making the White House a sort of living museum. Although the White House closed its doors to individual visitors for security reasons in 2001, groups may arrange for free self-guided tours of public areas. An off-site visitors center provides general information for everyone.

An artist from the 20th century imagined the scene (above, lower) of George Washington viewing the construction with architect James Hoban of what was first called simply the President's House. The modern White House (top, and see cutaway and key) serves as office and residence to the President and family. Its surrounding 18 acres are enjoyed by modern first families for horseback riding, croquet, tennis, horseshoes, golf, swimming, basketball, and jogging. The White House is shared with the nation through events like the annual Easter egg roll, when more than 25,000 children use spoons to roll colored eggs down the sloping lawn. During the War of 1812, invading British forces (right) destroyed all but the outer walls of the White House. Before setting it ablaze, they ate the dinner left behind by its fleeing residents. Later on, workers put a fresh coat of white paint on the building to hide scorch marks left by the fire.

FIRST FLOOR

* F6
F7
* F5
* F3
* F2
* F8
* F9
* F1
F4
G6
* G2
GROUND FLOOR
G5
G4
G1
G3

WHITE HOUSE CUTAWAY KEY

FIRST (STATE) FLOOR

* F1 EAST ROOM
* F2 GREEN ROOM
* F3 BLUE ROOM
  F4 SOUTH PORTICO
* F5 RED ROOM
* F6 STATE DINING ROOM
  F7 FAMILY DINING ROOM
* F8 CROSS HALL
* F9 ENTRANCE HALL

GROUND FLOOR

G1 LIBRARY
* G2 GROUND FLOOR
  CORRIDOR
G3 VERMEIL ROOM
G4 CHINA ROOM
G5 DIPLOMATIC
  RECEPTION ROOM
G6 MAP ROOM

ONLY SELECTED ROOMS ARE SHOWN.
* MARKS ROOMS OPEN FOR GROUP TOURS.

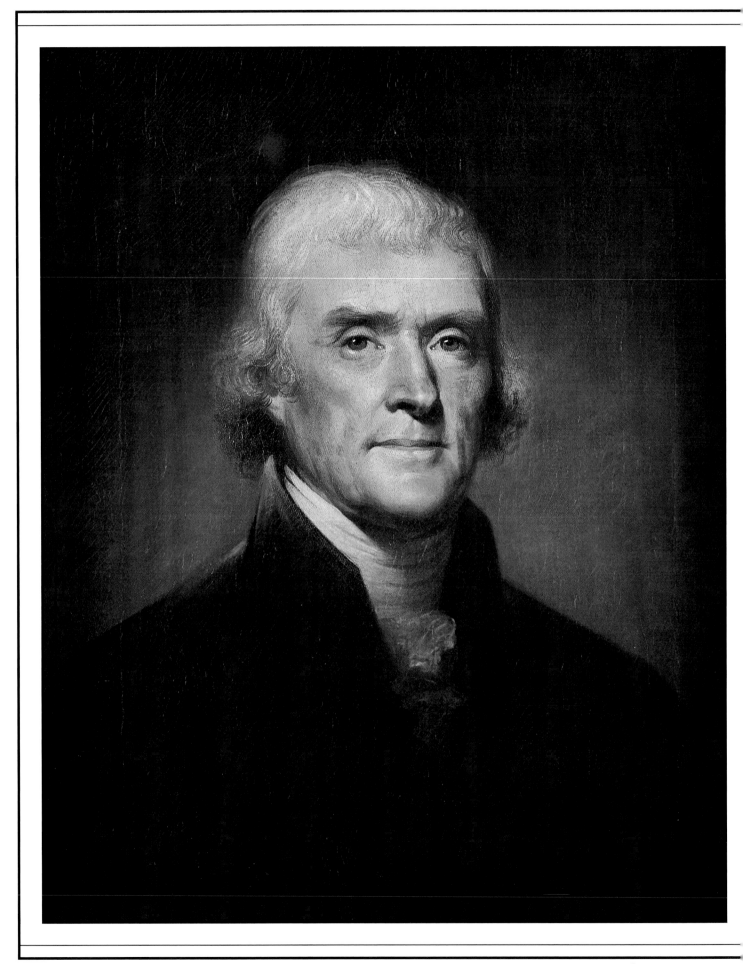

Thomas Jefferson

3RD PRESIDENT OF THE UNITED STATES ★ *1801 – 1809*

NICKNAME	Father of the Declaration of Independence
BORN	April 13, 1743, at Shadwell, Goochland (now Albemarle) County, Va.
POLITICAL PARTY	Democratic-Republican
CHIEF OPPONENTS	1st term: President John Adams, Federalist (1735–1826) and Aaron Burr, Democratic-Republican (1756–1836); 2nd term: Charles Cotesworth Pinckney, Federalist (1746–1825)
TERM OF OFFICE	March 4, 1801–March 3, 1809
AGE AT INAUGURATION	57 years old
NUMBER OF TERMS	two
VICE PRESIDENTS	1st term: Aaron Burr (1756–1836); 2nd term: George Clinton (1739–1812)
FIRST LADIES	Dolley Dandridge Payne Todd Madison (1768–1849), friend, and Martha "Patsy" Jefferson Randolph (1772–1836), daughter
WIFE	Martha Wayles Skelton Jefferson (1748–1782), married Jan. 1, 1772
CHILDREN	Martha, Mary, plus three daughters and a son died young
GEOGRAPHIC SCENE	16 states
NEW STATES ADDED	Ohio (1803)
DIED	July 4, 1826, at Monticello, Charlottesville, Va.
AGE AT DEATH	83 years old
SELECTED LANDMARKS	Monticello, Charlottesville, Va. (homestead and grave); Poplar Forest, Bedford County, Va. (homestead retreat); Jefferson Memorial, Washington, D.C.; Mount Rushmore National Memorial, Keystone, S. Dak.

BEFORE HIS DEATH, Thomas Jefferson listed the accomplishments he wanted carved on his gravestone. Serving as the nation's third President did not make his list. Nonetheless, Jefferson remains one of the most important Presidents in U.S. history. The Louisiana Purchase he made during his first term of office extended the country beyond the Mississippi River toward the Pacific.

Jefferson had the skills for many careers. However, because he came of age during the American Revolution, he devoted himself most notably to service as a statesman. Jefferson was born in 1743 near the western frontier of colonial Virginia. His father, a landowner, surveyor, and government official, died when his son was 14. From the age of nine, Jefferson studied some distance from home and boarded with his tutor. Later he enrolled at the College of William and Mary in Williamsburg, Virginia. His education was broad and comprehensive, including science,

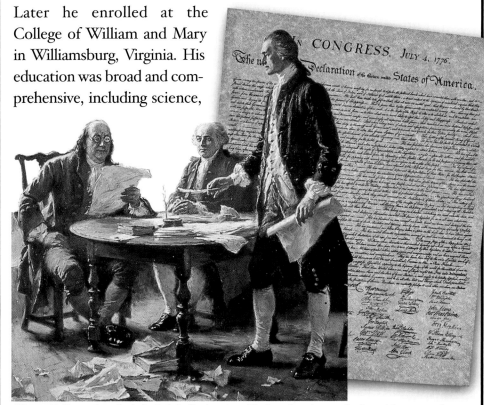

Thomas Jefferson (standing) drafted the Declaration of Independence in consultation with, among others, Benjamin Franklin (seated on left) and John Adams. Adams suggested that Jefferson compose the document. "You can write ten times better than I can," said Adams, plus "I am obnoxious, suspected, and unpopular."

In 1804 Aaron Burr, who was Thomas Jefferson's Vice President, killed Alexander Hamilton, a political rival, in a duel (left). During the Tripolitan War of 1801–1805, the U.S. fought with the Barbary pirates and their allies in North Africa (right) to stop lawlessness on the seas. French troops turned over New Orleans and the territory of Louisiana to U.S. forces on December 20, 1803. During the ceremony (below) the Stars and Stripes of the U.S. replaced the tricolor French flag at the Mississippi river port. Eventually all or parts of 15 states would be carved from Thomas Jefferson's Louisiana Purchase.

mathematics, philosophy, law, English language and literature, Latin, Greek, French, and even dancing.

After college Jefferson became an attorney. By age 26 he was a member of Virginia's House of Burgesses. Jefferson spoke out there against British policies during the final years of colonial government. On June 7, 1776, Jefferson and other delegates at the Second Continental Congress in Philadelphia were asked to consider whether "these United Colonies are, and of right ought to be, free and independent States."

Soon after, Jefferson, Benjamin Franklin, John Adams, and two others were appointed to draft a declaration, or statement, in favor of independence. Jefferson spent about two weeks putting their ideas on paper. On July 2 the delegates agreed to declare their independence. Two days later, after a few revisions, members approved Jefferson's official declaration. This document is treasured for its persuasive calls for freedom and equality. It is the first achievement Jefferson listed on his gravestone.

During the Revolutionary War, Jefferson tried to put his democratic dreams into action. He wrote the "Statute for Religious Freedom" while serving in the Virginia Legislature. This document called for the separation of church and state, a concept that says it is improper for religious groups and the government to interact. Later this idea was adopted as one of the

"We hold these truths to be self-evident, that all men are created equal, that they are endowed by their Creator with certain unalienable Rights, that among these are Life, Liberty and the pursuit of Happiness."

Thomas Jefferson, Declaration of Independence, July 4, 1776

basic principles of the national government. Jefferson listed this achievement on his gravestone, too.

Over the next 20 years Jefferson served as governor of Virginia, a representative to the Continental Congress, U.S. minister to France, secretary of state for George Washington, and Vice President for John Adams. These last two posts left Jefferson frustrated. Some government leaders, known as Federalists, favored a strong federal, or national, government ruled by the country's most prosperous and well-educated citizens. They patterned their beliefs and social customs after those of wealthy Britons. Jefferson opposed these stands. His supporters were called the Anti-Federalists, Democratic-Republicans, National Republicans, or eventually, the Democrats. Jefferson expressed his dislike of Federalism by resigning from Washington's administration. He chose not to powder his hair, too, and he encouraged states to disobey federal laws that they disliked.

When the electoral college voted in 1800, Jefferson and Aaron Burr tied for the Presidency. It took the House of Representatives 36 ballots and two months to decide that Jefferson should be the winner. The Constitution was amended by the time of the next presidential elections, so that separate votes were held for President and Vice President. Jefferson was then easily reelected.

As President, Jefferson reversed what he saw as the most offensive Federalist programs. He restored full freedom of speech to the press, reduced restrictions on immigration, increased land sales in the West, ended U.S. taxes, decreased the national debt, closed the national bank, and canceled the last-minute "midnight judges" appointments that Adams had made as he left office. During his second term he ended the practice of importing slaves into the United States from other countries.

Jefferson invented new codes of presidential behavior, too. He dressed casually around guests,

Thomas Jefferson is called a "Renaissance Man" because of his broad range of talents. He excelled as a farmer, an architect, an inventor, a lawyer, a writer, a musician, and an educator, as well as a statesman. Among his inventions were swivel chairs and the polygraph (right), a machine that duplicated an original document as it was being composed. He designed and founded the University of Virginia in Charlottesville (below) during his retirement years. Jefferson's personal library of 6,500 books became the foundation for a new Library of Congress after the Library's original collections were destroyed during the War of 1812.

Thomas Jefferson inspects the effectiveness of a plow he invented for use at his estate, Monticello. He depended on slaves to provide the labor there, both in the fields and in his house. Thomas Jefferson is the only person to serve two full terms as President after serving as Vice President. The Jefferson Memorial (below) was constructed in his honor 200 years after his birth.

even answered the White House door himself sometimes, and invited ordinary citizens to visit the President's home on New Year's Day and Independence Day. His administration, and the two like-minded ones that followed it, led to the end of the Federalist Party.

Jefferson's most noted presidential triumph was the Louisiana Purchase of 1803. When Jefferson tried to buy the port of New Orleans, the French offered to sell all of their western lands, not just the port. They were too busy preparing to fight the British to defend this distant territory. The price was 60 million francs, or about $15 million. The United States nearly doubled in size by gaining more than 800,000 square miles of territory west of the Mississippi River. Many Federalists failed to see the value of buying "a howling wilderness." Jefferson, however, was thrilled.

Even before the Louisiana Purchase, Jefferson had been planning an exploration of the West. He asked Meriwether Lewis, his personal secretary, to lead the trip. News of the Louisiana Purchase reached the U.S. on Independence Day in 1803, just as Lewis was about to set off from the East. Lewis joined forces with William Clark and a small corps of explorers in St. Louis, Missouri. The next spring they set off up the Missouri River in search of a water passageway to the Pacific. Instead they found the Rocky Mountains. They finally reached the Pacific Ocean by way of the Columbia River in December 1805. The Lewis and Clark expedition returned by a similar route to St. Louis the following fall. Their 8,000-mile trip helped open the Louisiana Purchase for settlement.

Thomas Jefferson married a young widow when he was 28 years old. She died 10 years later; no pictures of her survive. Their elder daughter, Martha (left), served sometimes as her father's First Lady. Jefferson spent five decades perfecting his beloved mountaintop home, Monticello. In Italian, Monticello (pronounced Mont-ti-chello) means "little mountain." Jefferson added clever details to his house (above) such as hiding beds, dumbwaiters, octagonal rooms, skylights, revolving storage space, a clock that kept track of the days of the week, and pairs of doors that opened when only one of them was pushed. As a naturalist, Jefferson enjoyed seeing a magpie and prairie dog (below) that were collected during the Lewis and Clark expedition.

Jefferson retired to Monticello at the end of his second term. For the remaining 17 years of his life he made improvements to his beloved home, surrounded himself with grandchildren, entertained distinguished guests, and juggled the mounting debts that came with his lavish lifestyle. He accomplished the third and final credit for his gravestone during these years: Jefferson is called the Father of the University of Virginia for designing and organizing this institution. Jefferson, like his old Revolutionary War friend John Adams, died 50 years to the day after the approval of the Declaration of Independence.

Jefferson left a complicated legacy. His estate was so in debt that Monticello had to be sold.

Modern genetic tests seem to confirm old rumors that Jefferson had a long-term relationship with one of his slaves, Sally Hemings, after his wife's death and that he fathered children with her. Jefferson freed only five slaves when he died (including some who were probably his children). The rest of his 200 slaves were sold to pay his bills.

From today's perspective it is hard to reconcile Jefferson's use of slavery with his passion for freedom. In truth, Jefferson's lavish lifestyle forced him to depend on slave labor. Jefferson, troubled by the institution of slavery, wrote: "I tremble for my country when I reflect that God is just." Jefferson knew it would be left for future generations to end slavery and that the process would most likely be painful.

"I shall not die without a hope that light and liberty are on a steady advance."

Thomas Jefferson, letter to John Adams, September 12, 1821

James Madison

4TH PRESIDENT OF THE UNITED STATES ★ *1809 – 1817*

NICKNAME	Father of the Constitution
BORN	March 16, 1751, at Belle Grove, Port Conway, Va.
POLITICAL PARTY	Democratic-Republican
CHIEF OPPONENTS	1st term: Charles Cotesworth Pinckney, Federalist (1746–1825); 2nd term: DeWitt Clinton, Federalist (1769–1828)
TERM OF OFFICE	March 4, 1809–March 3, 1817
AGE AT INAUGURATION	57 years old
NUMBER OF TERMS	two
VICE PRESIDENTS	1st term: George Clinton (1739–1812); 2nd term: Elbridge Gerry (1744–1814)
FIRST LADY	Dolley Dandridge Payne Todd Madison (1768–1849), wife (married Sept. 15, 1794)
CHILDREN	none
GEOGRAPHIC SCENE	17 states
NEW STATES ADDED	Louisiana (1812), Indiana (1816)
DIED	June 28, 1836, at Montpelier, Orange County, Va.
AGE AT DEATH	85 years old
SELECTED LANDMARKS	Montpelier, Orange County, Va. (homestead and grave); The Octagon, Washington, D.C. (temporary executive home after destruction of the White House)

Dolley Madison

JAMES MADISON IS REMEMBERED MOST for the hand he had in creating the basic rules for governing the United States—the Constitution and its Bill of Rights. Madison made sure that his new country had a strong and democratic government. Later, as President, he struggled to lead the United States safely through its first war since the American Revolution: the War of 1812.

Madison devoted his adult life to the creation of the United States. Born a British subject in the colony of Virginia, he completed his education at the college that became Princeton University. Madison was the smallest man in the history of the Presidency. He stood 5 feet 4 inches tall and weighed only 100 pounds.

After serving in the Virginia legislature and with the Continental Congress, Madison was sent to the Constitutional Convention of 1787. He and other delegates spent 86 days inventing the structure of the U.S. government, including its Congress, Presidency, and federal court system. His detailed notes remain a valuable record of the entire event. As one of the authors of *The Federalist Papers,* Madison helped influence states to ratify, or accept, the new Constitution. These 85 essays supported the idea of a strong federal, or national, government. As a Representative in the first U.S. Congress, Madison helped secure passage of the Bill of Rights. This companion document to the Constitution sets down the basic privileges of the nation's citizens and states. Because Madison played such a central role

James Madison had studied hundreds of books on history and government by the time delegates gathered at the Constitutional Convention of 1787 to organize a new government (above). Madison joked that he earned the scar on his nose in "defense of his country." Actually it resulted from the frostbite he suffered during a long ride home after a 1788 debate with James Monroe during a U.S. Congressional campaign.

Wars raged on many fronts during the Presidency of James Madison. U.S. soldiers were guided by future President William Henry Harrison in their repulse of an attack by Native Americans at the Tippecanoe River, Indiana Territory, in 1811 (left). Forced recruitment of its sailors by the British navy (right) helped draw the U.S. into the War of 1812 with Great Britain. This conflict featured many battles at sea (below).

in these events, he became known as the "Father of the Constitution." Madison thought otherwise. The Constitution was not "the off-spring of a single brain," he insisted, but "the work of many heads and many hands." Madison and George Washington are the only men who signed the Constitution and later became Presidents.

Madison served four terms in Congress, then worked in Virginia's state government before his friend Thomas Jefferson asked him to join his new presidential administration as secretary of state. At the end of his two terms, Jefferson favored Madison as his successor. Madison easily defeated his opponent, Charles Pinckney, in the electoral college voting. Pinckney, noting the popularity of Madison's wife, Dolley, observed that he "might have had a better chance had I faced Mr. Madison alone."

When Madison became President, the United States was being drawn into conflict with the British over their war with France. Americans were frustrated because the British were halting U.S. cargo ships bound for France and seizing U.S. sailors and goods. If modern forms of communication had existed in Madison's time, war might have been avoided. Not knowing that the British were ending these seizures, the U.S. declared war against Great Britain.

During the War of 1812 (which lasted until 1814), American forces were beaten regularly on land and at sea. The greatest humiliation occurred late in the war when the British entered Washington and set fire to the White House and the U.S. Capitol building. The final contest, the Battle of New Orleans, was fought after a peace treaty had been signed in Europe but

Scenes from the War of 1812: U.S. and British sailors compete for control of the Great Lakes in 1813 (above, left); Dolley Madison supervises the packing of White House valuables (above, right) as the British march on the nation's capital in 1814. Francis Scott Key (right) captures the drama of a British naval attack at Baltimore in 1814 by writing the poem that became the U.S. national anthem.

before that news could reach North America. Madison was praised after the war for having allowed others to criticize his wartime policies without fear of trial or imprisonment. He insisted it was important for the United States to be able to fight a war without limiting the constitutional rights of its citizens, including the right of free speech.

First Lady Dolley Madison gained lasting fame during the war. She rescued government documents and a famous portrait in the White House of George Washington, just hours before the British raided the capital. She was famous, too, for her role as a hostess. She gave lively parties, made pleasant conversation, and dressed lavishly, often topping her head with a turban, jewels, or feathers.

After eight years in the White House, Dolley and her husband, "Jemmey," returned to Montpelier, his family homestead. From there James Madison helped Jefferson create the University of Virginia, spoke out against slavery, argued against secession (the idea that a state could quit being part of the United States), helped create a colony in Africa for freed slaves, and organized his notes from the Constitutional Convention. He outlived all of the other Founding Fathers, the men who had influenced the American Revolution and written the U.S. Constitution. Madison died in 1836, six days shy of the nation's 60th Independence Day celebration.

"If men were angels, no government would be necessary."

James Madison, *The Federalist Papers*, #51, 1788

The Powers of the President

★ *The Executive Branch in Government* ★

THE STRUCTURE of the United States government was established by the Constitution in 1787. That document and its 27 amendments explain the basic organization of the nation. The three branches, or divisions, of government are the legislative, executive, and judicial forms of federal power. The legislative branch is represented by the U.S. Congress, which consists of the House of Representatives and the Senate. The judicial branch contains the federal court system, including its Supreme Court. The executive branch includes the President and the departments of the government. Originally there were three departments—State, War, and Treasury. Today (*see chart*) there are 15 departments.

The Constitution lists the central powers of the President: serve as Commander in Chief of the armed forces; make treaties with other nations; grant pardons; inform Congress on the state of the union; and appoint ambassadors, officials, and judges. Over time the government has evolved so the branches operate within a system of checks and balances. For example, most of the President's actions require the approval of Congress. Likewise, the laws passed in Congress must be signed by the President before they can take effect. This system prevents one area of government from becoming so powerful as to overly influence the business of the nation.

The powers of the President at work: Setting policy with cabinet officers from the earliest Presidency (left) to modern times with Ronald Reagan (right); directing the opinions of the judicial system by appointing new judges (top); asking Congress to declare war (far right, next page); and addressing Congress. John Adams (left, next page) was the last President to address Congress in person until Woodrow Wilson (right, next page). Other Presidents sent written messages instead.

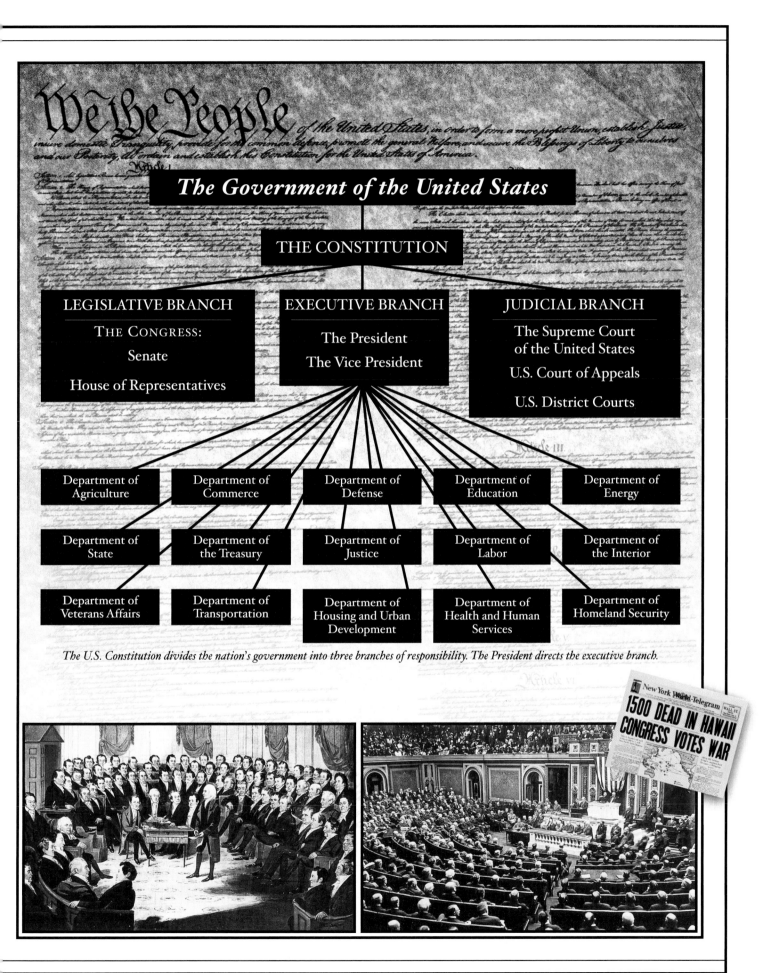

The Government of the United States

THE CONSTITUTION

LEGISLATIVE BRANCH

THE CONGRESS:

Senate

House of Representatives

EXECUTIVE BRANCH

The President

The Vice President

JUDICIAL BRANCH

The Supreme Court of the United States

U.S. Court of Appeals

U.S. District Courts

Department of Agriculture	Department of Commerce	Department of Defense	Department of Education	Department of Energy
Department of State	Department of the Treasury	Department of Justice	Department of Labor	Department of the Interior
Department of Veterans Affairs	Department of Transportation	Department of Housing and Urban Development	Department of Health and Human Services	Department of Homeland Security

The U.S. Constitution divides the nation's government into three branches of responsibility. The President directs the executive branch.

New York World-Telegram

1500 DEAD IN HAWAII CONGRESS VOTES WAR

James Monroe

5TH PRESIDENT OF THE UNITED STATES ★ 1817 – 1825

James Monroe

NICKNAME	Era of Good Feelings President
BORN	April 28, 1758, in Westmoreland County, Va.
POLITICAL PARTY	Democratic-Republican
CHIEF OPPONENTS	1st term: Rufus King, Federalist (1755–1827); 2nd term: none
TERM OF OFFICE	March 4, 1817–March 3, 1825
AGE AT INAUGURATION	58 years old
NUMBER OF TERMS	two
VICE PRESIDENT	Daniel D. Tompkins (1774–1825)
FIRST LADY	Elizabeth Kortright Monroe (1768–1830), wife (married Feb. 16, 1786)
CHILDREN	Eliza, Maria, plus a son died young
GEOGRAPHIC SCENE	19 states
NEW STATES ADDED	Mississippi (1817), Illinois (1818), Alabama (1819), Maine (1820), Missouri (1821)
DIED	July 4, 1831, in New York, N.Y.
AGE AT DEATH	73 years old
SELECTED LANDMARKS	Ash Lawn-Highland, Charlottesville, Va. (homestead); James Monroe Museum and Memorial Library, Fredericksburg, Va.; Hollywood Cemetery, Richmond, Va.

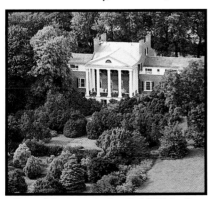

James Monroe retired to Oak Hill in 1825.

JAMES MONROE WAS THE LAST U.S. PRESIDENT who had been an adult during the Revolutionary War. He presided over a country in the midst of widespread change. New thinking was developing about the role of political parties, the issue of slavery, and the fate of European colonies in the Americas.

Monroe grew up during an earlier period of change. He was born in Virginia as tensions increased between the American colonists and their motherland, Great Britain. Although he entered the College of William and Mary, he interrupted his education to join in early revolutionary activities. At age 17 he raided the local armory with other students; the next year he dropped out of school to join the Continental Army. Monroe served under the command of General George Washington, rising in rank to major. He crossed the Delaware River with Washington's troops, was severely wounded during a heroic capture of British cannons in the Battle of Trenton, and wintered at Valley Forge.

Near the end of the war Monroe studied law in Thomas Jefferson's law practice and later opened his own. He also began his lifelong career of public service. Before being elected President, Monroe served in the Virginia Assembly, the Continental Congress, the U.S. Senate, and as governor of Virginia. He held foreign affairs

James Monroe was a tall President, just over six feet in height. He chose to be inaugurated outdoors (above) in 1817. Monroe added to his popularity as President by taking two extensive "goodwill tours" during his administration. In 1817 he traveled north and west as far as Maine and Michigan. Two years later he headed south to Georgia, went as far west as the Missouri Territory, and traveled back to Washington through Kentucky.

The White House (above, center) and adjacent federal office buildings as they appeared in 1820. The building of canals and locks expanded the opportunities for travel and commerce (below) during James Monroe's Presidency.

posts under three of the first four Presidents. He was Washington's minister to France, Jefferson's minister to Great Britain, and secretary of state and secretary of war for James Madison. In 1803 President Jefferson sent him to France to help negotiate the Louisiana Purchase.

Both Jefferson and outgoing President Madison favored Monroe's election as President in 1816. Some Democratic-Republicans spoke of their desire to pass over Monroe, a Virginian, and end the "Virginia Dynasty" of Presidents. (Three of the first four Presidents had come from Virginia. Eventually 7 of the first 12 would be Virginians.) Monroe's abilities were more important than concerns about his birthplace, though, and he was elected by a wide margin. Four years later he ran without opposition and earned all but one electoral vote. Legend says he lost this single vote because an elector wanted to preserve George Washington's record of unanimous election. Facts suggest, however, that the elector simply did not support Monroe and put forth another candidate (John Quincy Adams) instead. During his Presidency a newspaper credited

> "The American continents...are henceforth not to be considered as subjects for future colonization by any European powers."

James Monroe,
The Monroe Doctrine, December 2, 1823

As President, James Monroe (right, by globe) framed a new vision for the role of the U.S. government in the Western Hemisphere. During earlier diplomatic years, his wife, Elizabeth (below), influenced French radicals to free the condemned wife of the Marquis de Lafayette.

Monroe with bringing the nation an "era of good feelings." The phrase stuck and came to be associated with him like a nickname.

The United States underwent significant geographic changes during Monroe's leadership. Five new states joined the nation. Only one administration would add more. (Six states joined the nation during Benjamin Harrison's single term in office.) In addition, Monroe purchased Florida from Spain and resolved key border concerns with Canada. Most important, he stated a vital U.S. position about the Western Hemisphere: The American continents were off-limits for further colonizing by European nations. This policy came to be known as the Monroe Doctrine. It set the stage for the expansion of the United States westward to the Pacific Ocean during the next two decades.

The greatest controversy of Monroe's administration was whether Missouri should enter the Union as a state that permitted slavery. Politicians organized along regional lines—North against South—over this issue. In the end the Missouri Compromise admitted Missouri as a "slave state" with Maine entering as a "free state." Since each "side" in the debate gained one state, balance between opposing viewpoints was maintained. Legislators agreed to prohibit further expansion of slavery north and west of Missouri's southern border. This position would be reconsidered by future administrations during an increasingly tense debate over slavery.

In 1825 Monroe and his wife, Elizabeth, retired to their northern Virginia home, which was designed by Jefferson. When Elizabeth died in 1830, James moved to New York City. He lived there with his younger daughter, Maria, and her family. Within the year Monroe died, too. He was the last U.S. President to die on the Fourth of July. His death followed those of Presidents Jefferson and Adams by exactly five years.

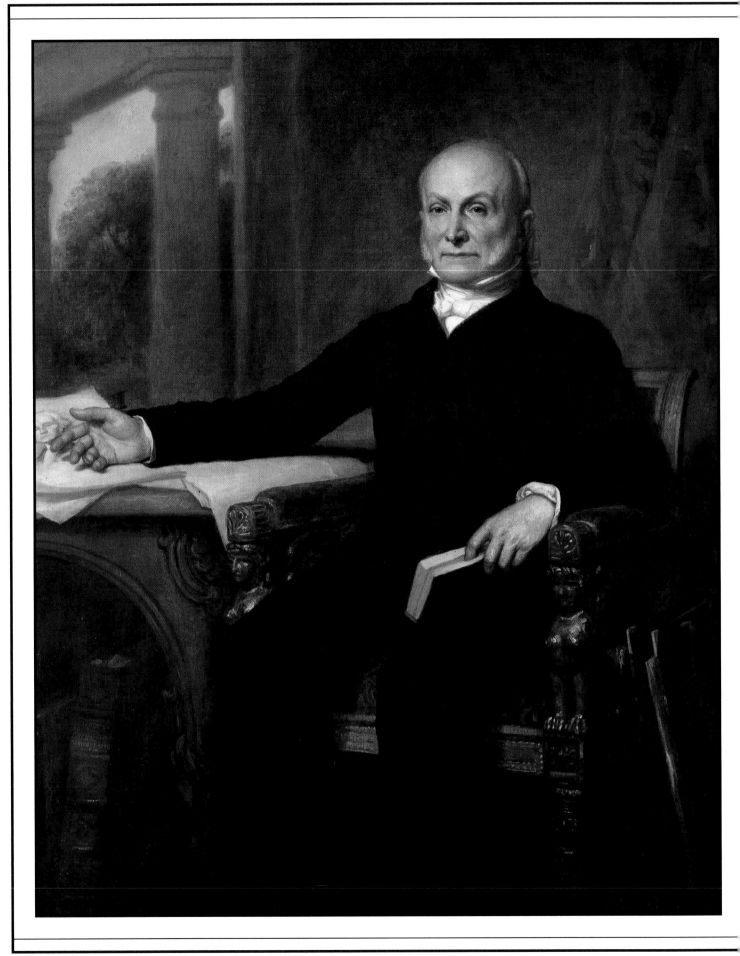

John Quincy Adams

NICKNAME	Old Man Eloquent
BORN	July 11, 1767, in Braintree (now Quincy), Mass.
POLITICAL PARTY	Democratic-Republican
CHIEF OPPONENT	Andrew Jackson, Democratic-Republican (1767–1845)
TERM OF OFFICE	March 4, 1825–March 3, 1829
AGE AT INAUGURATION	57 years old
NUMBER OF TERMS	one
VICE PRESIDENT	John Caldwell Calhoun (1782–1850)
FIRST LADY	Louisa Catherine Johnson Adams (1775–1852), wife (married July 26, 1797)
CHILDREN	George, John, Charles, plus a daughter died young
GEOGRAPHIC SCENE	24 states
NEW STATES ADDED	none
DIED	Feb. 23, 1848, at the U.S. Capitol, Washington, D.C.

The collapse of Congressman Adams

AGE AT DEATH	80 years old
SELECTED LANDMARKS	Adams National Historical Site, Quincy, Mass. (birthplace and family home); United First Parish Church, Quincy, Mass. (grave)

JOHN QUINCY ADAMS, like his father, earned more lasting fame for his accomplishments beyond the White House than for his Presidency. His single term of office took place following important overseas service and preceded a celebrated career in Congress. Adams was the only son of a Chief Executive to seek and gain the Presidency until George W. Bush did so in the 2000 election.

Adams grew up in Massachusetts during the American Revolution. He witnessed the Battle of Bunker Hill at age eight. He traveled abroad while his father was a diplomat and later earned a degree from Harvard University. After studying law, he served his country with each of the nation's first Presidents. He was a U.S. ambassador for George Washington and his father, a senator under Thomas Jefferson, an ambassador for James Madison, and secretary of state to James Monroe.

The 1824 electoral votes failed to give majority support to one candidate. After an ugly debate, the House of Representatives named Adams the victor. As Chief Executive, Adams ignored political strategy, stuck to his principles, and found himself generally miserable. It seemed that no one supported him. Jealous political rivals accused him of corruption. Congress refused to fund his plan for a national transportation system of roads and canals. Newspapers slandered him. Adams felt it was undignified to personally campaign for reelection and lost at the polls in 1828.

Adams is the only President to serve later in the House of Representatives. He won election to the chamber in 1830 at age 63. Adams earned the nickname "Old Man Eloquent" for his passionate arguments. He fought for eight years to overturn the 1836 "gag rule" that prohibited discussion of slavery. His speeches were fiery, both about the restrictions and, once lifted, about slavery itself. On February 21, 1848, Adams had a stroke at his desk on the House floor. Realizing he was deathly ill, Adams asked to be tended in a nearby office so he could die in his beloved Capitol building. He did so two days later.

John Quincy Adams enlivened his gloomy White House years by playing billiards, writing in his diaries, and exercising. Often he swam nude in the Potomac River. Once someone stole his clothes, and he had to ask a passing boy to fetch new ones for him from the White House.

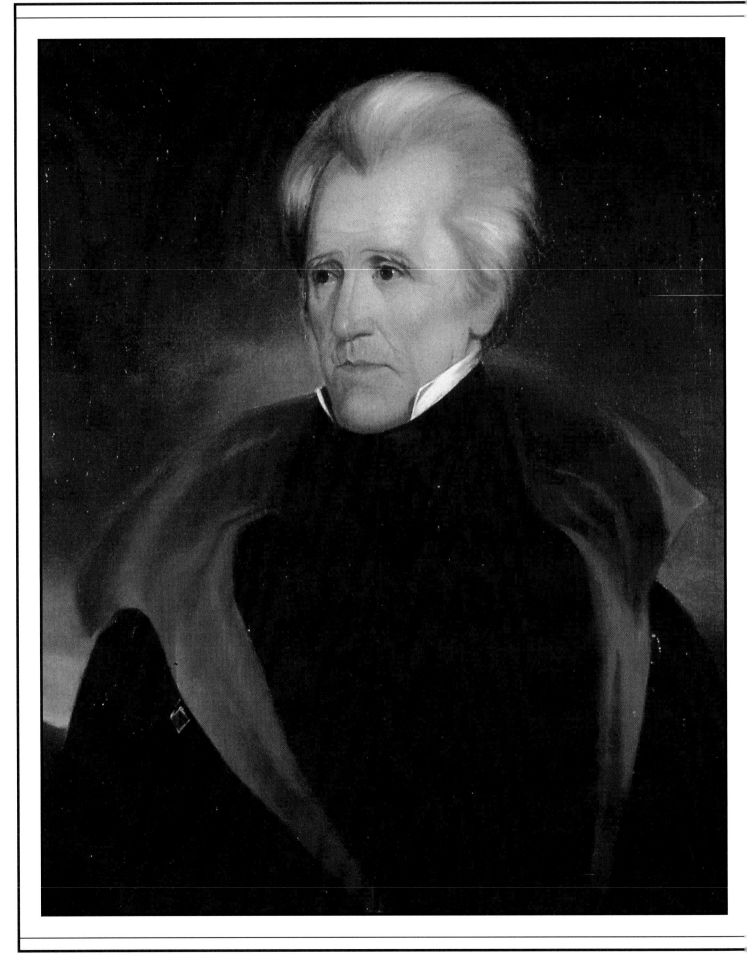

Andrew Jackson

7TH PRESIDENT OF THE UNITED STATES ★ *1829 – 1837*

The Inauguration of Andrew Jackson, 1829

THE ELECTION OF ANDREW JACKSON put in the White House for the first time a man who seemed to represent the background and ambitions of "ordinary" Americans. His leadership style differed from that of his predecessors, too. Jackson set new patterns for presidential power that continue to be used today.

Jackson grew up earning his "man-of-the-people" reputation. He was the son of Scotch-Irish immigrants, born to a family on the move following the sudden death of his father just a few days earlier. His exact birthplace remains uncertain. He is considered the first of the log cabin Presidents. Nonetheless, by 1776 he was able, at age nine, to read aloud the text of the new Declaration of Independence to nonreading neighbors. Although he never learned proper grammar and spelling, he was well-spoken.

Jackson's education was interrupted by the American Revolution. At 13 he served as a messenger for American troops and was captured by the British. Jackson is the only President who was a prisoner of war, and the last one who served in the Revolutionary War.

A British officer attacked Andrew Jackson (above) after he refused to polish the captor's boots during the Revolutionary War. Jackson's face bore a lifelong scar from his wound.

Andrew Jackson's reputation as a war hero made him a popular candidate for President (above). He had led troops against Indians (right) and the British during the War of 1812. Jackson's wife, Rachel, became ill when she learned that their marital history was a campaign issue. The couple had been married twice; the second ceremony occurred after they learned that their first wedding had taken place before she was properly divorced from an earlier husband. Rachel died of a heart attack before her husband became President.

Jackson tried several professions after the war before he took up the study of law and became an attorney. He settled in Tennessee. Jackson practiced law there and established a cotton plantation, worked by slaves, named the Hermitage. Later he served briefly in both the House and Senate of the U.S. Congress.

More than a decade later—during the War of 1812—Jackson earned the national reputation that carried him to the White House. He served as an officer for volunteers from Tennessee and became a U.S. general. General Jackson became famous for his leadership during the Battle of New Orleans, the last conflict in the War of 1812. Jackson's soldiers thought their leader was as tough as an old hickory tree. The nickname "Old Hickory" stuck with Jackson for life.

During the 1828 presidential election the opposition party sought to discredit Jackson. It issued a thick booklet about his "youthful indiscretions," or mistakes, including accounts of his numerous fights and duels. (Jackson lived the last four decades of his life with a bullet lodged near his heart from one of his duels.) Jackson's supporters dished out their own round of slander, and Jackson defeated his rival, President John Quincy Adams. Citizens stormed the White House during Jackson's Inaugural Reception. They

General Jackson (above) went on to become the first President to have his life threatened by an assassin. The unlucky assailant (who was later ruled insane) fired two guns at the President from close range in the U.S. Capitol rotunda, but neither one fired properly. Jackson was so angry that he beat the gunman with his cane.

General Andrew Jackson became the "hero of New Orleans" after his forces killed or wounded 2,000 British soldiers who were attacking the city at the end of the War of 1812. U.S. casualties were only 71. Jackson's fame helped earn him the Presidency 14 years later.

were eager to see the "People's President." Muddy boots climbed on silk chairs, fists flew, china crashed, and ladies fainted in the crush of visitors. Jackson escaped out a back door to the safety of a hotel. Finally, staff members placed tubs of punch on the White House lawn to lure the crowd outside, then locked the doors.

Jackson marked his two terms of office by assuming greater powers of leadership than any prior President. Critics nicknamed him "King Andrew the First." Future Presidents would thank him for setting standards that fortified their own administrations. Jackson insisted the President could hire and fire his own Cabinet members by replacing ones who refused to follow his orders. He upheld the authority of the U.S. government over state governments by insisting it was treasonous for

South Carolina to ignore federal import tax law. He encouraged the practice of awarding federal jobs to political supporters. He defied the Supreme Court by ignoring its support of Cherokee Indians. Jackson insisted that Native Americans living east of the Mississippi should be relocated to new land in the West.

Although his bold actions shocked many politicians, they were generally popular with citizens. Jackson was the last two-term President until Abraham Lincoln. After his second term he retired to the Hermitage, where he continued to influence politics. He took particular pleasure in the presidential elections of two of his protégés—his own Vice President, Martin Van Buren, and, later on, James K. Polk, a fellow Tennessean. "Old Hickory" died shortly after Polk became President.

Andrew Jackson, who grew up in a simple log cabin (left), was called "a barbarian who...hardly could spell his own name" by political rival John Quincy Adams. Jackson's final home, the Hermitage (right), reflected the advances he had made during his lifetime. In 1833 Jackson responded playfully to his introduction, delivered in Latin, at a Harvard University ceremony in his honor. He joked: "All the Latin I know is E pluribus unum." (This motto on the U.S. seal means "out of many, one.") The crowd applauded with delight.

FROM SEA TO SHINING SEA

★ *1837 – 1861* ★

1845

Frederick Douglass increased public concern over the treatment of slaves when he published his autobiography. He worked with abolitionists to end slavery.

circa 1846

By 1846 large parties of settlers were traveling the Oregon Trail from Missouri to the western United States. They rested at Independence Rock before crossing the Rocky Mountains.

1846–1848

The Mexican War began with battles at disputed Texas border spots such as Palo Alto. By the end of the war, U.S. boundaries stretched to California.

1849

The discovery of gold in California triggered a massive gold rush to the territory. Prospectors flocked to the region in search of the valuable metal.

Presidents faced a delicate balancing act before the Civil War. Efforts to expand U.S. land holdings always seemed to spark renewed debate over whether to expand slavery as well. Presidents had greater success at adding land than at resolving what to do about slavery. Native Americans suffered when they were pushed from their homelands by new waves of settlers. None of the Presidents from this era served more than one term in office. Rather, they left by choice, lost reelection bids, or died in office.

1850s

The number of miles of railroad track in use throughout the United States tripled during the 1850s. A spreading web of routes moved people and freight across vast distances.

1854

Commodore Matthew C. Perry, backed up by a strong show of military might, established trading rights between the United States and Japan during his visit there.

1860

By 1860 more than one-third of all Southerners—some 3.5 million people—were slaves. Disagreement over the expansion of slavery erupted into the Civil War a year later.

1860–1861

Pony Express riders could deliver mail between Missouri and California in ten days or less. Rides ceased after telegraph wires spanned the continent in October 1861.

Martin Van Buren

8TH PRESIDENT OF THE UNITED STATES ★ *1837 – 1841*

NICKNAME	Little Magician
BORN	Dec. 5, 1782, in Kinderhook, N.Y.
POLITICAL PARTY	Democrat
CHIEF OPPONENT	William Henry Harrison, Whig (1773–1841)
TERM OF OFFICE	March 4, 1837–March 3, 1841
AGE AT INAUGURATION	54 years old
NUMBER OF TERMS	one
VICE PRESIDENT	Richard M. Johnson (1780–1850)
FIRST LADY	Angelica Singleton Van Buren (1816–1878), daughter-in-law
WIFE	Hannah Hoes Van Buren (1783–1819), married Feb. 21, 1807
CHILDREN	Abraham, John, Martin, Smith
GEOGRAPHIC SCENE	26 states
NEW STATES ADDED	none
DIED	July 24, 1862, in Kinderhook, N.Y.
AGE AT DEATH	79 years old
SELECTED LANDMARKS	Lindenwald, Kinderhook, N.Y. N.Y. (homestead); Kinderhook Cemetery, Kinderhook, N.Y.

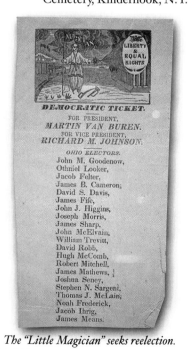

The "Little Magician" seeks reelection.

MARTIN VAN BUREN EARNED THE RESPECT and support of the Democratic Party by inventing new ways to expand political influence. The financial panic that began soon after he entered the White House in 1837 clouded his bright prospects as President. This popular Vice President of Andrew Jackson failed to win election to a second term.

Van Buren was an unlikely President to lose a reelection bid. He had spent his adult life creating the political system that earned him his first term in office. A native of New York, he was the first President born as a citizen of the United States. (Earlier Presidents, although born as British subjects, were considered U.S. citizens by their association with the new nation.) Van Buren, the descendant of Dutch immigrants, completed his formal schooling before his 14th birthday. He then took up the study of law. By age 21 he was a practicing attorney.

A successful political career followed. Between 1812 and 1829 Van Buren—originally a Democratic-Republican—served as a member of the New York State Senate, then as a U.S. senator, and briefly as governor of his home state. Along the way he revolutionized party politics.

Martin Van Buren's birthplace (above) was in Kinderhook, New York. Van Buren earned many nicknames because of his political cleverness and success. He was called the "Little Magician," "Enchanter," "Wizard," and "Red Fox of Kinderhook." In 1840 Democrats in New York City formed the "O.K. Club," after "Old Kinderhook," another Van Buren nickname. Soon "OK" came to mean "all right."

A HARD ROAD TO HOE!

"The less government interferes with private pursuits the better for the general prosperity."

Martin Van Buren, 1837

Martin Van Buren's Presidency was troubled by obstacles (left), such as how to manage the federal money supply and how to overcome the popular frontier-style image, complete with hard cider, of his 1840 political opponent, William Henry Harrison. When Martin Van Buren became President, the nation's population had almost quadrupled to over 15 million people since the start of George Washington's administration nearly 50 years earlier.

Van Buren wanted to defeat those who held office as a result of their personal wealth and influence. He worked with others who shared this view to stir up popular support over issues such as the costly construction of canals. He and his supporters identified themselves by displaying the tail of a buck deer on their hats. The "Bucktail" Democrats gained broad influence by unseating their aristocratic rivals.

Once in power, the Bucktails rewarded their supporters with thousands of state jobs, thus assuring continued loyalty to the party. This practice came to be known as the "spoils system" because it distributed the riches, or spoils, of office among party members. It was these supporters who helped Van Buren get elected to the U.S. Senate. Later, Andrew Jackson gained his place in the White House thanks, in part, to the practice of Van Buren-style politics. Jackson rewarded Van Buren for his support by naming him secretary of state. When Jackson ran for reelection, he chose Van

Buren as his Vice President. He supported Van Buren's own bid for the Presidency four years later.

Van Buren gained Jackson's post in the election of 1836, but he did not enjoy the same popularity as his predecessor. Nor did his administration enjoy the same prosperity. Soon after his Inauguration, the national economy collapsed in what became known as the Panic of 1837. Banks failed, businesses closed, and tens of thousands of workers lost their jobs. In some cities, angry residents rioted and stole food. It was the worst financial crisis the nation had ever experienced, and it lasted for five years. Van Buren handled the problem poorly. He continued Jackson's financial policies without realizing they were making matters worse, not better.

Van Buren had better luck managing other threats to the nation. Using diplomacy, he quieted tensions with Mexico over the newly independent republic of Texas. His antistatehood position on Texas helped reduce North-South concerns over

During Martin Van Buren's Presidency, federal troops drove some 15,000 Cherokees out of their homes in or near Georgia to the Indian Territory in present-day Oklahoma. Close to a third of these Native Americans died because of the harsh conditions along what became known as the Trail of Tears.

the possible expansion of slavery there. He avoided war with Great Britain in two disputes, one over the Maine-Canada border and the other regarding American support of rebels from Ontario, Canada.

Van Buren continued the Indian Removal Act policies of the Jackson administration. As a result, the United States waged a vicious war against Seminole Indians in Florida, forcing survivors to move west. These battles and other Indian removal efforts cost the federal government some $50 million. This flow of money unexpectedly helped improve the economy, although not early enough before the election to earn Van Buren a second term in office. The "Little Magician" found himself out of tricks when faced for the second time with a challenge by William Henry Harrison. Van Buren was defeated by someone whose own party had grown stronger using the same tactics Van Buren had promoted earlier with the Democrats.

Van Buren returned to his hometown in upstate New York. He lived at Lindenwald, an estate he had purchased there some years earlier. Van Buren made two more unsuccessful runs for the White House, most notably in 1848 with the short-lived Free Soil Party. He supported President Abraham Lincoln's pro-Union policies during the Civil War but died before the end of the conflict.

Martin Van Buren (far left) became a widower in 1819 after the death of his wife, Hannah (right), at age 35. He never remarried.

William Henry Harrison

9TH PRESIDENT OF THE UNITED STATES ★ *1841*

W. H. Harrison (signature)

NICKNAME	Tippecanoe
BORN	Feb. 9, 1773, in Charles City County, Va.
POLITICAL PARTY	Whig
CHIEF OPPONENT	President Martin Van Buren, Democrat (1782–1862)
TERM OF OFFICE	March 4, 1841–April 4, 1841
AGE AT INAUGURATION	68 years old
NUMBER OF TERMS	one (cut short by death)
VICE PRESIDENT	John Tyler (1790–1862)
FIRST LADY	Jane Irwin Harrison (dates unknown), daughter-in-law
WIFE	Anna Tuthill Symmes Harrison (1775–1864), married Nov. 25, 1795
CHILDREN	Elizabeth, John, Lucy, William, John, Benjamin, Mary, Carter, Anna, plus a son died young
GEOGRAPHIC SCENE	26 states
NEW STATES ADDED	none
DIED	April 4, 1841, in the White House, Washington, D.C.
AGE AT DEATH	68 years old
SELECTED LANDMARKS	Berkeley Plantation, Charles City County, Va. (birthplace); Grouseland, Vincennes, Ind. (family home); Harrison Tomb State Memorial, North Bend, Ohio

Harrison defeated Tecumseh in 1813.

WILLIAM HENRY HARRISON had a Presidency of extremes. At 68 he was the oldest man to become President until Ronald Reagan. He gave the longest Inaugural Address ever—one hour and 40 minutes, and he was the first President to die in office. But Harrison is remembered most for having the shortest term of office: one month.

Harrison was also the last President born before the start of the American Revolution. Harrison's father signed the Declaration of Independence when William Henry was three years old. Harrison attended Hampden-Sydney College in Virginia before studying medicine and becoming a soldier. He battled Indians at the Tippecanoe River (hence his nickname) and fought in the War of 1812. He was the governor of Indiana Territory, an Ohio state senator, the ambassador to Colombia, and a U.S. representative and senator before seeking the Presidency. Harrison represented the Whigs, a new party that evolved from the Federalists. He and his 1840 presidential running mate were billed as the ticket of "Tippecanoe and Tyler Too." They won.

Harrison delivered his lengthy Inaugural Address outdoors in brisk weather, yet he refused to wear a hat or coat. He caught cold soon after, perhaps because of this mistake. Several weeks later, still recovering from his cold, he was soaked in a sudden downpour. His illness worsened, and he developed pneumonia. "I am ill, very ill," he concluded. Harrison died five days later, exactly one month after taking office. His death triggered the first promotion of a Vice President to the Presidency without benefit of an election. Years later Harrison's grandson, Benjamin Harrison, became the nation's 23rd President.

The Whig Party urged voters to "keep the ball rolling on to Washington" by supporting its candidate.

John Tyler

NICKNAME	His Accidency
BORN	March 29, 1790, in Charles City County, Va.
POLITICAL PARTY	Whig
CHIEF OPPONENT	none; succeeded William Henry Harrison
TERM OF OFFICE	April 6, 1841–March 3, 1845
AGE AT INAUGURATION	51 years old
NUMBER OF TERMS	one (partial)
VICE PRESIDENT	none
FIRST LADIES	Letitia Christian Tyler (1790–1842), first wife (married March 29, 1813); Priscilla Cooper Tyler (1816–1889), daughter-in-law; Letitia Tyler Semple (1821–1907), daughter; Julia Gardiner Tyler (1820–1889), second wife (married June 26, 1844)
CHILDREN	Mary, Robert, John, Letitia, Elizabeth, Alice, Tazwell, David, John, Julia, Lachlan, Lyon, Robert, Pearl, plus a daughter died young
GEOGRAPHIC SCENE	26 states
NEW STATES ADDED	Florida (1845)
DIED	Jan. 18, 1862, in Richmond, Va.
AGE AT DEATH	71 years old
SELECTED LANDMARKS	Sherwood Forest Plantation, Charles City County, Va. (homestead); Hollywood Cemetery, Richmond, Va.

The first telegraph message was sent in 1844.

JOHN TYLER WAS THE FIRST VICE PRESIDENT to complete a different Chief Executive's term. He took firm command of the office immediately after the death of William Henry Harrison. This confident action set the standard for future midterm successions.

A Virginian like his predecessor, Tyler was a graduate of the College of William and Mary in Williamsburg. Before being named to the 1840 presidential ticket, he had served Virginia in the state legislature, as governor, and in the U.S. House and Senate.

Tyler was dubbed "His Accidency" after Harrison's unexpected death. The Constitution was vague about how a Vice President should take over as President. Tyler insisted that he was a true President, not an acting one. He took the oath of office, moved into the White House, and prepared to serve out Harrison's term. He even delivered a brief Inaugural Address (and did not catch cold).

As President, Tyler favored greater power for state governments and less for the federal government. His policies added to North-South tensions and helped lead the country to civil war later on. Tyler supported settlement of the West, helped resolve a dispute with Great Britain over Canada's boundaries with Maine, and led efforts to bring the Republic of Texas (then an independent country) into the Union.

Tyler was kicked out of the Whig Party after he vetoed its pro-banking legislation. Without the backing of a party, he had no easy way to seek reelection. He and his family retired to Virginia. When civil war seemed likely, Tyler, who was a slaveholder, encouraged his state to leave the Union. He was elected to serve in the Confederate Congress, but he died before he could take office.

John Tyler fathered more offspring than any other President: 15 children by two wives. He and his fiancée, Julia, escaped harm in 1844 when a cannon misfired during their visit to the warship Princeton *(above). After Julia hosted a popular White House ball at the end of her husband's Presidency, Tyler, who had been kicked out of his political party, joked: "They cannot say now that I am a President without a party."*

The Vice Presidents

FORTY-SIX MEN have served as Vice President of the United States since 1789. Fourteen have eventually become President, starting with John Adams, the first Vice President. The others, although important political figures in their day, have tended to fade from popular memory.

The Vice Presidency was created at the same time as the Presidency with the writing of the U.S. Constitution in 1787. The office received only brief definition. It took two Constitutional amendments to clarify how Vice Presidents should be chosen and what role they should play when a President becomes ill or dies in office.

The earliest Vice Presidents earned their posts by being the runners-up in the voting for President by the Electoral College. By the late 1820s, after the expansion of popular elections, political parties began identifying their own candidates for the two offices. Today such selection is directed by each presidential nominee. Then and now vice presidential nominees often balance and broaden the appeal of an election ticket by representing, for example, a different geographic region or age.

Early Vice Presidents were not seen as Presidents-in-waiting the way they are today. In fact, lawmakers disagreed over whether the Vice President even had this responsibility. It was not until the death of President William Henry Harrison in 1841 that this uncertainty was resolved. John Tyler, Harrison's Vice President, insisted that he deserved all the rights and responsibilities of President. His

Aaron Burr was among the most notorious Vice Presidents, particularly after he shot Alexander Hamilton in an 1804 duel (far left). Hamilton later died, leaving Burr open to murder charges while serving in Thomas Jefferson's administration. Modern Vice Presidents juggle a growing set of duties, whether ceremonial (left, Hubert Humphrey with Martin Luther King, Jr., during Lyndon B. Johnson's administration), advisory (right, Al Gore with President Bill Clinton), or directive (far right, Dick Cheney during the 43rd Presidency). They support favored legislation, too. Their official residence (top) lies a short drive from the White House.

decisive example set the pattern for future presidential successions.

The Constitution spells out one main responsibility for the Vice President: to preside over the U.S. Senate. In that role the Vice President is expected to cast deciding votes whenever the tally of senators' ballots results in a tie. Vice President John Adams was called upon to fulfill this duty on 29 occasions, more than any other Vice President.

With such a limited job description, early Vice Presidents often spent little time in the nation's capital, especially when the Senate was out of session. Many returned to their home states and took up old responsibilities. It was not until the 1970s that the Vice President even earned an official residence. The home is a 33-room house on the grounds of the U.S. Naval Observatory, a short drive from the White House. Walter Mondale, second in command to Jimmy Carter, became the first Vice President to inhabit this space.

Over the years Vice Presidents have shared similar backgrounds with Presidents, starting with a common average age, about 55 years old. New York State, a popular home for Presidents, gave more Vice Presidents to the country than any other state. Eight were born there, and 11 lived there prior to taking office. Like Presidents, many Vice Presidents served first as governors (15 of them did) or members of Congress (in 33 cases) before running for national office. Many had presidential ambitions of their own but settled for the post of Vice President, perhaps with the hope that the

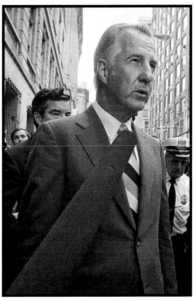

Only two Vice Presidents, John C. Calhoun and Spiro T. Agnew, have resigned from office. Calhoun left Andrew Jackson's administration to become a U.S. senator. Agnew was forced from office (above) during Richard M. Nixon's Presidency for failing to properly pay his income taxes. Ten months later scandal forced Nixon to resign.

job would serve as a stepping stone to the Presidency later on.

About half of the Vice Presidents served at least one four-year term in office, only seven have completed two terms as Vice President. Others either succeeded to the Presidency by death (on eight occasions), or because of resignation (once), died in office themselves (in seven instances), resigned from their duties (twice), or filled unexpired terms of other Vice Presidents (once). The end of their terms has often signaled the end of their political careers, though some have gone on to win seats in Congress. Five gained election directly to the Presidency itself.

Until the U.S. Constitution was amended in 1967, vacancies in the office of Vice President remained unfilled until the next presidential election. Now the 25th Amendment asks the President to nominate someone to serve as Vice President, subject to approval by a majority of the members of Congress. Richard M. Nixon was the first President to use this provision. All together there have been 19 occasions totaling nearly 38 years when the nation has had no one serving as Vice President.

The role a Vice President plays in an administration is set by each individual President. During the 20th century, Vice Presidents gained greater influence and were given increasingly important duties. Today's Vice Presidents juggle a growing range of responsibilities. At the same time they live each day knowing they are but a heartbeat away from becoming President of the United States.

James K. Polk

11TH PRESIDENT OF THE UNITED STATES ★ *1845 – 1849*

NICKNAME	Young Hickory
BORN	Nov. 2, 1795, near Pineville, Mecklenburg County, N.C.
POLITICAL PARTY	Democrat
CHIEF OPPONENT	Henry Clay, Whig (1777–1852)
TERM OF OFFICE	March 4, 1845–March 3, 1849
AGE AT INAUGURATION	49 years old
NUMBER OF TERMS	one
VICE PRESIDENT	George Mifflin Dallas (1792–1864)
FIRST LADY	Sarah Childress Polk (1803–1891), wife (married Jan. 1, 1824)
CHILDREN	none
GEOGRAPHIC SCENE	27 states
NEW STATES ADDED	Texas (1845), Iowa (1846), Wisconsin (1848)
DIED	June 15, 1849, at Nashville, Tenn.
AGE AT DEATH	53 years old
SELECTED LANDMARKS	Pineville, N.C. (reconstructed birthplace); State Capitol Grounds, Nashville, Tenn. (grave)

Polk camps with his father on a surveying trip.

USING A COMBINATION OF WAR AND ROUGH DIPLOMACY, James Knox Polk increased the nation's size by two-thirds. By the end of his single term, he had secured the land that would form all 48 contiguous United States. However, disagreements over the possible expansion of slavery into the new territories left the nation more divided than ever.

Polk came to Washington with the nickname "Young Hickory" because of his ties to Andrew Jackson, the famed "Old Hickory" President. Like Jackson, Polk was born in the Carolinas and settled in Tennessee. He was the son of a prosperous landowner, planter, and slaveholder. Polk's formal education began at age 17. He earned a degree with honors from the University of North Carolina, studied law, became an attorney, and sought a career in politics.

After a few years in the Tennessee Legislature, Polk gained election to the U.S. House of Representatives. He served there for 14 years and

James K. Polk grew up in the backwoods of North Carolina and Tennessee. Polk pushed the U.S. boundaries to the Pacific Ocean. The first U.S. postage stamps, the U.S. Naval Academy, and the Smithsonian Institution all began during his administration.

Posters compare the candidates for President in 1844 (left). James K. Polk was a "dark horse," or unexpected choice, for his political party. When word of his nomination reached Washington, D.C., by the new Morse telegraph, some doubted that the machine was working correctly. A political cartoon (right) questions whether trouble caused by President Polk's policies will collapse on him like a house of cards. An artist illustrated his policy of Manifest Destiny by showing the symbolic figure of Columbia (below) leading settlers westward.

was eventually elected Speaker, or leader, of the House. He earned Andrew Jackson's friendship in those years by supporting the President's policies. Later Polk served as governor of Tennessee.

Despite this record of public service, the nomination of Polk for President in 1844 came as a surprise. Most Democrats had expected the party to renominate former President Martin Van Buren, with Polk as a possible vice presidential candidate. Van Buren, however, had lost favor because of his antislavery stand against Texas statehood. Polk, a slaveholder, supported bringing Texas into the Union as a slave state and became the compromise nominee. He narrowly defeated the noted statesman Henry Clay at the polls.

Polk came into office determined, as were many citizens then, to expand his country's borders to the Pacific Ocean.

"The people of this continent alone have the right to decide their own destiny."

James K. Polk, Message to Congress, December 2, 1845

This belief—that the U.S. had the right to take over lands to the West—was called Manifest Destiny, which means something that is expected to happen without question.

Polk started with the Oregon Territory. Previously this Northwestern region, which included parts of present-day Oregon, Idaho, Washington State, and Canada's British Columbia, had been settled by British and Americans alike. U.S. pioneers traveled to it by way of the Oregon Trail. Polk bluffed that he expected the British to give up all land south of latitude 54° 40', the southern border of Russia's Alaskan Territory. Otherwise he would fight to take it. Hence the popular slogan: "Fifty-four forty, or fight." In the end Polk was delighted to settle on the 49th parallel, which still forms most of the U.S.-Canada border.

Next Polk concentrated on the southern U.S. border. Texans had won their independence from Mexico in 1836. Polk angered Mexico by granting Texas statehood soon after he became President. Then a boundary dispute erupted over the new state's southern border. Mexico insisted the Nueces River, the boundary of Texas as a Mexican state, was still its southern border. The U.S. claimed territory all the way to the Rio Grande—about half of the country of Mexico.

On Polk's instructions, U.S. soldiers provoked the Mexicans to attack by crossing into the disputed region in early 1846. From then on, U.S. forces never lost a battle in a war that ultimately took them all the way to Mexico City. When the Mexican War ended in the fall of 1847, the United States had gained not only the border it wanted for Texas but considerable other new land as well. Eventually, some or all of the states of Arizona, California, Colorado, Nevada, New Mexico, Utah, and Wyoming would take shape in the extra territory. Mexico was paid

$15 million for its loss of land. Ulysses S. Grant, the future Civil War general and U.S. President, was among those who fought in the war. He described it as "one of the most unjust ever waged by a stronger against a weaker nation."

In all, Polk added 1.2 million square miles of territory to the United States. It came with a heavy price. Northerners opposed to slavery and Southerners who supported it debated furiously over whether slavery had a place in the vast new lands. The two sides seemed ready to come to blows over the issue, and they finally did when the Civil War erupted some dozen years later.

Polk left the White House after one term, fulfilling an election promise not to run again. He enjoyed the shortest retirement of any President— three months—in part because he had literally exhausted himself on the job. Polk became ill, possibly with cholera, and died. His wife, Sarah, lived in their Tennessee home 42 years longer, remaining neutral during the Civil War.

James K. Polk and his wife, Sarah (right), had no children. They retired to "Polk Place" (left) after his Presidency. Sarah was well educated, and she devoted her energies to her husband's career. She traveled with him, helped with his speeches, reviewed newspapers for him, and served as the White House hostess. Because of her religious beliefs, she disapproved of alcohol, gambling, and dancing. When she entered the room for her husband's Inaugural Ball, the dancing ended. The Polks started the White House traditions of an annual Thanksgiving dinner and the playing of "Hail to the Chief" for the President's arrival.

Presidential Campaigns

A Blend of Party Politics and Hard Work

★ ★

THE PRESIDENTIAL campaigns of modern times are vastly different from those waged by earlier candidates for President. In fact, the concept of presidential campaigning did not even gain favor until well into the 19th century. Prior to that time supporters spoke on behalf of candidates. Sitting Presidents with reelection hopes were particularly reluctant to mix the politics of campaigning with their work as chief executive.

Candidate participation grew with time. Front-porch campaigns gained popularity during the last half of the 19th century. Candidates hosted large groups of supporters from their own front porches. Whistle-stop campaigns came into style during the early 1930s. Candidates traveled by train, giving speeches from the rear car, even at the smaller whistle-stop stations. By mid-century, airplanes were a preferred form of travel, and campaigning had become an essential step to becoming President.

Today candidates begin their official presidential campaigns more than a year before Election Day. Exploratory campaigns occur even earlier. Some potential candidates spend millions of dollars but become discouraged and withdraw from the race before any votes

Campaign scenes: A 1920 whistle-stop with Warren G. Harding (top), Franklin D. Roosevelt on tour with mine workers (left), and, in 1960, the first televised presidential debates (right). John F. Kennedy (at right), who made a more favorable impression in the match up, went on to defeat his opponent, Richard M. Nixon.

Enthusiasm is a hallmark of political campaigns, from the smile of a supporter (below, a fan of Dwight D. Eisenhower) to the cheers of a hall full of convention delegates (above, Democrats in 1996). Conventions showcase a party's strengths; they confirm its presidential nominees, too, with ceremonial state-by-state balloting.

are ever cast. Those who persevere face their first challenges in a series of statewide contests that take place in the opening months of election year. These primaries and caucuses determine which of any competing candidates will be supported by their political parties. Votes earned at the state level determine how many delegates will support each candidate during summer nominating conventions.

Prior to the 1950s, many rounds of voting and deal-making often took place at the Democratic and Republican conventions before a candidate could earn enough support to gain a party's nomination. Similar negotiating went into the choice of the vice presidential "running mate." Today the presidential nominee is determined during the spring season of primaries and caucuses. Candidates usually name their preferred running mate by early summer.

Each innovation in communications technology—from radio to television to the Internet—draws use during presidential campaigns. New technologies make it easier for candidates to influence voter decisions. They also offer increasing challenges to voters who must sort out factual stories from fanciful ones.

The increased use of advertising during campaigns, particularly television commercials, has vastly increased the cost of presidential elections. As a result, candidates must now raise millions and millions of dollars to finance their election bids. This fund-raising effort may discourage some candidates from running for office. Others may find it hard not to be influenced by the special interests of donors, either during their campaigns or after winning an election. Although laws now restrict the size of direct gifts from individuals, there are still ways for wealthy donors, businesses, and groups to use their money to influence a candidate's campaign. In 1974 Congress members established the Federal Election Commission to oversee the increasingly complex business of campaigning for office. Congress continues to pass laws that regulate campaign fund-raising practices, too.

Zachary Taylor

NICKNAME	Old Rough-and-Ready
BORN	Nov. 24, 1784, in Orange County, Va.
POLITICAL PARTY	Whig
CHIEF OPPONENT	Lewis Cass, Democrat (1782–1866)
TERM OF OFFICE	March 4, 1849–July 9, 1850
AGE AT INAUGURATION	64 years old
NUMBER OF TERMS	one (cut short by death)
VICE PRESIDENT	Millard Fillmore (1800–1874)
FIRST LADIES	Margaret Mackall Smith Taylor (1788–1852), wife (married June 21, 1810); Mary Elizabeth Taylor Bliss (1824–1909), daughter
CHILDREN	Ann, Sarah, Mary, Richard, plus two daughters died young
GEOGRAPHIC SCENE	30 states
NEW STATES ADDED	none
DIED	July 9, 1850, in the White House, Washington, D.C.
AGE AT DEATH	65 years old
SELECTED LANDMARKS	Zachary Taylor National Cemetery, Louisville, Ky.

General Zachary Taylor often wore old farm clothes into battle. He made a straw hat part of his standard battle dress.

ZACHARY TAYLOR WAS A SOLDIER BY TRAINING, not a politician, but he discovered unexpected similarities between those two professions after becoming President. Politicians in the nation's capital could become as combative as soldiers, he learned, particularly when the matter of slavery was discussed. He threatened to use military force to settle the debate over slavery; then he died in office before he could.

Taylor was the first President who had never held another elected office. In fact, he had never even voted in a presidential election because he felt his loyalty as a soldier for the U.S. government required him to stay above politics. Born in Virginia, Taylor was raised on a plantation in Kentucky and was one of the last slave owners to become President. He never attended college. Instead he entered into a 40-year career as an officer in the U.S. Army. His relaxed style of military dress, reputation for bravery, and consistent victories earned him the nickname "Old Rough-and-Ready."

Being a military hero helped Taylor win the election, but his Army career was poor training for the national debate on slavery. When he suggested that new states should decide for themselves whether to be slave or free, all sides protested. Northerners wanted Taylor to restrict slavery, not expand it. Southerners feared new antislavery states would diminish their own pro-slavery influence in Congress. When Southerners threatened to secede from, or leave, the Union, Taylor offered to lead the U.S. Army against them. We must "preserve the Union at all hazards," he said.

Then Taylor died. An Independence Day snack of iced buttermilk and cherries was probably contaminated with bacteria. He developed cholera and succumbed to his illness five days later.

Zachary Taylor's legs were so short that he needed help mounting a horse. He liked to ride sidesaddle. Eventually both Taylor and his 1848 running mate (above) served as President of the nation.

Millard Fillmore

13TH PRESIDENT OF THE UNITED STATES ★ *1850 – 1853*

NICKNAME	Last of the Whigs
BORN	Jan. 7, 1800, in Cayuga County, N.Y.
POLITICAL PARTY	Whig
CHIEF OPPONENT	none; succeeded Taylor
TERM OF OFFICE	July 10, 1850–March 3, 1853
AGE AT INAUGURATION	50 years old

Millard Fillmore failed to be elected in 1856.

NUMBER OF TERMS	one (partial)
VICE PRESIDENT	none
FIRST LADIES	Abigail Powers Fillmore (1798–1853), wife (married Feb. 5 1826); Mary Abigail Fillmore (1832–1854), daughter
SECOND WIFE	Caroline Carmichael McIntosh Fillmore (1813–1881), married Feb. 10, 1858
CHILDREN	Millard, Mary
GEOGRAPHIC SCENE	30 states
NEW STATES ADDED	California (1850)
DIED	March 8, 1874, in Buffalo, N.Y.
AGE AT DEATH	74 years old
SELECTED LANDMARKS	Fillmore Glen State Park, Moravia, N.Y. (reconstructed birthplace); The Millard Fillmore House, East Aurora, N.Y.; Forest Lawn Cemetery, Buffalo, N.Y.

MILLARD FILLMORE OFFERED COMPROMISE, in contrast to the threatening style of his predecessor, as a way to end the ongoing tense debate over slavery. Despite being born a Northerner, Fillmore seemed to sympathize with Southern concerns. In the end, the compromises he signed only delayed civil war between North and South.

Born in a log cabin in upstate New York, Fillmore fulfilled the American dream of rising from simple beginnings to national importance. He was poorly educated. He is said to have seen his first map of the United States upon entering school at age 19. (Later he married his schoolteacher.) He never attended college, but he trained himself to be a lawyer. He won election to government posts in New York State and the U.S. House of Representatives before agreeing to run as Vice President for Zachary Taylor's ticket in 1848.

When Fillmore became President after Taylor died in office, he chose to compromise with lawmakers over quarrelsome debates about slavery. Their five agreements became known as the Compromise of 1850. These deals admitted California as a free state, settled border disputes between Texas and New Mexico, gave territory status to New Mexico, closed the slave markets in the nation's capital, and allowed federal law officers to return runaway slaves to their owners. Each side gained something, and war seemed less likely.

Fillmore showed little interest in the next election, so the Whigs selected a different candidate and lost in 1852. The party then fell into confusion and disappeared, earning Fillmore the nickname "Last of the Whigs." Fillmore retired to Buffalo, New York. In 1856 he ran for President with the new Know-Nothing Party, but he came in third. He died in 1874.

Millard Fillmore was tall, handsome, and well mannered, in striking contrast with the rough-and-ready image of his predecessor. He and his wife, Abigail, established the first permanent library at the White House. Abigail traveled in an elegant carriage (above). Sadly, she caught cold and died after attending the Inauguration of her husband's successor.

Franklin Pierce

14TH PRESIDENT OF THE UNITED STATES ★ 1853 – 1857

NICKNAME	Handsome Frank
BORN	Nov. 23, 1804, in Hillsborough (now Hillsboro), N.H.
POLITICAL PARTY	Democrat
CHIEF OPPONENT	Winfield Scott, Whig (1786–1866)
TERM OF OFFICE	March 4, 1853–March 3, 1857
AGE AT INAUGURATION	48 years old
NUMBER OF TERMS	one
VICE PRESIDENT	William Rufus De Vane King (1786–1853)
FIRST LADY	Jane Means Appleton Pierce (1806–1863), wife (married Nov. 10, 1834)
CHILDREN	Frank, Benjamin, plus a son died young
GEOGRAPHIC SCENE	31 states
NEW STATES ADDED	none
DIED	Oct. 8, 1869, in Concord, N.H.
AGE AT DEATH	64 years old
SELECTED LANDMARKS	Hillsboro, N.H. (boyhood home); Concord, N.H. (adult home); Old North Cemetery, Concord, N.H.

Benjamin Pierce (above, with mother) died in a train crash shortly before his father's Inauguration.

When Franklin Pierce became President, the national debate about slavery had quieted. Pierce, a man with an undistinguished record in public office, carelessly renewed the controversy by supporting the option of slavery in Kansas. This stand re-opened the slavery issue and helped push the country closer to civil war.

In large part Pierce was nominated for President because he had not made many political enemies or taken a firm stand about slavery. His party decided it would be easier to elect "Handsome Frank" than other, more controversial Democrats. Pierce had been born in a log cabin in New Hampshire. A graduate of Maine's Bowdoin College, he took up law and served in the New Hampshire Legislature. Later he spent 10 years in Washington, D.C., as a representative and a senator. While there Pierce earned more notice for his heavy drinking than for his lawmaking. Democrats campaigned for his Presidency with the slogan: "We Polked you in 1844; we shall Pierce you in 1852."

As President, Pierce infuriated Northerners by supporting the Kansas-Nebraska Act of 1854. This measure ended the Missouri Compromise of 1820 by permitting slavery to spread north of Missouri's southern border. Using a policy called popular sovereignty, the act suggested that residents of new states should determine for themselves whether to permit slavery within their borders. Casualties climbed to about 200 in "Bleeding Kansas" after both pro-slavery and antislavery settlers rushed to the territory and began fighting.

The Democratic Party was so embarrassed by the scene that it did not renominate Pierce for a second term. Pierce retired to New Hampshire in disgrace. His death in 1869 went largely unrecognized.

Franklin Pierce seemed to find trouble wherever he turned during the stormy pre–Civil War years of his Presidency. Debates over slavery turned particularly ugly in "Bleeding Kansas" (above). Improving the White House, with hot and cold running water and a hot-water-based heating system, proved more manageable than policymaking.

James Buchanan

15TH PRESIDENT OF THE UNITED STATES ★ 1857 – 1861

NICKNAME	Ten-Cent Jimmy
BORN	April 23, 1791, in Cove Gap, Pa.
POLITICAL PARTY	Democrat
CHIEF OPPONENT	John C. Frémont, Republican (1813–1890)
TERM OF OFFICE	March 4, 1857–March 3, 1861
AGE AT INAUGURATION	65 years old
NUMBER OF TERMS	one
VICE PRESIDENT	John Cabell Breckinridge (1821–1875)
FIRST LADY	Harriet Lane (1830–1903), niece
WIFE	never married
CHILDREN	none
GEOGRAPHIC SCENE	31 states
NEW STATES ADDED	Minnesota (1858), Oregon (1859), Kansas (1861)
DIED	June 1, 1868, in Lancaster, Pa.
AGE AT DEATH	77 years old
SELECTED LANDMARKS	Mercersburg Academy, Mercersburg, Pa. (relocated boyhood home); Wheatland, Lancaster, Pa. (homestead); Woodward Hill Cemetery, Lancaster, Pa.

"Don't fire 'til I get out of office," exclaims James Buchanan in this political cartoon. The departing President told his successor, Abraham Lincoln: "If you are as happy, my dear sir, on entering this house as I am on leaving it and returning home, you are the happiest man on earth."

JAMES BUCHANAN, in an effort to hold the Union together, offered concession after concession to the South, regardless of the anger his actions provoked in the North. When Southern states began to secede anyway, he protested but claimed to have no constitutional authority to force them to come back.

Buchanan's unhappy single term in the White House followed a distinguished, 40-year career of public service in the United States and abroad. Buchanan was born in a log cabin in Pennsylvania. The son of an Irish immigrant, he graduated from Dickinson College, studied law, and entered public service. He served briefly in the state legislature, then spent a decade each in the U.S. House and Senate. In addition, he was minister to Russia under Andrew Jackson, James K. Polk's secretary of state, and minister to Great Britain for Franklin Pierce. This final post helped earn him the presidential nomination. By being abroad he had avoided the latest slavery debates.

Shortly after Buchanan's Inauguration, the Supreme Court issued its *Dred Scott* ruling. The slave Dred Scott had argued he should be free if his master moved with him to a free state. The Court disagreed, saying slaves were property, not citizens, and remained slaves anywhere. Although Buchanan disliked slavery (he even bought slaves in order to free them), he hated breaking laws even more. (His nickname recalled his insistence on precise bookkeeping, for example.) Buchanan stood by the ruling, infuriating Northerners. He could not resolve the financial Panic of 1857 or the secession of Southern states from the Union. Having stated he would serve only one term, Buchanan was delighted to leave office. Buchanan, the only President who never married, retired to Pennsylvania to write his memoirs. He died in 1868.

Dred Scott

James Buchanan had one good eye for each type of vision—close up and distant. In order to see well he cocked his head to one side or the other depending on which eye he needed to use.

A NEW BIRTH OF FREEDOM

★ *1861 – 1897* ★

1863

Union forces defeated Confederate troops at the Battle of Gettysburg after the Southern Army crossed over onto Northern soil. The four-year-long Civil War ended in 1865.

1865–1870

Many Northerners who moved South after the Civil War carried their belongings in suitcases made from carpets. These "carpetbaggers" tried to influence the Reconstruction of the South.

1871

Fires burned across Chicago for more than 24 hours beginning on October 8. The city rebuilt itself into a vibrant midwestern business center, complete with early skyscrapers.

1879

Thomas Edison invented the electric lightbulb. Other inventions by Edison included the phonograph, microphone, and motion pictures. He developed the scientific research laboratory, too.

Years of disagreement between Northerners and Southerners over slavery and related issues finally led to Civil War between the two regions. After the four-year war ended in 1865, a series of Presidents struggled with Reconstruction, the process of reuniting and rebuilding the splintered nation. Post–Civil War Presidents more often found themselves watching history unfold than shaping it. The growth of industry in the East and the expansion of western settlement drove the United States toward its modern form.

1886

The Statue of Liberty became a beacon of welcome to immigrants after its dedication. Within a decade, more than 350,000 newcomers were arriving annually. The figure had more than doubled by 1906.

1889

When the federal government opened up central Oklahoma for settlement in April, some 50,000 "sodbusters" rushed to stake their claims in the new territory on one day.

1890

Susan B. Anthony spent half a century trying without success to earn women the right to vote. In 1890 she became president of the National American Woman Suffrage Association.

1893

The Duryea brothers built the first successful gasoline-powered car in the United States. Within a dozen years more than 1.5 million cars were being produced in the country.

Abraham Lincoln

16TH PRESIDENT OF THE UNITED STATES ★ *1861 – 1865*

First Lady Mary Todd Lincoln

WHEN ABRAHAM LINCOLN WAS INAUGURATED in 1861, he became President of states that were not united. In fact, after arguing for years about slavery and states' rights, Northerners and Southerners were on the brink of civil, or internal, war. Lincoln has been called the greatest U.S. President because he reunited the country. He was assassinated just after the end of the Civil War in 1865.

Lincoln's humble beginnings are a schoolbook legend. He was born in a log cabin in Kentucky to parents who could neither read nor write. The sum of his schoolhouse education was about one year's time, but he educated himself by reading books he borrowed from others. When Lincoln was nine years old, his mother died. His father, a carpenter and farmer, remarried and moved his family farther west, eventually settling in Illinois. Lincoln was taller (at six feet four inches) than any other President. His high-pitched voice and thick frontier accent (saying "git" for "get" or "thar" for "there") made an odd contrast with his thin but strong and dignified figure.

Lincoln worked as a flatboat navigator, storekeeper, soldier, surveyor, and postmaster before being elected at age 25 to the Illinois Legislature in Springfield. Once there, he taught himself law, opened a law practice, and earned the nickname of Honest Abe. He served one term in the U.S. House of Representatives during 1847–49 but lost two U.S. Senate races in the 1850s. However, the debates he had about slavery with his 1858 opponent, Stephen Douglas, helped him earn the presidential nomination two years later. In the

Abraham Lincoln's lifelong love of reading whenever and wherever he could (above) began in his youth, when books often took the place of school. Favorite reading included U.S. history, Aesop's Fables, Robinson Crusoe, *the* Bible, *and Shakespeare.*

four-way presidential race of 1860, Lincoln was the top vote-getter.

Lincoln grew strong by splitting logs into thousands of rails for fences. At 21, he "paid" 400 rails a yard for pants fabric.

Lincoln was elected on a platform that considered it treason for Southern states to secede, or withdraw, from the nation. It agreed to continue slavery in the South but outlawed its spread elsewhere. Southern leaders threatened to secede rather than accept this Republican plan. After Lincoln's victory, but before his inauguration, these states began to act on their threat to leave the Union. The Civil War officially began on April 12, 1861, at Fort Sumter, South Carolina, when forces from the new Confederate States of America attacked this U.S. fort.

Lincoln had promised in his Inaugural oath to "preserve, protect, and defend" the Union. Now he began to act, competing with Confederate leaders for the allegiance of states not yet committed to either side. With Congress out of session until July, Lincoln broke laws when they stood in his way of protecting the Constitution. "Often limb must be amputated to save a life," he reasoned. Lincoln expanded the size of the Army and Navy, jailed people who might encourage secession of border states, stopped trade with the Confederacy, and spent government funds without the approval of lawmakers. His efforts strengthened the Northern cause; later they were approved by Congress and the courts. In the end, 11 states joined the Confederacy and 23 remained in the Union, including the crucial border states of Missouri, Kentucky, and Maryland.

The outcome of the Civil War remained unclear during the early years of fighting. While the North held the upper hand on the seas, the South generally beat Union forces on land. It was not until the Battle of Gettysburg, in July 1863, that Southern dominance of the battlefield ended. Through speeches such as his Gettysburg Address, Lincoln encouraged Northerners to keep fighting whatever the costs. In this famous three-minute dedication of the battlefield cemetery, he urged citizens to assure "that these dead shall not have died in vain—that this nation, under God, shall have a new birth of freedom—and that government of the people, by the people, for the people, shall not perish from the earth." Earlier that same year Lincoln called for the end of slavery in his Emancipation Proclamation.

Consistent military victories, including the capture of Atlanta, Georgia, in September 1864, helped Lincoln win reelection. His selection of Southern-born Andrew Johnson as his new running mate balanced his ticket. Only Union states participated in the election. By the following March, Union victory in the war was certain; the only question was when. Lincoln's second Inaugural Address made it clear that the Northern states would keep fighting "until every drop of blood drawn with the lash, shall be paid by another drawn with the sword."

Lincoln joked that he mostly battled mosquitoes during the Black Hawk War of 1832. The war pushed Native Americans farther west.

Lincoln and his running mate, Hannibal Hamlin, won the 1860 election even though many Southern states left them off their ballots.

Seeing the Union successfully through the Civil War was Lincoln's greatest presidential responsibility, but it was not his only accomplishment. Together with Congress, he inaugurated a national banking system, established the Department of Agriculture, standardized paper currency, supported the development of a transcontinental railroad, enacted the Homestead Act, which opened up vast holdings of federal land to settlers, and crafted the 13th Amendment, which ended slavery.

> "A house divided against itself cannot stand."
>
> Abraham Lincoln, June 1858

Yet Lincoln urged citizens to end the war free from bitterness, "with malice toward none; with charity for all." Victory came on April 9, 1865, at Appomattox Court House, Virginia, when Confederate General Robert E. Lee surrendered to Union General Ulysses S. Grant. More than 600,000 soldiers had died during the four-year conflict.

Lincoln's personal life in the White House revolved around his wife, Mary, and two young sons, William and Thomas, known as Willie and Tad. (Son Robert was already away at

Northerners and Southerners differed for years over whether the federal government had the right to control the practice of slavery. Disagreement about matters such as returning runaway slaves to their owners (above) caused Southern states to secede from the Union and led to the Civil War.

Citizens saw the toll war took on their President (left) and their countrymen thanks to early photographs made during the nation's four-year Civil War.

school.) Lincoln often romped with his sons and their friends. A teenage guest recalled how she once entered a room to find the President flattened on the floor with four boys holding down his limbs. "Come quick and sit on his stomach," invited Tad. Lincoln forgave the boys their wildness. "It's a diversion," he told a visitor, "and we need diversion at the White House." Lincoln told jokes, tall tales, anecdotes, and stories to relieve wartime tensions.

In 1862 humor lost its place for a while when

Left to right: Mary, Willie, Robert, Tad, and Abraham Lincoln. By 1871 only Mary and Robert remained alive.

Willie became the only child to die in the White House. He was a victim of typhoid fever. Mary, already saddened by criticism of her performance as First Lady, grieved deeply and long. First falsely accused of being sympathetic to the Confederacy (she had relatives in the South), then scolded for her lavish spending, she was now chided by the public for neglecting her official duties. The subsequent deaths of her husband and Tad left her so griefstricken that some people considered her insane.

Lincoln spent much of the final weeks of his life away from the White House. He met with military commanders, such as Ulysses S. Grant (who would become the 18th President), and discussed surrender terms. Lincoln's plans for Reconstruction, or the reunion, of the United States were flexible and generous. However, he would barely live to enjoy the end of the war, much less shape its peace. He became the first President to be assassinated when he was shot on April 14, 1865.

Lincoln had received thousands of death threats since 1860. The day he was shot, he confided to his daytime bodyguard that he

> "That on the 1st day of January, A.D. 1863, all persons held as slaves...shall be then, thenceforward, and forever free."

Abraham Lincoln,
from the Emancipation Proclamation,
January 1, 1863

had dreamed for the three previous nights of being assassinated. His nightmare became a reality that evening when he went out to see a play. His nighttime bodyguard left Lincoln's box seat unguarded so he could watch the performance too. John Wilkes Booth, an actor familiar with the theater, was thus able to enter the President's box unnoticed. Booth hoped to revive the Confederate cause by killing the President. He shot Lincoln in the back of the head, then jumped to the stage floor, breaking his

leg in the process. He escaped the theater nonetheless and remained on the loose for nearly two weeks. Eventually he was shot and killed while being captured.

The wounded and unconscious President was carried to a boardinghouse across the street. His long body had to be placed diagonally across the standard-size bed in order to recline properly. He died the following morning, said to be wearing an expression of happiness and repose on his face. His body lay in state at the U.S. Capitol and at other sites in the North before traveling home for burial in Illinois.

From the Lincoln-Douglas Debates of 1858 to the Emancipation Proclamation and Gettysburg Address of 1863 (top), Lincoln promoted freedom and unity. He was silenced by gunshot in 1865 (bottom left). The President's death at the end of the Civil War (bottom right) unsettled the fragile nation.

Andrew Johnson

Andrew Johnson

NICKNAME	The Veto President
BORN	Dec. 29, 1808, in Raleigh, N.C.
POLITICAL PARTY	Democrat
CHIEF OPPONENT	none; succeeded Lincoln
TERM OF OFFICE	April 15, 1865–March 3, 1869
AGE AT INAUGURATION	56 years old
NUMBER OF TERMS	one (partial)
VICE PRESIDENT	none
FIRST LADIES	Eliza McCardle Johnson (1810–1876), wife (married May 17, 1827); Martha Johnson Patterson (1828–1891), daughter
CHILDREN	Martha, Charles, Mary, Robert, and Andrew, Jr.
GEOGRAPHIC SCENE	36 states
NEW STATES ADDED	Nebraska (1867)
DIED	July 31, 1875, in Carter's Station, Tenn.
AGE AT DEATH	66 years old
SELECTED LANDMARKS	Mordecai Historic Park, Raleigh, N.C. (relocated birthplace); Andrew Johnson National Historic Site, Greenville, Tenn. (includes two residences and grave)

Andrew Johnson opened a tailor's shop (above) when he was 17. He continued to make his own clothes even after becoming a legislator. During his Presidency the U.S. purchased the Alaskan Territory from Russia. In 1875 the retired President returned to the U.S. Senate. No other President has gone on to become a senator. At his request he was buried wrapped in a U.S. flag with his head resting on his copy of the Constitution.

THE CRISIS OF WAR BETWEEN THE STATES was followed by a crisis within the U.S. Presidency. It began with the assassination of Abraham Lincoln and continued through the Presidency of his successor, Andrew Johnson. The climax came with Johnson's impeachment and near removal from office by Congress.

Johnson grew up with more poverty and hardship than any other President. His parents were illiterate laborers; his father died when Andrew was three. He never attended a day of school. Nonetheless, by age 20 Johnson had been elected to be an alderman, or city legislator. Later he became a mayor, then a Tennessee state senator, U.S. representative, Tennessee governor, and U.S. senator. Johnson was the only Southern legislator who stayed on to work in the U.S. Senate during the Civil War. Southerners branded him a traitor, but Lincoln rewarded him by making him the military governor of Tennessee.

Although Johnson was a Democrat, Republicans put him on Lincoln's 1864 presidential ticket as a representative from the South. Thus, the party allegiance of the Presidency changed with Lincoln's death. Johnson was the last slave owner to become President. He argued with politicians about how to "reconstruct" the United States after the Civil War. He routinely vetoed, or rejected, Congress's ideas and became known as "The Veto President."

His leadership style angered legislators so much that, in 1868, the House of Representatives impeached him, or charged that he should be removed from office. House members identified 11 articles, or reasons, for removal. Nine of them dealt with the President's controversial firing of his secretary of war, an ally of Congress. The Senate considered the House charges but fell one vote short of convicting Johnson, so he completed his term of office.

Andrew Johnson—the first President ever impeached—received a summons (above) for his Senate trial.

U. S. Political Parties

★ The Two-Party System ★

THE FOUNDING FATHERS hoped that representatives of the new United States government would work together in harmony without dividing into opposing groups called parties. Yet, soon after George Washington became President, political parties began to form. Leaders partnered with others who shared their geographic background, foreign policy beliefs, or other ideas for governing the country.

Today, as then, the party with the largest number of elected members in the U.S. House of Representatives and the U.S. Senate holds a majority of influence over those chambers. Its members outnumber those of the minority, or opposing, parties. Occasionally the same party will control both chambers of Congress and the Presidency. With that much political power, it can significantly influence the nature of government. Usually each party will control only one or two of these three areas. In that case, political parties will have to compromise and cooperate with one another in order to enact new laws and policies.

During George Washington's Presidency, lawmakers divided into two groups. They became known as either Federalists or as Anti-Federalists, depending on whether or not they believed that a strong federal government should oversee weaker state governments. Ever since, although names and opinions may change, two political parties have dominated the U.S. government. Today's leaders are primarily members of the Democratic and Republican parties. Each group can trace its origins well back into the 19th century.

The Democratic Party evolved from the early Anti-Federalists. Leaders such as Thomas Jefferson shaped the Anti-Federalists into a group of members known variously as the Democratic-Republicans, the National Republicans, or, eventually, the Democrats.

The modern Republican Party was formed during the 1850s to combat the spread of slavery. Its first successful presidential candidate was Abraham Lincoln. Sometimes it is referred to as the Grand Old Party (GOP).

The Democratic and Republican Parties have shared fairly equally in the control of the White House. There have been several occasions, however, when one party has had a long period of domination. From Lincoln's election in 1860 through the election of 1908, for example, all but two

A campaign banner (center) promotes the 1920 ticket of the Democratic Party. A 19th-century political cartoonist popularized the use of animals to symbolize the Republican and Democratic Parties. He drew an elephant (left) to represent the colossal size of Republican Party support in 1874. He chose a donkey (right) for the Democrats, knowing that Andrew Jackson had adopted that symbol after being called a jackass during the feisty campaign of 1828.

The Republican Party was founded in Ripon, Wisconsin (far left), in 1854. It is still going strong more than 150 years later. Future President Gerald Ford and his wife, Betty, posed with party supporters during the 1960s (left). There have been many attempts to start new parties over the years. These range from the Free Soil and Know-Nothing Parties of the 19th century to the Reform and Green Parties of modern times. These third parties may try to offer an alternative to the established parties on all fronts or may form around a single issue.

Presidents were Republicans. The Democratic Party earned its longest streak of control—20 years—from 1933 to 1953. Its predecessor, the Democratic-Republican Party, had an even longer streak—28 years, from 1801–1829.

Two other political parties had members become Chief Executives, too. Washington and his successor, John Adams, were associated with the Federalist Party. The Whig Party evolved from these early Federalists. Four of its members became President. Two Whigs won outright election: William Henry Harrison and Zachary Taylor. Both of them died in office. Their Whig Vice Presidents, John Tyler and Millard Fillmore, replaced them.

Often the presidential ballot will include candidates from third parties, those groups that exist beyond the two major parties. Occasionally a candidate will run for office as an "independent," that is, without the support of a political party. No independent or third-party candidates have ever made it to the White House. Even so, these candidates may influence an election by dividing the support of voters or by directing attention to a particular issue or cause. In recent elections, third party and independent candidates have frequently siphoned support away from Republican and Democratic candidates in ways that helped secure a victory for the opposing major party. In 2000, for example, the Green Party attracted just enough support away from the Democratic Party to place the Republican Party's candidate in office.

Andrew Jackson (left) was the first President to campaign under the banner of the same Democratic Party that exists today. Former Republican President Theodore Roosevelt (right) tried to return to the White House as the nominee of the Progressive, or Bull Moose, Party. He finished second in the 1912 election, ahead of the sitting Republican President William Howard Taft. In no other presidential election has a third party surpassed one of the two major parties.

Ulysses S. Grant

18TH PRESIDENT OF THE UNITED STATES ★ *1869 – 1877*

NICKNAME	Unconditional Surrender Grant
BORN	April 27, 1822, in Point Pleasant, Ohio
POLITICAL PARTY	Republican
CHIEF OPPONENTS	1st term: Horatio Seymour, Democrat (1810–1886); 2nd term: Horace Greeley, Democrat (1811–1872)
TERM OF OFFICE	March 4, 1869–March 3, 1877
AGE AT INAUGURATION	46 years old
NUMBER OF TERMS	two
VICE PRESIDENTS	1st term: Schuyler Colfax (1823–1885); 2nd term: Henry Wilson (1812–1875)
FIRST LADY	Julia Boggs Dent Grant (1826–1902), wife (married Aug. 22, 1848)
CHILDREN	Frederick, Ulysses, Ellen, Jesse
GEOGRAPHIC SCENE	37 states
NEW STATES ADDED	Colorado (1876)
DIED	July 23, 1885, in Mount McGregor, N.Y.
AGE AT DEATH	63 years old
SELECTED LANDMARKS	Point Pleasant, Ohio (birthplace); Georgetown, Ohio (boyhood home); General Grant National Memorial, New York, N.Y. (grave)

Birthplace of Ulysses S. Grant (above). As a child Grant imagined becoming a farmer or a river trader.

BY THE END OF THE CIVIL WAR, Ulysses Simpson Grant was the highest ranking U.S. general since George Washington. He was a national hero, too. Grant's popular appeal helped him become President in the first post–Civil War national election. Mastery of military tactics did not prepare him for the world of politics, however. His administration is remembered more for its scandals than for its accomplishments.

As a child, Grant seemed an unlikely person to triumph on the battlefield. He disliked hunting, got sick in his father's tanning shop, and later resisted attending the U.S. Military Academy at West Point. Once there, however, Grant distinguished himself as a horseman and excelled at math. Within a few years, Grant was on active duty in the Mexican War. His subsequent attempts at civilian life yielded little financial success, and he was happy to return to the military when the Civil War began.

Grant entered the fighting as a brigadier general of Illinois troops in Missouri. His aggressive assault on Fort Donelson, Tennessee, during February 1862, gave the Union its first notable victory in the Civil War. Citizens boasted that his initials stood for "Unconditional Surrender," the terms he had set for the Southern rebels at the fort. When

The name of the nation's 18th President was accidentally changed from Hiram Ulysses Grant to Ulysses Simpson Grant when he was enrolled at the U.S. Military Academy. (His local congressman incorporated the maiden name of Grant's mother into his appointment recommendation by mistake.) Classmates nicknamed him "Uncle Sam," like the already popular patriotic character. Grant distinguished himself during the Civil War (above). By the end he was commander of all Union armies.

A scene from the Inauguration of Ulysses S. Grant (left). Passage of the 15th Amendment in 1870 permitted large numbers of African Americans to begin voting (above). In 1872 Victoria Claflin Woodhull became the first woman presidential candidate. She suggested that Frederick Douglass, the former slave, run as Vice President. He declined, and her campaign fizzled. Grant won instead. Ulysses S. Grant was an expert handler of horses (bottom, left). While a student at West Point, he set a horse-jumping record that stood for 25 years. While President he was stopped for speeding in his horse-drawn carriage; Grant walked back to the White House after the officer confiscated his vehicle.

Northerners learned he had smoked a cigar during the assault, they sent him as many as 10,000 boxes of them to help guarantee future victories. (Thus developed Grant's custom of smoking some 20 cigars a day, a habit that probably helped cause his death.) Some called him "Butcher Grant" for the

casualties that came with his victories, but Abraham Lincoln was impressed. "I cannot spare this man—he fights," he said. Lincoln named him commander of all Federal troops in March 1864. Grant, who was superstitious about retracing his steps, did not like to retreat. He persisted on the battlefield, and, supported by Union commanders fighting aggressively elsewhere, he wore down the Confederate side until it was forced to surrender.

After the embarrassing political arguments of Andrew Johnson's administration, voters were enthusiastic about electing Grant—the respected war hero—as their President. He was the only man to complete two presidential terms during the 76-year span between Andrew Jackson and Woodrow Wilson. Under Grant's leadership the government established the world's first national park (Yellowstone, founded in 1872), avoided war with Great Britain about Civil War damage claims, established the Department of Justice, and passed the 15th Amendment. This legislation granted voting rights regardless of "race, color, or previous condition of servitude" to all men. (Women did not gain voting rights until 1920.)

Ulysses S. Grant retired after an administration tainted by scandal (left). During his post-presidential years, Grant mixed quiet time (bottom right) with family, business, and travel. Grant found he had much in common with the Viceroy of China (above, seated at right) when they met during a world tour after his Presidency. Both leaders had defended their countries as generals during civil wars. Both liked to eat—the Viceroy hosted an eight-hour, 70-course dinner for his guest.

These accomplishments were overshadowed, however, by controversies. The federal government was unable to prevent white Southerners from using violence and political tricks to limit the rights of former slaves. The financial Panic of 1873 put millions of laborers out of work. Worst of all were the scandals of Grant's administration—from corrupt banking and currency deals to the stealing of federal liquor taxes by manufacturers and public officials. Although none of these crimes involved Grant directly, his reputation as a leader suffered.

Grant failed to win nomination for a third presidential term. (A constitutional amendment in 1951 limited a President to two elected terms of office, but no such barrier existed before then.) After leaving the White House, Grant, his wife, and teenage son embarked on a 30-month tour of the world. Along the way he met Queen Victoria in England and became the first person ever allowed to shake hands with a Japanese emperor. In 1880 he failed to win the Republican nomination for President. Grant invested in a family business venture during his retirement in New York City, but a dishonest business partner brought financial ruin to the project. Congress provided Grant with much-needed income by putting him back on the Army payroll as a general, although he was not on active duty.

At the suggestion of author and publisher Mark Twain, Grant decided to make even more money by writing his autobiography. Grant raced to complete the book before his life could be claimed by throat cancer. He finished only days before his death. The book became a best-seller and earned his family a small fortune. Grant and his wife, Julia, who died 17 years after him, are buried in the New York City landmark popularly known as Grant's Tomb.

"No terms except an unconditional and immediate surrender can be accepted."

Ulysses S. Grant,
during the assault of Fort Donelson, Tennessee,
February 16, 1862

Rutherford B. Hayes

19TH PRESIDENT OF THE UNITED STATES ★ *1877 – 1881*

NICKNAME	His Fraudulency
BORN	Oct. 4, 1822, in Delaware, Ohio
POLITICAL PARTY	Republican
CHIEF OPPONENT	Samuel Jones Tilden, Democrat (1814–1886)
TERM OF OFFICE	March 4, 1877–March 3, 1881
AGE AT INAUGURATION	54 years old
NUMBER OF TERMS	one
VICE PRESIDENT	William Almon Wheeler (1819–1887)
FIRST LADY	Lucy Ware Webb Hayes (1831–1889), wife (married Dec. 30, 1852)
CHILDREN	Sardis, James, Rutherford, Frances, Scott, plus three sons died young
GEOGRAPHIC SCENE	38 states
NEW STATES ADDED	none
DIED	Jan. 17, 1893, in Fremont, Ohio
AGE AT DEATH	70 years old
SELECTED LANDMARKS	Spiegel Grove National Historic Landmark, Fremont, Ohio (adult home, memorial library, museum, grave)

Lucy Hayes, shown with her children Fanny and Scott and a friend, was the first First Lady to finish college. She was nicknamed "Lemonade Lucy" for supporting temperance by serving soft drinks instead of alcohol at the White House.

RUTHERFORD BIRCHARD HAYES started his administration amid controversy. Politicians argued about how to count the national election returns. In the end, Hayes won office by one electoral vote, the narrowest presidential victory in history. He went on to bring dignity, honesty, and reform to the government.

Hayes came to the White House with a solid background of service to his country. He was born in Delaware, Ohio, graduated from Kenyon College in Ohio, and earned a law degree from Harvard University. In 1861 Hayes interrupted law practice in his home state to join the Union army. He rose to the rank of major general by the end of the Civil War and survived having four horses shot out from under him. Hayes declined to leave the battlefield after he was nominated for a seat in Congress. He wrote home that soldiers who campaigned for office "ought to be scalped" for deserting their posts. (These patriotic words assured his election.) Later he served three times as Ohio's governor.

Widespread ballot fraud, or illegal vote-casting, clouded the results of the popular and electoral voting in the 1876 presidential election. Victory belonged to the person with the greatest number of electoral votes, and Congress was left to determine the most accurate tally of them. The debate split along party lines and lasted for months. Finally, three days before the Inauguration, Congress confirmed Hayes as President. In exchange Republicans apparently promised Democrats, who were concentrated in the South, that Reconstruction would end. The dealmaking earned Hayes the offensive nicknames of "His Fraudulency" and "Ruther*fraud* B. Hayes." As President, Hayes left scandal behind. He actually worked to increase the standards of behavior for civil servants, or government employees.

Having always planned to serve only one term, Hayes retired to Ohio where he took an active role in local and state causes. He died in 1893.

Alexander Graham Bell personally installed the first White House telephone while Rutherford B. Hayes was President. Another inventor, Thomas Edison, visited the First Family to demonstrate his new phonograph. The Hayes family held the first public Easter egg roll on the White House lawn.

Presidential Landmarks

★ *From Log Cabins to Libraries* ★

THE PRESIDENCY has led every Chief Executive to Washington, D.C. Even George Washington, who never lived there, visited the site of the nation's new capital as it was being planned and built. But all of the Presidents have left footprints in other parts of the country, too. Their birthplaces, homes, graves, museums, libraries, and memorials offer a trail of history for others to follow.

The oldest presidential landmarks lie along the eastern seaboard of the U.S. They remind us of the modest size of the new country and the role key states like Virginia and Massachusetts played in providing early national leaders. As citizens pushed the U.S. boundaries westward, new states, particularly in the Midwest, became an important homebase for Presidents. By the 20th century, the West Coast had begun to foster future Presidents, too.

The lives of some Presidents are commemorated at multiple sites. Abraham Lincoln probably lays claim to having more memorials than any other President, in part because he lived in and visited so many spots during his lifetime. Other Presidents leave little more than a gravesite behind. Birthplaces, boyhood homes, even adult residences can fall into disrepair or give way to new

The U.S. landscape is dotted with markers (top) and landmarks connected to the personal histories of the U.S. Presidents. See the accompanying map for a listing of key sites. Among those represented are (above, left to right) the tomb of James K. Polk in Nashville, Tenn., the brand-new Abraham Lincoln Presidential Library and Museum in Springfield, Ill., and the Franklin Delano Roosevelt Memorial in Washington, D.C., which opened in 1997.

Presidential Landmarks

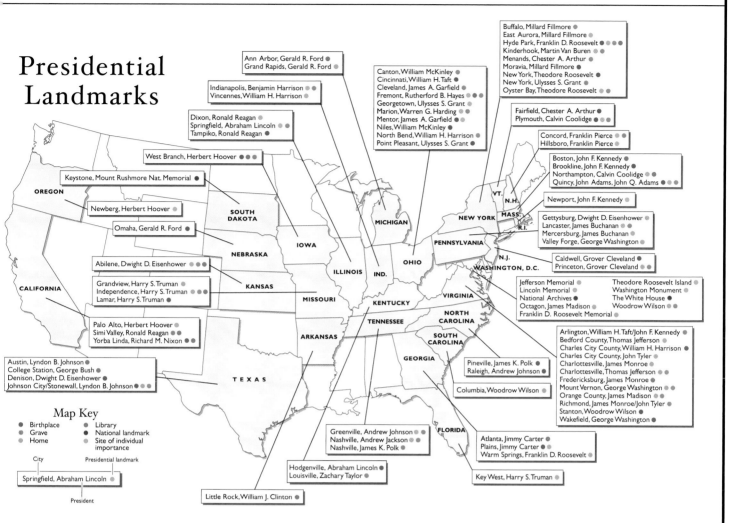

Map Key
- ● Birthplace
- ● Grave
- ● Home
- ● Library
- ● National landmark
- ● Site of individual importance

City   Presidential landmark

Springfield, Abraham Lincoln ●

President

Ann Arbor, Gerald R. Ford ●
Grand Rapids, Gerald R. Ford ●

Indianapolis, Benjamin Harrison ● ●
Vincennes, William H. Harrison ●

Dixon, Ronald Reagan ●
Springfield, Abraham Lincoln ● ●
Tampiko, Ronald Reagan ●

West Branch, Herbert Hoover ● ● ●

Keystone, Mount Rushmore Nat. Memorial ●

Newberg, Herbert Hoover ●

Omaha, Gerald R. Ford ●

Abilene, Dwight D. Eisenhower ● ● ●

Grandview, Harry S. Truman ●
Independence, Harry S. Truman ● ● ●
Lamar, Harry S. Truman ●

Palo Alto, Herbert Hoover ●
Simi Valley, Ronald Reagan ● ●
Yorba Linda, Richard M. Nixon ● ●

Austin, Lyndon B. Johnson ●
College Station, George Bush ●
Denison, Dwight D. Eisenhower ●
Johnson City/Stonewall, Lyndon B. Johnson ● ● ●

Canton, William McKinley ●
Cincinnati, William H. Taft ●
Cleveland, James A. Garfield ●
Fremont, Rutherford B. Hayes ● ● ●
Georgetown, Ulysses S. Grant ●
Marion, Warren G. Harding ● ●
Mentor, James A. Garfield ● ●
Niles, William McKinley ●
North Bend, William H. Harrison ●
Point Pleasant, Ulysses S. Grant ●

Buffalo, Millard Fillmore ●
East Aurora, Millard Fillmore ●
Hyde Park, Franklin D. Roosevelt ● ● ●
Kinderhook, Martin Van Buren ● ●
Menands, Chester A. Arthur ●
Moravia, Millard Fillmore ●
New York, Theodore Roosevelt ● ●
New York, Ulysses S. Grant ●
Oyster Bay, Theodore Roosevelt ● ●

Fairfield, Chester A. Arthur ●
Plymouth, Calvin Coolidge ● ● ●

Concord, Franklin Pierce ● ●
Hillsboro, Franklin Pierce ●

Boston, John F. Kennedy ●
Brookline, John F. Kennedy ●
Northampton, Calvin Coolidge ● ●
Quincy, John Adams, John Q. Adams ● ● ●

Newport, John F. Kennedy ●

Gettysburg, Dwight D. Eisenhower ●
Lancaster, James Buchanan ●
Mercersburg, James Buchanan ●
Valley Forge, George Washington ●

Caldwell, Grover Cleveland ●
Princeton, Grover Cleveland ● ●

Jefferson Memorial ●
Lincoln Memorial ●
National Archives ●
Octagon, James Madison ●
Franklin D. Roosevelt Memorial ●
Theodore Roosevelt Island ●
Washington Monument ●
The White House ●
Woodrow Wilson ● ●

Arlington, William H. Taft/John F. Kennedy ●
Bedford County, Thomas Jefferson ●
Charles City County, William H. Harrison ●
Charles City County, John Tyler ●
Charlottesville, James Monroe ●
Charlottesville, Thomas Jefferson ● ●
Fredericksburg, James Monroe ●
Mount Vernon, George Washington ● ●
Orange County, James Madison ●
Richmond, James Monroe/John Tyler ●
Stanton, Woodrow Wilson ●
Wakefield, George Washington ●

Pineville, James K. Polk ●
Raleigh, Andrew Johnson ●

Columbia, Woodrow Wilson ●

Greenville, Andrew Johnson ●
Nashville, Andrew Jackson ● ●
Nashville, James K. Polk ●

Atlanta, Jimmy Carter ●
Plains, Jimmy Carter ● ●
Warm Springs, Franklin D. Roosevelt ●

Hodgenville, Abraham Lincoln ●
Louisville, Zachary Taylor ●

Key West, Harry S. Truman ●

Little Rock, William J. Clinton ●

construction before their value is ever recognized.

Some presidential landmarks are actually replicas of original structures. They may even be located on different ground than the first buildings. Most log cabin homes are copies, for example. The furnishings in landmark buildings may not be original either, although they may mimic known pieces of furniture, wallpaper designs, and so on. Even with these modifications, the sites help visitors imagine what life might have been like for the Presidents.

In 1940, while still President, Franklin D. Roosevelt began the tradition of creating presidential libraries. Every President since then has established a presidential library, either during or following his administration. Presidential libraries have also been established for two earlier Presidents, Abraham Lincoln (in Illinois) and Herbert Hoover (in Iowa).

Presidential libraries may be located near important home sites, at academic institutions, or in major cities of importance to the President. These sites hold the presidential papers, or the important documents of a leader's administration. Historians and other visitors study the thousands of pages of paper that make up each collection. The libraries acquire other material from the personal, professional, and family history of the Presidents, too. Collections include everything from Dwight D. Eisenhower's military souvenirs to Presidents' favorite artworks to official gifts received while in office to Herbert Hoover's fishing gear. Staff members use these extensive holdings to create exhibits for the general public about the Presidents' lives.

James A. Garfield

NICKNAME	Preacher President
BORN	Nov. 19, 1831, near Orange, Ohio
POLITICAL PARTY	Republican
CHIEF OPPONENT	Winfield Scott Hancock, Democrat (1824–1886)
TERM OF OFFICE	March 4, 1881–Sept. 19, 1881
AGE AT INAUGURATION	49 years old
NUMBER OF TERMS	one (cut short by assassination)
VICE PRESIDENT	Chester A. Arthur (1829–1886)
FIRST LADY	Lucretia Rudolph Garfield (1832–1918), wife (married Nov. 11, 1858)
CHILDREN	Harry, James, Mary, Irvin, Abram, plus a son and a daughter died young
GEOGRAPHIC SCENE	38 states
NEW STATES ADDED	none
DIED	Sept. 19, 1881, in Elberon, N.J.
AGE AT DEATH	49 years old
SELECTED LANDMARKS	Lawnfield, Garfield National Historic Site, Mentor, Ohio (birthplace and replica homestead); Lake View Cemetery, Cleveland, Ohio

James A. Garfield became the second President to die by assassination, and the fourth to die in office. X rays, surgery, and antibiotics might have saved him, had they been available.

J AMES A. GARFIELD, like William Henry Harrison, barely had a chance to establish himself as President before death removed him from office. He was shot by an assassin early in his term and died 79 days later.

Garfield was the last President born in a log cabin. His election followed notable service as an educator, soldier, and statesman. A graduate of Williams College in Massachusetts, Garfield returned to his home state of Ohio to be a college professor. Later he became a lawyer, Ohio state senator, Civil War colonel, and U.S. congressman. Garfield served 18 years in the House of Representatives before receiving his unexpected nomination for President in 1880. He became known as the "Preacher President" for his talents at public speaking.

As President, Garfield surprised legislators by how diligently he sought to end political corruption, or improper influence, especially among his own Republican Party. He refused to be bullied by powerful party leaders in the Senate when making political appointments; in the end, two senators resigned, and he got his own way. Garfield fought similar battles on a smaller scale at the White House. The place swarmed with job hunters. People expected to be rewarded with posts in Garfield's administration because they had supported the Republican Party.

One disappointed and mentally ill job hunter shadowed Garfield and his staff for weeks. He shot the President at a Washington, D.C., train station on July 2, 1881. Although Garfield survived the initial wound, the bullet could not be removed, and he died from complications two and a half months later. His assassin was tried and hanged. Reacting to Garfield's murder, lawmakers wrote new rules for how to fill many government posts. These jobs were to be given as a reward for talent and experience, not political favors.

James A. Garfield was the nation's first left-handed President. He was actually ambidextrous, or able to write with either hand. Friends said he could write Latin with one hand and Greek with the other hand—at the same time! Garfield had considered a career as a sailor until he fell overboard while working on a canal boat and caught a bad cold. A nonswimmer, he decided to teach instead.

Chester A. Arthur

21ST PRESIDENT OF THE UNITED STATES ★ 1881 – 1885

NICKNAME	Elegant Arthur
BORN	Oct. 5, 1829, in Fairfield, Vt.
POLITICAL PARTY	Republican
CHIEF OPPONENT	none; succeeded Garfield
TERM OF OFFICE	Sept. 20, 1881–March 3, 1885
AGE AT INAUGURATION	51 years old
NUMBER OF TERMS	one (partial)
VICE PRESIDENT	none
FIRST LADY	Mary Arthur McElroy (1842–1917), sister
WIFE	Ellen Lewis Herndon Arthur (1837–1880), married Oct. 25, 1859
CHILDREN	Chester, Ellen, plus a son died young
GEOGRAPHIC SCENE	38 states
NEW STATES ADDED	none
DIED	Nov. 18, 1886, in New York, N.Y.
AGE AT DEATH	57 years old
SELECTED LANDMARKS	Fairfield, Vt. (reconstructed birthplace); Albany Rural Cemetery, Menands, N.Y.

Chester Arthur's wife died the year before he became President. His sister served as First Lady and helped him care for his younger child, 13-year-old Nell (above). "Elegant Arthur" changed clothes for each occasion of the day; he was said to own 80 pairs of pants.

MANY CITIZENS WERE AS SHOCKED at the thought of Chester Alan Arthur becoming President as they were by the shooting of his predecessor, James A. Garfield. Once again—as with John Tyler, Millard Fillmore, and Andrew Johnson—a Vice President chosen for political reasons instead of leadership skills became President.

Arthur had never been elected to public office until he became James Garfield's Vice President. Born in Vermont, Arthur was a graduate of Union College in New York and an attorney. In 1871 he was made collector of the port of New York City and was responsible for collecting import fees for goods arriving at the nation's busiest harbor. Arthur built his personal and political fortune there by using the "spoils system" and "machine politics." He awarded jobs, raises, and favorable regulations (the spoils) to employees and businesses who supported his political candidates with their votes and donations (the vote-buying "machine" that influenced elections). This favoritism led the *New York Times* to call his pre-White House career a "mess of filth."

Arthur was deeply shocked that Garfield had been shot by someone caught up in the greed of machine politics. As President, he angered old friends and surprised the nation by supporting passage of the Pendleton Act. This legislation created a Civil Service Commission to oversee the government's civilian (nonmilitary) workers. It established procedures to ensure that a core of basic federal jobs were filled by competitive exam, not presidential appointment. It also protected these employees from being fired because of their political views.

After Arthur learned that he suffered from a fatal kidney disease, he did not care if he was renominated for a second term (he was not). Arthur retired to New York City. He died 20 months later.

Chester Arthur visited Yellowstone National Park (right) in 1883. Arthur modernized the U.S. Navy by ordering the construction of four steel warships.

Grover Cleveland

22ND AND 24TH PRESIDENT OF THE UNITED STATES
1885 – 1889 ★ 1893 – 1897

NICKNAME	Uncle Jumbo
BORN	March 18, 1837, in Caldwell, N.J.
POLITICAL PARTY	Democrat
CHIEF OPPONENTS	1st administration: James Gillespie Blaine, Republican (1830–1893); 2nd administration: President Benjamin Harrison, Republican (1833–1901)
TERM OF OFFICE	1st administration: March 4, 1885–March 3, 1889; 2nd administration: March 4, 1893–March 3, 1897
AGE AT INAUGURATION	1st administration: 47 years old; 2nd administration: 55 years old
NUMBER OF TERMS	two (nonconsecutive)
VICE PRESIDENTS	1st administration: Thomas Andrews Hendricks (1819–1885); 2nd administration: Adlai Ewing Stevenson (1835–1914)

The Clevelands aboard the presidential train

FIRST LADIES	Rose Elizabeth Cleveland (1846–1918), sister; Frances Folsom Cleveland (1864–1947), wife (married June 2, 1886)
CHILDREN	Ruth, Esther, Marion, Richard, Frances
GEOGRAPHIC SCENE	1st administration: 38 states; 2nd administration: 44 states
NEW STATES ADDED	Utah (1896)
DIED	June 24, 1908, in Princeton, N.J.
AGE AT DEATH	71 years old
SELECTED LANDMARKS	Caldwell, N.J. (birthplace); Westland (home) and Princeton Cemetery, Princeton, N.J.

GROVER CLEVELAND WAS THE FIRST DEMOCRAT to be elected President after the Civil War. Although he lost his reelection bid in 1888 to Benjamin Harrison, he returned to the White House four years later after winning a rematch in the 1892 election. Thus, Cleveland is the only President to serve two nonconsecutive terms of office. His disregard of popular and political opinion cost him reelection after each term.

Cleveland's political career developed rapidly; he went from county sheriff to U.S. President in only 11 years. Although born in New Jersey, he grew up in New York State, the son of a Presbyterian minister. His school years ended at age 16 with the death of his father. Eventually Cleveland studied law and entered into private practice in Buffalo, New York. His firm hand as the local sheriff led citizens to elect him mayor. Cleveland succeeded so well at ending corruption, waste, and scandal that he was nominated for governor of New York. He won by a landslide. His popularity in New York State made him a natural candidate for President in 1884.

Gossip and scandal fueled the presidential campaign. Republicans were delighted to discover that the bachelor Cleveland might have fathered a child. They chanted: "Ma, Ma, where's my Pa? Gone to the White House, ha, ha, ha!" However, the public seemed less concerned about Cleveland's private life than about the professional actions of his opponent. Democrats joked about "James Blaine, James Blaine the continental liar from the state of Maine." Cleveland claimed "Public Office Is a Public Trust." Republican "Mugwumps" (an Indian word meaning "big chief") deserted their own party's candidate and favored him instead. Cleveland narrowly won the race.

During his first administration, Cleveland vetoed more than twice as many pieces of legislation (413 total) as had all previous Presidents combined. As with Andrew Johnson two decades earlier,

Grover Cleveland, who weighed 250 pounds, was nicknamed "Uncle Jumbo." He was the first President since the Civil War who had not fought in that conflict. Cleveland avoided military service then by paying a Polish immigrant $150 to take his place. Although this practice was legal, it was not considered admirable. As a presidential candidate, Cleveland was criticized for avoiding combat.

Grover Cleveland's campaign banner (above) emphasized his party's ties to well-known Democratic Presidents of the past, such as Thomas Jefferson and Andrew Jackson. His two administrations were interrupted by the single term of Benjamin Harrison. Cleveland delivered his Inaugural Addresses from the East Portico of the U.S. Capitol (right).

critics called him "The Veto President." Children sang: "A fat man once sat in the President's chair, singing 'Ve-to,' 'Ve-to.'" Although Cleveland worked hard to hire loyal Democrats to fill government posts, other party members were often angered by his choices. He was more popular for his unexpected marriage, at age 49, to 21-year-old Frances Folsom, the daughter of a deceased friend.

During the election of 1888, Cleveland again won a greater share of the popular vote than his opponent. However, the Presidency went to Benjamin Harrison because he earned the most electoral votes. The story goes that the departing First Lady assured the White House staff that she and her husband would return after the next election. They did. Cleveland won by a sizable margin in both popular and electoral voting when he faced Harrison in 1892.

Grover Cleveland became the only President to marry at the White House (left) when he wed Frances Folsom during his first administration. The couple changed their wedding vows so Frances could pledge to "love, honor, and keep" her husband instead of agreeing to "love, honor, and obey" him. Their first child, nicknamed "Baby Ruth," had a candy bar named after her. Their second child, Esther (right), was the only child of a President born in the White House.

> "What is the use of being elected or reelected unless you stand for something?"
>
> Grover Cleveland, 1887

Grover Cleveland hunted with a rifle he nicknamed "Death and Destruction." The President was forced to take a break from outdoor recreation in 1893 after developing mouth cancer. To avoid media attention, Frances Cleveland arranged for doctors to operate on the President aboard a private yacht. Doctors removed the tumor and part of Cleveland's jaw, then inserted a rubber shape to take the place of the missing bone. They left no visible scars. Some two dozen years passed before news of the operation leaked out.

Public support of Cleveland began to fall soon after his reelection, however, with the start of a new round of economic hard times. The Panic of 1893 lasted for the rest of Cleveland's Presidency and brought widespread suffering. Cleveland argued with Congress over what, if anything, to do. Should the government issue more money, or less money, or should it do nothing? Should paper money continue to be worth a standard amount of gold? Should extra money be created in the form of silver coins? Was it better for the government to hoard precious metals or to share them? No one was quite sure how all the elements of national finance influenced one another, so it was hard to know what might help end the panic. Meanwhile, politicians gave little thought to the suffering of the nation's citizens. Some people joked that if a hungry man started eating grass on the White House lawn, Cleveland, instead of offering him food, would suggest he move to the backyard, where the grass was taller.

By the next election, Democrats were ready for a new candidate, and the public was ready for an entirely different party. Republicans, who had dominated the Presidency since the Civil War, became the favored party again. Except for Cleveland and Woodrow Wilson, Republicans controlled the White House from 1861 until 1933.

Cleveland retired to New Jersey and became a lecturer and trustee for Princeton University. His dying words, 11 years after leaving the White House, were: "I have tried so hard to do right."

The Clevelands (from left to right: Esther, Frances, Mrs. Cleveland, Ruth, Richard, and the former President) posed for a family snapshot on the porch of the President's retirement home in New Jersey. Frances outlived her husband by 39 years. She became the first widow of a President to remarry when she wed a professor in 1913.

Presidential Facts and Comparisons

★ *A Look at the Stats* ★

George Washington tried false teeth of silver, ivory, cow's teeth, and more. Contrary to legend, wood was never used.

FORTY-TWO MEN have served their nation as President in 43 administrations. (Grover Cleveland is counted twice—once for each of his two separate Presidencies.) The oldest President on taking office was Ronald Reagan, age 69; the youngest was Theodore Roosevelt, age 42. The nation's second oldest President, William Henry Harrison, served the shortest term in office—32 days. Franklin D. Roosevelt served the longest term; he was elected four times and was President for 12 years before dying in office at age 63.

Eight Presidents were born in Virginia, earning that state the nickname "Mother of Presidents." Many Presidents have come from Massachusetts, New York, and Ohio, too. In all, 23 Presidents were born in one of those four states. Some half-dozen Presidents were born in log cabins; Jimmy Carter was the first President born in a hospital. About half of the Presidents were sons of farmers.

Warren G. Harding throws out the first pitch of the baseball season. William Howard Taft began this presidential tradition in 1910.

Nine Presidents have failed to complete their terms of office. Eight died on the job. One, Richard M. Nixon, resigned from office because of political scandal.

During the course of the nation's history, the presidential salary has grown from $25,000 a year (for George Washington) to $400,000 a year (for George W. Bush). Each President receives a significant expense allowance, too.

All but nine of the Presidents attended college; 30 were college graduates. More than half of all Presidents were members of the armed services, although not all witnessed combat. Eleven

In 1974 Richard M. Nixon (far left) became the only U.S. President to resign from office. In the previous century, members of Congress had tried unsuccessfully to remove Andrew Johnson from office. Special tickets to his impeachment trial (left) allowed visitors to watch the proceedings at the U.S. Capitol.

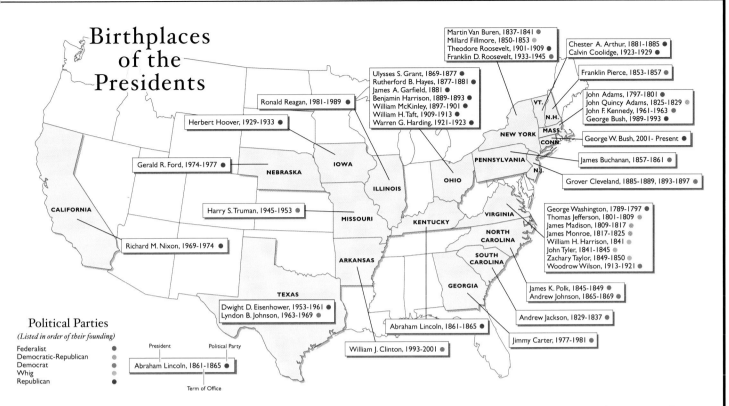

Birthplaces of the Presidents

Martin Van Buren, 1837-1841 ●
Millard Fillmore, 1850-1853 ●
Theodore Roosevelt, 1901-1909 ●
Franklin D. Roosevelt, 1933-1945 ●

Chester A. Arthur, 1881-1885 ●
Calvin Coolidge, 1923-1929 ●

Franklin Pierce, 1853-1857 ●

Ulysses S. Grant, 1869-1877 ●
Rutherford B. Hayes, 1877-1881 ●
James A. Garfield, 1881 ●
Benjamin Harrison, 1889-1893 ●
William McKinley, 1897-1901 ●
William H. Taft, 1909-1913 ●
Warren G. Harding, 1921-1923 ●

John Adams, 1797-1801 ●
John Quincy Adams, 1825-1829 ●
John F. Kennedy, 1961-1963 ●
George Bush, 1989-1993 ●

George W. Bush, 2001- Present ●

Ronald Reagan, 1981-1989 ●

Herbert Hoover, 1929-1933 ●

VT.

N.H.

NEW YORK

MASS.

CONN.

James Buchanan, 1857-1861 ●

Gerald R. Ford, 1974-1977 ●

NEBRASKA

IOWA

ILLINOIS

OHIO

PENNSYLVANIA

N.J.

Grover Cleveland, 1885-1889, 1893-1897 ●

CALIFORNIA

Harry S. Truman, 1945-1953 ●

MISSOURI

KENTUCKY

VIRGINIA

NORTH CAROLINA

George Washington, 1789-1797 ●
Thomas Jefferson, 1801-1809 ●
James Madison, 1809-1817 ●
James Monroe, 1817-1825 ●
William H. Harrison, 1841 ●
John Tyler, 1841-1845 ●
Zachary Taylor, 1849-1850 ●
Woodrow Wilson, 1913-1921 ●

Richard M. Nixon, 1969-1974 ●

ARKANSAS

SOUTH CAROLINA

James K. Polk, 1845-1849 ●
Andrew Johnson, 1865-1869 ●

GEORGIA

Andrew Jackson, 1829-1837 ●

TEXAS

Dwight D. Eisenhower, 1953-1961 ●
Lyndon B. Johnson, 1963-1969 ●

Abraham Lincoln, 1861-1865 ●

Jimmy Carter, 1977-1981 ●

William J. Clinton, 1993-2001 ●

Political Parties
(Listed in order of their founding)

Federalist ●
Democratic-Republican ●
Democrat ●
Whig ●
Republican ●

President　　　　Political Party

Abraham Lincoln, 1861-1865 ●

Term of Office

Presidents were former generals. Fourteen Presidents were first Vice President of the country. Two dozen had served in the U.S. Congress. Seventeen were governors before becoming President. Twenty-five had studied law and become attorneys. Other prepresidential occupations include farmer, teacher, journalist, college professor, actor, engineer, and tailor.

Presidents have enjoyed hobbies including fishing, golf, and stamp collecting. Two played the piano (Harry S. Truman and Richard M. Nixon); two played the violin (Thomas Jefferson and John Tyler). Calvin Coolidge's instrument was the harmonica. Bill Clinton played the saxophone.

Most Presidents have been affiliated with Protestant churches, including 12 Episcopalians and 7 Presbyterians. Three Presidents, including Thomas Jefferson and Abraham Lincoln, listed no preferred religious affiliation. No one of non-Christian faith has yet served as President.

Some Presidents have enjoyed only brief retirements: James K. Polk died 103 days after his term ended. Herbert Hoover enjoyed the longest retirement: 31 years. Ronald Reagan lived to be older than any other President: 93 years. John F. Kennedy died at the youngest age: 46. Three Presidents died on Independence Day: John Adams, Thomas Jefferson, and James Monroe.

Gerald R. Ford is the only Eagle Scout to become a U.S. President. Folding the national flag (right) was one of his duties while camping with other Boy Scouts during his youth.

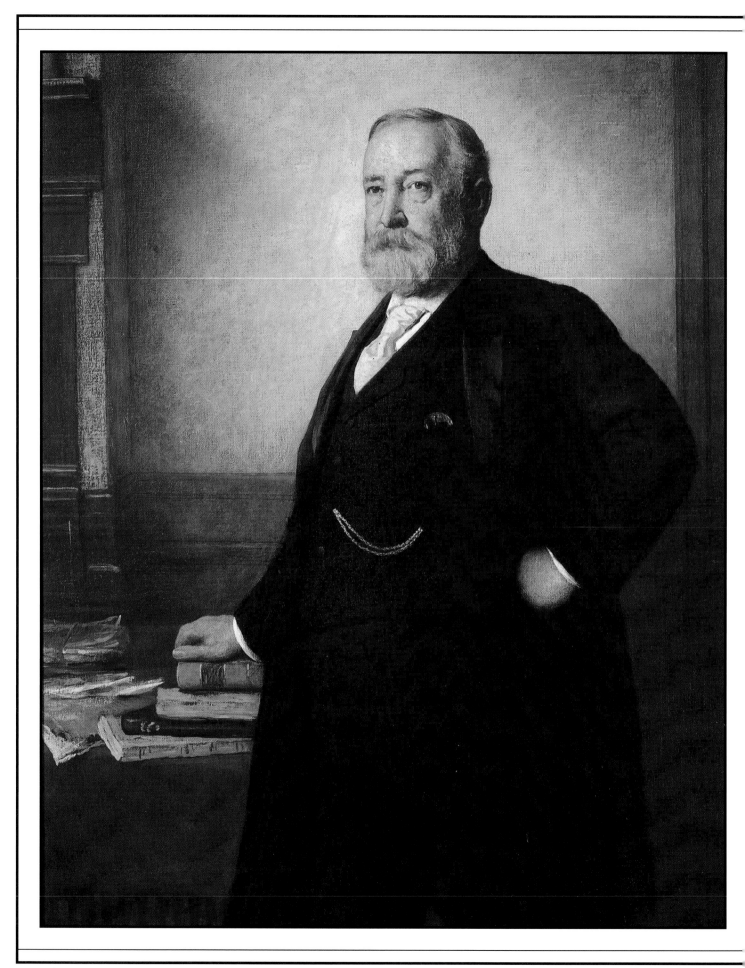

Benjamin Harrison

23RD PRESIDENT OF THE UNITED STATES ★ *1889 – 1893*

NICKNAME	Little Ben
BORN	Aug. 20, 1833, in North Bend, Ohio
POLITICAL PARTY	Republican
CHIEF OPPONENT	President Grover Cleveland, Democrat (1837–1908)
TERM OF OFFICE	March 4, 1889–March 3, 1893
AGE AT INAUGURATION	55 years old
NUMBER OF TERMS	one
VICE PRESIDENT	Levi Parsons Morton (1824–1920)
FIRST LADIES	Caroline Lavinia Scott Harrison (1832–1892), wife (married Oct. 20, 1853); Mary Scott Harrison McKee (1858–1930), daughter
SECOND WIFE	Mary Scott Lord Dimmick Harrison (1858–1948), married April 6, 1896
CHILDREN	Russell, Mary, Elizabeth
GEOGRAPHIC SCENE	38 states
NEW STATES ADDED	Montana, North Dakota, South Dakota, and Washington (1889); Idaho and Wyoming (1890)
DIED	March 13, 1901, in Indianapolis, Ind.
AGE AT DEATH	67 years old
SELECTED LANDMARKS	Indianapolis, Ind. (home); Crown Hill Cemetery, Indianapolis, Ind.

Harrison facing the latest round of office seekers

BENJAMIN HARRISON'S SINGLE TERM of office was sandwiched between the two presidential terms of Grover Cleveland. Harrison and Cleveland competed for the Presidency in the consecutive elections of 1888 and 1892. In both cases Cleveland won the popular vote. However, Harrison was awarded the Presidency in 1888 after receiving a majority of electoral college votes.

Harrison grew up in the shadow of another resident of the White House—his grandfather. "Little Ben" was a seven-year-old boy living in Ohio when William Henry Harrison became President. The younger Harrison went on to graduate from Ohio's Miami University and become an attorney in Indiana. He served one term in the U.S. Senate before being nominated for President.

Harrison, as was customary at the time, chose to run a low-key campaign. He spoke only to the crowds who were encouraged to gather at his home in Indianapolis. For one campaign stunt, 40,000 drummers from 11 states were organized to visit him. Harrison's well-financed campaign earned him victories in enough key states so that he topped his opponent in the electoral college. Cleveland's slim lead in popular votes—about 90,000—became irrelevant.

As President, Harrison authorized the first peacetime federal budget to reach the $1 billion mark. This money improved harbors, established naval fleets on both U.S. coasts, and helped pay the costs of building steamship lines. More states were added to the nation during Harrison's single administration than during any other Presidency.

Harrison lost his reelection bid to Cleveland. He returned to Indianapolis a widower, his wife having died of tuberculosis the previous year. He resumed his law practice and married his late wife's niece. He died of pneumonia five years later.

As a Union officer in the Civil War (above), Harrison fought in more battles in one month than his famous grandfather had in a lifetime. They are the only grandfather-grandson pair of Presidents.

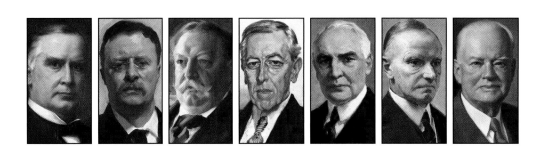

AMERICA TAKES CENTER STAGE

★ *1897 – 1933* ★

circa 1890s

By the late 19th century, labor-saving inventions such as the mechanical washing machine were changing the way families handled routine household chores.

1903

Wilbur and Orville Wright made the first successful airplane flight—12 seconds long—on December 17. Only two dozen years later, Charles Lindberg would fly solo across the Atlantic.

1906

An earthquake and subsequent fires leveled much of San Francisco. Neighboring communities were hit, too; 50 miles away the Santa Rosa Courthouse collapsed.

1912

The "unsinkable" Titanic went down on its first voyage after it struck an iceberg in the North Atlantic Ocean on April 14. More than 1,500 people died.

U.S. Presidents took firm control of the federal government at the start of the 20th century. They helped develop the United States into a global power, both economically and politically. The era featured fantastic advances in science, technology, transportation, and exploration. Leaders were challenged to expand the rights of citizens and curb the power of businesses. They struggled to cope with worldwide war and widespread economic suffering, too. Public opinion of federal policies played a central role in national elections.

1913–1920

Women intensified their efforts to gain suffrage, or voting rights. In 1920 an amendment finally granted all female U.S. citizens the right to vote.

1914–1918

U.S. forces entered World War I during 1917. Their presence helped win the war. Nearly 10 million people, including 100,000 Americans, died worldwide.

1920s

People celebrated increased peace and prosperity during the "Roaring Twenties." Flappers danced the Charleston as fashions, behaviors, and outlooks changed.

1930s

A decade of economic suffering followed the stock market collapse of October 1929. Citizens who had lost their jobs and even their homes sought free food in breadlines.

William McKinley

NICKNAME	Idol of Ohio
BORN	Jan. 29, 1843, in Niles, Ohio
POLITICAL PARTY	Republican
CHIEF OPPONENT	1st and 2nd terms: William Jennings Bryan, Democrat (1860–1925)
TERM OF OFFICE	March 4, 1897–Sept. 14, 1901
AGE AT INAUGURATION	54 years old
NUMBER OF TERMS	two (cut short by assassination)
VICE PRESIDENTS	1st term: Garret Augustus Hobart (1844–1899); 2nd term: Theodore Roosevelt (1858–1919)
FIRST LADY	Ida Saxton McKinley (1847–1907), wife (married Jan. 25, 1871)
CHILDREN	two daughters died young
GEOGRAPHIC SCENE	45 states
NEW STATES ADDED	none
DIED	Sept. 14, 1901, in Buffalo, N.Y.
AGE AT DEATH	58 years old
SELECTED LANDMARKS	National McKinley Birthplace Memorial, Niles, Ohio; McKinley Museum and McKinley National Memorial (grave), Canton, Ohio

When McKinley was Ohio's governor, each day at 3 p.m. he waved to his wife from his office window, and Ida McKinley replied from their home across the street.

WILLIAM MCKINLEY WAS THE LAST CHIEF EXECUTIVE who fought in the Civil War. However, McKinley's witness of an earlier era did not stop him from pushing the nation and his office into modern times. He did everything from use telephones on a regular basis to expand the political influence of the United States around the globe. Early in his second term, McKinley became the fifth President to die in office, and the third one to be assassinated.

The state of Ohio sent five of her sons, including McKinley, to the White House in 28 years. (Two more followed him over the next 24 years.) As a youth, McKinley played Army games with friends or went fishing, ice skating, and horseback riding. He attended public schools where he excelled at speech making, and he studied briefly at Allegheny College in Pennsylvania. He served in the Civil War under future President Rutherford B. Hayes. Despite four years of duty, he escaped all injury and illness. Twice he won promotions for acts of bravery. After the war McKinley took up the study of law and became an attorney. His final wartime rank of major remained his nickname among close friends for years.

"The Major" spent a dozen years in the U.S. House of Representatives and gained national notice for his McKinley Tariff legislation. Once implemented, however, this tax on imported goods brought unexpectedly high prices to consumer goods at home. Many Republicans, including McKinley and President Benjamin Harrison, lost their elected posts as a result. Nonetheless, McKinley persuaded Ohioans to elect him as their governor two years later. He served two terms before being nominated for President in 1896. McKinley

---

William McKinley (above, on election banner) was the only President between Andrew Johnson and Woodrow Wilson not to have facial hair. He liked to wear a red carnation in the buttonhole of his jacket. Ohio went so far as to make this bloom its official flower in honor of the "Idol of Ohio." McKinley liked cigars, too. Sometimes he broke one in two and chewed the halves instead of smoking the whole cigar.

defeated his opponent, William Jennings Bryan, in part because he spent five times as much money during the campaign as his rival. Bryan, a noted orator, traveled 18,000 miles around the country during a three-month-long speaking tour. McKinley, as Benjamin Harrison had done in 1888, ran a "front porch" campaign from his home in Ohio and relied on others to campaign for him nationally.

As President, McKinley focused on U.S. relations with foreign countries. He started with Spain. This European nation still ruled Cuba and other Caribbean islands near the United States as well as the Philippine Islands in the Pacific. Diplomatic talks gave way to war in 1898 after the suspicious destruction of the U.S. battleship *Maine* while it was anchored near Cuba. Future President Theodore Roosevelt rode to national fame at the head of the Rough Riders once the fighting began. Meanwhile, the U.S. Navy destroyed Spain's Atlantic and Pacific fleets during the four-month-long Spanish-American War.

Combat ended when Spain withdrew its claim to Cuba. Spain put Puerto Rico, Guam, and the Philippine Islands under U.S. control in exchange for a $20 million settlement.

Americans pledged to "Remember the Maine!" (top) by going to war with Spain soon after the ship's destruction. William McKinley helped lead the United States to victory in the Spanish-American War of 1898. Two years later, McKinley gathered with dignitaries to celebrate his second Inauguration (above).

William McKinley proposed linking the Atlantic and Pacific Oceans through Central America by canal (left). President McKinley made full use of new technologies while in office. He communicated with the war front by telegraph, kept in touch with newspaper editors by telephone, and established the first White House press room. He even had telegraph lines installed there so reporters could easily dispatch stories to their newspaper offices. He controlled the slant reporters gave to news by putting his own twist on details released to them. Sometimes he completely censored, or kept secret, certain facts.

Guam and the Philippines gave the United States a Pacific base from which to influence Asian affairs, particularly in China. McKinley further increased the U.S. presence in the Pacific by annexing, or taking over, the Hawaiian Islands. In addition he initiated plans to build the Panama Canal, linking the Atlantic and Pacific Oceans through Central America.

McKinley's first Vice President died in office. Theodore Roosevelt was nominated to fill the job during the election of 1900. Roosevelt talked himself hoarse while campaigning for "Four More Years of the Full Dinner Pail." Buoyed by a strong economy and public satisfaction with the outcome of the war, McKinley triumphed over Bryan again. This time he won by an even greater margin of support.

In the fall of 1901, barely six months into his second administration, McKinley attended the Pan-American Exposition in Buffalo, New York. During the events a lone assassin joined a crowd of spectators waiting to shake the President's hand. When McKinley reached out to greet him, the man fired two shots at the President from a

hidden gun. McKinley died eight days later after developing gangrene from his wounds. The assailant, an unemployed laborer, said he was an anarchist, someone who works to destroy the systems of government. He was convicted of murder and executed.

"War should never be entered upon until every agency of peace has failed."

William McKinley,
First Inaugural Address, March 4, 1897

William McKinley often charmed strangers by presenting them with the carnation he wore on his jacket. Once, when two brothers were introduced to him, he carefully replaced the flower in his buttonhole with a fresh one so each boy could receive a bloom from the President. McKinley had just presented his lapel flower to a young girl when he was shot (right). The President died eight days later.

Theodore Roosevelt

26TH PRESIDENT OF THE UNITED STATES ★ *1901 – 1909*

Theodore Roosevelt

NICKNAME	T.R.
BORN	Oct. 27, 1858, in New York, N.Y.
POLITICAL PARTY	Republican
CHIEF OPPONENTS	1st term: none, succeeded McKinley; 2nd term: Alton Brooks Parker, Democrat (1852–1926)
TERM OF OFFICE	Sept. 14, 1901–March 3, 1909
AGE AT INAUGURATION	42 years old
NUMBER OF TERMS	one, plus balance of William McKinley's term
VICE PRESIDENTS	1st term: none; 2nd term: Charles Warren Fairbanks (1852–1918)
FIRST LADY	Edith Kermit Carow Roosevelt (1861–1948), second wife (married Dec. 2, 1886)
FIRST WIFE	Alice Hathaway Lee Roosevelt (1861–1884), married Oct. 27, 1880
CHILDREN	Alice, Theodore, Kermit, Ethel, Archibald, Quentin
GEOGRAPHIC SCENE	45 states
NEW STATES ADDED	Oklahoma (1907)
DIED	Jan. 6, 1919, in Oyster Bay, N.Y.
AGE AT DEATH	60 years old
SELECTED LANDMARKS	New York, N.Y. (birthplace); Sagamore Hill National Historic Site (homestead) and Young's Memorial Cemetery, Oyster Bay, N.Y.; Theodore Roosevelt Island, Washington, D.C.; Mount Rushmore National Memorial, Keystone, S. Dak.

Theodore Roosevelt wrote more than 30 books.

THEODORE ROOSEVELT TOOK CHARGE of the White House after the assassination of William McKinley. He filled it with his own personality and vision. He was the first "accidental" President to later win outright election to the office. During his tenure he expanded the reach of the U.S. government into such areas as industry, labor, the environment, consumer rights, and foreign affairs.

Few Presidents, if any, could compete with the unique background that Roosevelt brought to the White House. He was the son of a wealthy New York family. Sickly and asthmatic, he was schooled at home. Finally "Teedie's" father encouraged him to improve his health through vigorous physical exercise. By the time he attended Harvard University he was fit enough to compete in the campus boxing program. Roosevelt graduated with honors, married, and became a member of New York's state assembly.

Then tragedy struck. Roosevelt's mother and wife both died from illnesses on the same October day in 1884. Roosevelt took his grief to the western United States and worked as a cowboy and a rancher. Locals came to respect "Four Eyes" as the East Coast "dude" whose strongest curse was "By Godfrey!" Roosevelt did not hesitate to punch out an offensive cowboy, fire a dishonest ranch hand, or capture thieves.

In the fall of 1886 Roosevelt returned to East Coast life. He remarried, took up writing, and reentered public service. He worked on the U.S. Civil Service Commission for Benjamin Harrison, headed the

Not since Thomas Jefferson had a President enjoyed as many talents and diverse interests as Theodore Roosevelt. He loved being active outdoors (above). Roosevelt would swim through shark-infested waters to explore a shipwreck or lead cross-country hikes on an unwavering straight course, taking each obstacle as a fresh challenge. After being wounded by an assassin during his 1912 presidential campaign, Roosevelt insisted on speaking for nearly an hour, dripping blood, before seeking medical care. The folded copy of his speech and his metal eyeglass case had slowed the path of the bullet and prevented the wound from being too severe.

New York City Police Board, and served as William McKinley's assistant secretary of the Navy. When the Spanish-American War broke out, Roosevelt recruited a volunteer company of cowboys, college football players, New York City police officers, and Native Americans. Roosevelt's "Rough Riders" became famous for their charge near San Juan Hill in Cuba. Roosevelt was elected governor of New York after the war. In 1901 Roosevelt became Vice President and then President. He won outright election to the post in 1904.

Theodore Roosevelt posed with his Rough Riders atop San Juan Hill after their famous charge during the Spanish-American War.

> ## "Speak softly and carry a big stick; you will go far."
>
> Theodore Roosevelt's version of an African saying

Roosevelt's political background as an administrator prepared him to take aggressive charge of the office. He expanded the role of the national government in protecting the lives of its citizens. He went head to head with large corporations that had formed monopolies, called trusts, in railroad, beef, oil, tobacco, and other industries. Trusts had become so powerful from lack of competition that citizens and workers were suffering from high prices, low wages, and poor working conditions. Roosevelt became known as a "trustbuster" for breaking up these monopolies.

In other domestic affairs Roosevelt forced coal mine owners to settle labor disputes with 150,000 striking miners by threatening to have the government take control of the mines. He set aside vast areas of the country for conservation and resource development. He increased safety standards for the preparation of meat, other food products, and medicine.

In foreign policy Roosevelt outlined what became known as "Big Stick Diplomacy." He declared that the United States would serve as "an international police power" throughout the Western

Seven Rough Riders helped Theodore Roosevelt campaign to become governor of New York. At campaign stops (left), a bugler even sounded the cavalry charge. Roosevelt's second wife, Edith (below), served as his personal secretary when he was President. She gathered information to help her husband during the treaty negotiations that earned him a Nobel Peace Prize.

Theodore Roosevelt continued the work started by his predecessor for the construction of the Panama Canal, a waterway connecting the Atlantic and Pacific Oceans across Central America. He visited the construction site in 1906 (left). During his retirement years he spent seven months exploring the River of Doubt in the jungles of Brazil (right). He suffered periodically from malaria and other ailments during the trip and for the rest of his life.

Hemisphere of the globe if it felt threatened by other nations. He proved an effective mediator in disputes among other nations, too. He won the Nobel Peace Prize in 1905 for his role in negotiating an end to war between Russia and Japan.

Roosevelt, the youngest man ever to become President, was very much a family man when he entered the White House. His eldest daughter, Alice, was married there. His younger children grew up in its corridors and on its grounds. Once a son and his friends disrupted work at a nearby government building by using mirrors to bounce sunlight through the windows. When informed about the problem, Roosevelt, always playful, arranged for someone at the office building to send the boys a

message with signal flags: "Attack on this building must immediately cease...." A friend observed: "You must always remember that the President is about six."

Roosevelt left the White House in 1909. On an extended safari in Africa he collected hundreds of animals for the Smithsonian Institution. He made an unsuccessful attempt to regain the White House in 1912 by running as a third-party candidate for the Progressive, or Bull Moose, Party. Roosevelt's offer to raise a fighting force during World War I was refused, but all four of his sons joined the service. The combat death of his youngest son, Quentin, left Roosevelt shaken. With his health deteriorating, he died the following year.

Theodore Roosevelt (above with envoys of Japan and Russia) is known for being first at many things, both great and trivial. He was the first President to travel by car and submarine while in office. During his retirement years, he became the first President to ride in an airplane. He was the first President to have his initials become his nickname. He made the first overseas trip by a sitting President (to Panama). He was the first President and American to be awarded a Nobel Peace Prize. The teddy bear was named after Roosevelt by a toymaker who heard how he had spared the life of a bear cub during a hunting trip.

Kids in the White House

★ At Home in the Spotlight ★

THE FIRST RESIDENTS of the White House—John and Abigail Adams—were also the first occupants to bring children to the President's home. Their four-year-old granddaughter, Susanna, traveled with her grandmother to stay at the residence in 1800. A parade of children has continued to live there off and on ever since.

In 1806 Thomas Jefferson's grandson James became the first baby born in the President's home. Grover Cleveland is the only President to have one of his own children born in the White House. His daughter Esther was born there in 1893.

In 1861 the Lincolns were the first family to bring young children of their own to live in the White House. Among other antics, Tad Lincoln set up a White House refreshment stand, shot his toy cannon at the President's office door, and rode through a tea party in the East Room on a chair pulled by his pet goats.

Theodore Roosevelt brought five young children with him to the White House in 1901. These youngsters roller-skated in the East Room, "sledded" down White House staircases on serving trays, and surrounded themselves with pets—including snakes, a badger, raccoons, pigs, parrots, baby bears, and a young lion. Their father noted: "I don't think that any family has ever enjoyed the White House more than we have."

Theodore Roosevelt's youngest sons, Archie and Quentin, liked to join the daily roll call for the White House police (above). Willie and Tad Lincoln were an earlier pair of brothers who roamed freely in the President's home. They knew just how to cause chaos there by ringing various bells to call White House servants.

James A. Garfield's sons had pillow fights aboard velocipedes in the White House East Room (left). Quentin Roosevelt rode his pony, Algonquin (center), while growing up in the Executive Mansion. Once he brought his pet on the White House elevator so the pair could visit his brother, Archie, who was laid up with measles. The grandchildren of Benjamin Harrison took wagon rides behind a goat on the White House lawn (right).

The children of most Presidents are already grown up or are away in college by the time their parents move into the White House. Some of these young adults have been active campaigners for their fathers. In recent years, three Presidents—John F. Kennedy, Jimmy Carter, and Bill Clinton—have brought younger children with them to the White House. As parents they sheltered their children from public attention while encouraging them to "just be kids" in their home. Caroline Kennedy rode the grounds on her pony, Macaroni, and Amy Carter played in her own tree house. Since the days of Woodrow Wilson, Secret Service agents have acted as bodyguards for children of the Presidents—even out on dates! If the public spotlight ever gets too bright, presidential children can always find refuge back home in the White House.

In 1971 Tricia Nixon became the eighth and most recent presidential daughter to marry at the White House; Maria Monroe was the first in 1820. John F. Kennedy, Jr., liked to hide under his father's desk in the Oval Office (left). Chelsea Clinton accompanied her parents on some of their official trips abroad (below, left). Even family pets earn notice, like Barney (below, right) who gained his own Web site during George W. Bush's presidency.

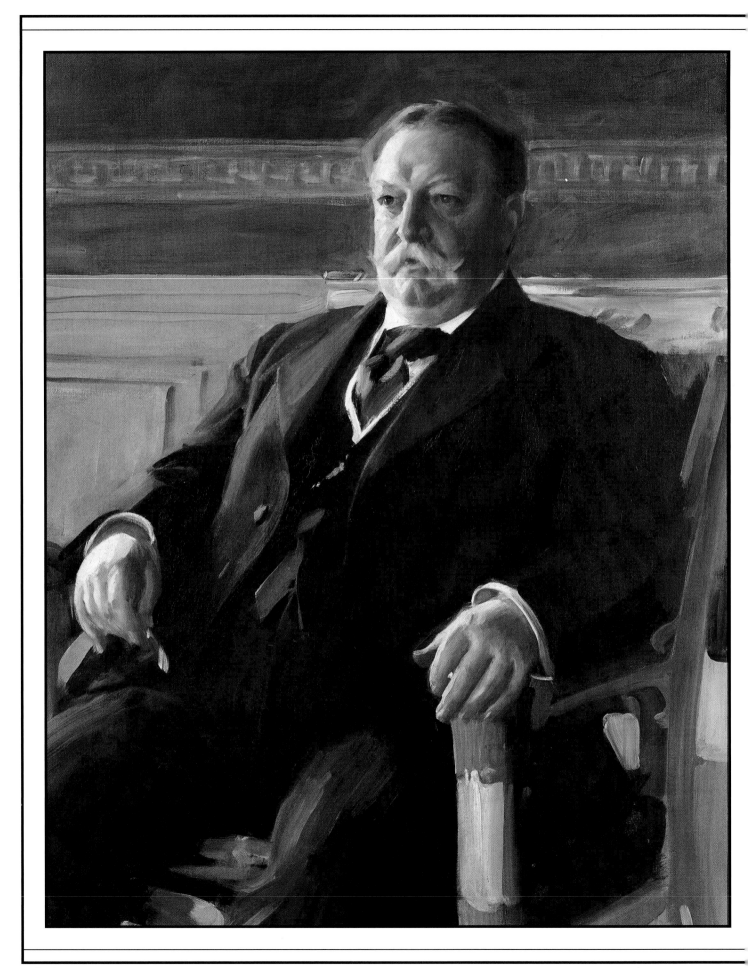

William Howard Taft

NICKNAME	Big Bill
BORN	Sept. 15, 1857, in Cincinnati, Ohio
POLITICAL PARTY	Republican
CHIEF OPPONENT	William Jennings Bryan, Democrat (1860–1925)
TERM OF OFFICE	March 4, 1909–March 3, 1913
AGE AT INAUGURATION	51 years old
NUMBER OF TERMS	one
VICE PRESIDENT	James Schoolcraft Sherman (1855–1912)
FIRST LADY	Helen Herron Taft (1861–1943), wife (married June 19, 1886)
CHILDREN	Robert, Helen, Charles
GEOGRAPHIC SCENE	46 states
NEW STATES ADDED	New Mexico, Arizona (1912)
DIED	March 8, 1930, in Washington, D.C.
AGE AT DEATH	72 years old
SELECTED LANDMARKS	Cincinnati, Ohio (birthplace); Arlington National Cemetery, Arlington, Va.

William Howard Taft relaxed by playing golf.

WILLIAM HOWARD TAFT WAS ELECTED PRESIDENT in 1908 as Theodore Roosevelt's hand-picked successor. He lacked Roosevelt's charisma and administrative talent, however, and lost popularity as his term progressed. Taft was defeated during his reelection bid, a three-way race that included a challenge by Roosevelt on a third-party ticket. Later, Taft served with distinction on the U.S. Supreme Court, the only man to be both a U.S. President and a Supreme Court justice.

Taft was the sixth Ohioan to become a U.S. President. His father, a lawyer and public servant, had served in the administrations of Ulysses S. Grant and Chester A. Arthur. Young Taft attended public schools and graduated second in his class from Yale University. By then "Big Bill" already weighed at least 225 pounds. Taft studied law, opened a practice, worked as a judge, and taught law.

In 1900 President William McKinley sent Taft to administer the Philippine Islands. He became governor of this new U.S. territory in the Pacific. Four years later Theodore Roosevelt made him secretary of war, responsible for the construction of the Panama Canal. Although Taft was eager to return to the bench as a judge, he turned down three opportunities to join the Supreme Court during these years. He felt he had to finish work assigned to him by Presidents instead.

Taft was encouraged by his wife, Helen, and Roosevelt to run for President in 1908. With some hesitation, he did. He won election easily because of his association with Roosevelt. Taft tried to continue the progressive reforms begun by his predecessor. In one term

Baseball was one of William Howard Taft's childhood pastimes. However, "Big Lub," as children called the sizable Taft, was better at batting than at running bases. Taft was the first President who played golf. He also rode horses, played tennis, and liked to dance. The "Taft March" (above) was written for his presidential campaign.

Taft served as governor of the Philippines (left) and supervised the construction of the Panama Canal (right) before he became President. He was famous for installing an oversize bathtub in the White House (below) after getting stuck in its standard-size one. At 332 pounds he was the heaviest President ever.

of office he broke twice as many trusts as Roosevelt had done in eight years, including major monopolies in tobacco and petroleum. During Taft's administration, the federal government took control of railroad freight fares, established a parcel post delivery service, initiated a postal savings system, created the Department of Labor, and added new lands to the federal conservation program. Congress passed two amendments to the Constitution, too. One created the structure for a federal income tax; the other called for the direct election of U.S. senators by citizens. (Previously, state legislatures had elected senators.) Taft was the first person to be President of 48

states. Nearly 50 years would pass before the nation added Alaska and Hawaii, its last two states.

These accomplishments were overshadowed in the minds of others by Taft's shortcomings. His efforts to reduce the tariff, or tax, on imports divided his party into warring factions. Many leaders at home and abroad disapproved of his "Dollar Diplomacy," a program that substituted "dollars for bullets" in an effort to influence foreign policy. He was ridiculed for trivial things such as not remembering names, needing an oversize bathtub, and falling asleep at awkward moments. (Once he even slept through his own parade while riding in an open car through the streets of New York City.) Voters rejected his reelection bid more firmly than that of any other major candidate in history. He won 23 percent of the popular vote, and just 8 electoral votes. Even his former ally Roosevelt won more votes running on a third-party ticket.

"Political considerations have never weighed heavily with me."

William Howard Taft

"No one candidate was ever elected ex-President by such a large majority," joked William Howard Taft after losing his reelection bid to Woodrow Wilson. Taft and Wilson rode together to the U.S. Capitol when it was time for the new President to be inaugurated (left). Taft was the first former Chief Executive to become a trustee of the National Geographic Society (right); he wrote more than a dozen articles for its magazine.

After leaving the White House, Taft became a law professor at his alma mater, Yale University. Then, in 1921, President Warren G. Harding named him Chief Justice of the United States Supreme Court. Taft wrote 253 Court opinions during his nine years on the bench. Even more important than his rulings was the work he did persuading Congress to construct the Supreme Court building. (Previously, the Court met in a separate chamber of the U.S. Capitol building.)

Taft enjoyed his post so much that he remarked: "I don't remember that I ever was President."

Taft retired from the Supreme Court in 1930 when his health began to fail. He died a few weeks later. He was the first President to be buried in Arlington National Cemetery. His wife, Helen, was laid to rest beside him following her death 13 years later. John F. Kennedy and his wife, Jacqueline, are the only other presidential couple buried at Arlington.

"I have tried to do in each case what seemed to me the wisest thing."

William Howard Taft

Helen Taft (above) was the first President's wife to accompany her husband during his Inaugural Parade (left). As First Lady she coordinated the planting of ornamental Japanese cherry trees in the nation's capital. She took an active interest in government business, supported women's rights, and wrote the first memoir by a President's wife of her years in the White House.

Woodrow Wilson

28TH PRESIDENT OF THE UNITED STATES ★ 1913 – 1921

NICKNAME	Professor
BORN	Dec. 29, 1856, in Staunton, Va.
POLITICAL PARTY	Democrat
CHIEF OPPONENTS	1st term: Theodore Roosevelt, Progressive (1858–1919) and President William Howard Taft, Republican (1857–1930); 2nd term: Charles Evans Hughes, Republican (1862–1948)

Wilson was reelected by being antiwar.

TERM OF OFFICE	March 4, 1913–March 3, 1921
AGE AT INAUGURATION	56 years old
NUMBER OF TERMS	two
VICE PRESIDENT	Thomas Riley Marshall (1854–1925)
FIRST LADIES	Ellen Louise Axson Wilson (1860–1914), first wife (married June 24, 1885); Margaret Woodrow Wilson (1886–1944), daughter; Edith Bolling Galt Wilson (1872–1961), second wife (married Dec. 18, 1915)
CHILDREN	Margaret, Jesse, Eleanor
GEOGRAPHIC SCENE	48 states
NEW STATES ADDED	none
DIED	Feb. 3, 1924, in Washington, D.C.
AGE AT DEATH	67 years old
SELECTED LANDMARKS	Staunton, Va. (birthplace); Columbia, S.C. (boyhood home); Woodrow Wilson House Museum and Washington National Cathedral (grave), Washington, D.C.

As PRESIDENT, WOODROW WILSON ushered important legislation through Congress. However, World War I became the greatest challenge of his two terms in office. When he failed to keep the United States out of the conflict, he used the nation's resources to help win it. He sought to secure lasting peace afterward with a new international governing body called the League of Nations.

Wilson grew up in the shadow of an earlier war—the Civil War. He was born in Virginia and raised in Georgia and the Carolinas. His first childhood memory was of hearing that Abraham Lincoln had been elected President and that war would follow. He watched Confederate troops march off to battle, saw soldiers die from their wounds, and, after the war, glimpsed Confederate General Robert E. Lee being paraded through Augusta, Georgia, under Union guard.

Wilson struggled with dyslexia, a learning disorder that delayed his mastery of basic skills in reading, writing, and math. He went on to graduate from the College of New Jersey (renamed Princeton University in 1896). Wilson practiced law, earned a graduate degree from Johns Hopkins University, and became a college professor. By 1902 he was president of Princeton University. Wilson stepped from

By 1917 intensified fighting in Europe (above) had forced Woodrow Wilson to change his first-term antiwar stance and enter the United States into World War I. Within 18 months some two million U.S. soldiers had joined the front lines and helped turn the tide of the Great War.

Program for the Peace of the World

By PRESIDENT WILSON January 8, 1918

I. Open covenants of peace, openly arrived at, after which there shall be no private international understandings of any kind, but diplomacy shall proceed always frankly and in the public view.

II. Absolute freedom of navigation upon the seas, outside territorial waters, alike in peace and in war, except as the seas may be closed in whole or in part by international action for the enforcement of international covenants.

III. The removal, so far as possible, of all economic barriers and the establishment of an equality of trade conditions among all the nations consenting to the peace and associating themselves for its maintenance.

IV. Adequate guarantees given and taken that national armaments will reduce to the lowest point consistent with domestic safety.

V. Free, open-minded, and absolutely impartial adjustment of all colonial claims, based upon a strict observance of the principle that in determining all such questions of sovereignty the interests of the population concerned must have equal weight with the equitable claims of the government whose title is to be determined.

VI. The evacuation of all Russian territory and such a settlement of all questions affecting Russia as will secure the best and freest cooperation of the other nations of the world in obtaining for her an unhampered and unembarrassed opportunity for the independent determination of her own political development and national policy, and assure her of a sincere welcome into the society of free nations under institutions of her own choosing; and, more than a welcome, assistance also of every kind that she may need and may herself desire. The treatment accorded Russia by her sister nations in the months to come will be the acid test of their good will, of their comprehension of her needs as distinguished from their own interests, and of their intelligent and unselfish sympathy.

VII. Belgium, the whole world will agree, must be evacuated and restored, without any attempt to limit the sovereignty which she enjoys in common with all other free nations. No other single act will serve as this will serve to restore confidence among the nations in the law which they have themselves set and determined for the government of their relations with one

another. Without this healing act the whole structure and validity of international law is forever impaired.

VIII. All French territory should be freed and the wrong done to France by Prussia in 1871 in the matter of Alsace-Lorraine, which has unsettled the peace of the world for nearly fifty years, should be righted, in order that peace may once more be made secure in the interest of all.

IX. A readjustment of the frontiers of Italy should be effected along clearly recognizable lines of nationality.

X. The peoples of Austria-Hungary, whose place among the nations we wish to see safeguarded and assured, should be accorded the freest opportunity of autonomous development.

XI. Rumania, Serbia and Montenegro should be evacuated; occupied territories restored; Serbia accorded free and secure access to the sea; and the relations of the several Balkan States to one another determined by friendly counsel along historically established lines of allegiance and nationality; and international guarantees of the political and economic independence and territorial integrity of the several Balkan States should be entered into.

XII. The Turkish portions of the present Ottoman Empire should be assured a secure sovereignty, but the other nationalities which are now under Turkish rule should be assured an undoubted security of life and an absolutely unmolested opportunity of autonomous development, and the Dardanelles should be permanently opened as a free passage to the ships and commerce of all nations under international guarantees.

XIII. An independent Polish State should be erected which should include the territories inhabited by indisputably Polish populations, which should be assured a free and secure access to the sea, and whose political and economic independence and territorial integrity should be guaranteed by international covenant.

XIV. A general association of nations must be formed under specific covenants for the purpose of affording mutual guarantees of political independence and territorial integrity to great and small States alike.

that post to the White House after brief service as governor of New Jersey. He was the top vote-getter in the three-way presidential race of 1912 that included President William Howard Taft and former President Theodore Roosevelt.

Wilson packed his first term of office with significant legislation. He established the Federal Reserve system that continues to control the nation's money supply today. In addition he reduced import taxes, established graduated income taxes, created a Federal Trade Commission to monitor business practices, supported labor practices such as strikes, discouraged the use of child labor, and promoted the eight-hour workday. He was the first President to hold periodic press conferences and to speak on the radio.

Wilson was reelected thanks to this record and because, as his campaign slogan put it, "He Kept Us Out of War." The Great War had begun in Europe in August 1914. The United States was

drawn into the fight soon after Wilson's 1916 reelection. November 11, 1918, became Armistice Day (later renamed Veteran's Day) when a truce ended World War I.

Wilson became the first U.S. President to visit Europe while in office when he traveled to Paris to help establish terms for peace. The final treaty supported Wilson's idea of creating a League of Nations that would settle future disputes using words and economic influence, not weapons. Wilson could not persuade Congress to accept his plan, though, and the League formed without support from the United States. Nonetheless, in 1919 Wilson earned the Nobel Peace Prize for his efforts. The United Nations took the place of the League after World War II.

Wilson's first wife, Ellen, was a talented artist. As First Lady she worked to improve housing for residents in the nation's capital. Two of the Wilsons' three daughters were wed in White

The son of a Presbyterian minister, Woodrow Wilson thought it was God's will that he had become President. He devoted himself to ending World War I (center) as if it were a charge from heaven. Wilson's "Fourteen Points" for lasting peace (top center), outlined in January 1918, formed the basis for peace settlements after the war ended. Wilson campaigned so intensely (top left and top right) for U.S. support of the treaty that his health suffered.

U.S. citizens helped secure a victory in World War I (above) by taking part in a nationwide rationing program during the war. Woodrow and Edith Wilson (right) set a positive example for others by going without gas on Sundays, meat on Mondays, and wheat on Tuesdays. They even let sheep roam on the White House lawns so they could "mow" the grass naturally, saving gas and labor. Nationwide sacrifices helped make scarce resources available to U.S. soldiers overseas. The war proved deadly and expensive to nations everywhere. Nearly 10 million soldiers died worldwide in a conflict that cost more than $300 billion.

House ceremonies during his first term of office. Wilson was devastated when Ellen became ill and died in 1914. He even told friends he would welcome being assassinated. The following spring Wilson was introduced to a widow. He liked her so much at first sight that he invited her to stay for tea at the White House. He married his new friend, Edith, before the end of the year.

Wilson, who had suffered for years from minor strokes, had a major stroke in October 1919, which ended his campaign to win congressional support of the League of Nations. Edith took charge of her husband's recovery. She kept details of her husband's health a secret, overruled the idea that he should resign, and controlled what official business could be brought to his attention.

Although her boldness drew criticism, it helped Wilson recover the strength he needed to serve out his term.

Wilson's retirement was relatively brief, and his health remained poor. He died in 1924, six months after the death of his successor, Warren G. Harding. Both Woodrow and Edith Wilson are buried at the Washington Cathedral. He is the only President buried in the nation's capital.

"The world must be made safe for democracy."

Woodrow Wilson,
Request that Congress declare war on Germany, April 2, 1917

Presidents at War

★ Serving as the Commander in Chief ★

DURING WARTIME, U.S. Presidents take on the added responsibility of Commander in Chief for the nation's armed forces. Two of the country's earliest Presidents took this duty literally. During the Whiskey Rebellion of 1794, George Washington rode at the head of more than 10,000 soldiers to silence protests over a new federal tax on liquor. Likewise, when the British threatened the nation's capital near the end of the War of 1812, James Madison actually took command of scattered troops in an attempted defense.

Since then many wartime Presidents have visited troops near combat zones, even at the risk of being in harm's way. Most participate in debates about military strategy, too. All Presidents at least direct the nature of the fight by choosing military commanders. They often play a role in shaping the peacetime that follows war, too.

Ironically some of the nation's most prominent wartime leaders had no personal combat experience themselves. Woodrow Wilson and Franklin D. Roosevelt, for example, grew up during peacetime. In all 11 U.S. Presidents never served in the military. Others include John Adams and John Quincy Adams (who were foreign diplomats instead of soldiers during the Revolutionary War), Grover Cleveland (who paid someone else to take his place during the Civil War, a legal option at the time), and Bill Clinton (who pursued his education, not military service, during the Vietnam War). Even Abraham Lincoln, one of the most important commanders in chief, had served in the military for just a few months during a frontier Indian war.

Commanders in chief through the centuries of the Presidency: George Washington (top) led federal troops during the Whiskey Rebellion of 1794. During the Civil War of the 1860s, Abraham Lincoln (above left) began the practice of visiting battlefront troops. During the 20th century, Woodrow Wilson (above, right at far right) worked with leaders from France, Great Britain, and Italy to draft the peace treaty that ended World War I.

Nonetheless, wartime service is often seen as a measure of fitness for presidential candidates. Those with little or no experience may be criticized, particularly if it appears that service was deliberately avoided. Those with more experience are often more favorably received. A number of Presidents have gained election, in part at least, because of famous military performances. They include George Washington, Andrew Jackson, Ulysses S. Grant, Theodore Roosevelt, and Dwight D. Eisenhower. Ironically most of these leaders presided over periods of national peace after they were elected.

Presidential popularity tends to rise during times of national crisis. Approval ratings soared for Franklin D. Roosevelt after the bombing of Pearl Harbor, for Jimmy Carter during the early months of the Iran hostage crisis, and for George W. Bush following the 2001 terrorist attacks on U.S. soil. Such popularity inevitably falls if conflicts remain unresolved or if presidential leadership becomes questioned.

If presidential elections occur during times of war, voters often choose to "stay the course" instead of changing leaders. Such was the case for Franklin D. Roosevelt; he was reelected twice during World War II. George W. Bush was also returned to the White House in 2004 with the help of wartime support. On the other hand, if a wartime leader is perceived to be failing as Commander in Chief, that issue alone can end a Presidency. For example, wartime unpopularity forced Lyndon B. Johnson to cancel his 1968 reelection bid.

Wartime Presidents often choose to reduce Constitutional freedoms in the name of national defense. At the outset of the Civil War, for example, Abraham Lincoln jailed potential traitors and restricted freedom of speech. During World War II, Franklin D. Roosevelt authorized the detention in restricted camps of more than 100,000 Japanese American citizens. Concerns over terrorist threats prompted George W. Bush to permit greater surveillance of U.S. residents. Not all Presidents have chosen this tack, however. James Madison insisted during the War of 1812 that civil liberties like free speech remain unchecked in order to demonstrate the nation's commitment to liberty.

  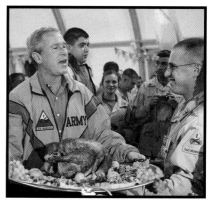

President Harry S. Truman's decision to have the Enola Gay *(top) drop an atomic bomb on Japan during World War II continues to be much-debated. Eleanor Roosevelt (above left), often visited World War II troops on behalf of her husband. Vietnam anti-war protests (above center) affected the popularity of two U.S. Presidents, Lyndon B. Johnson and Richard M. Nixon. In 2003 George W. Bush (above, right) paid a surprise Thanksgiving trip to soldiers in Iraq.*

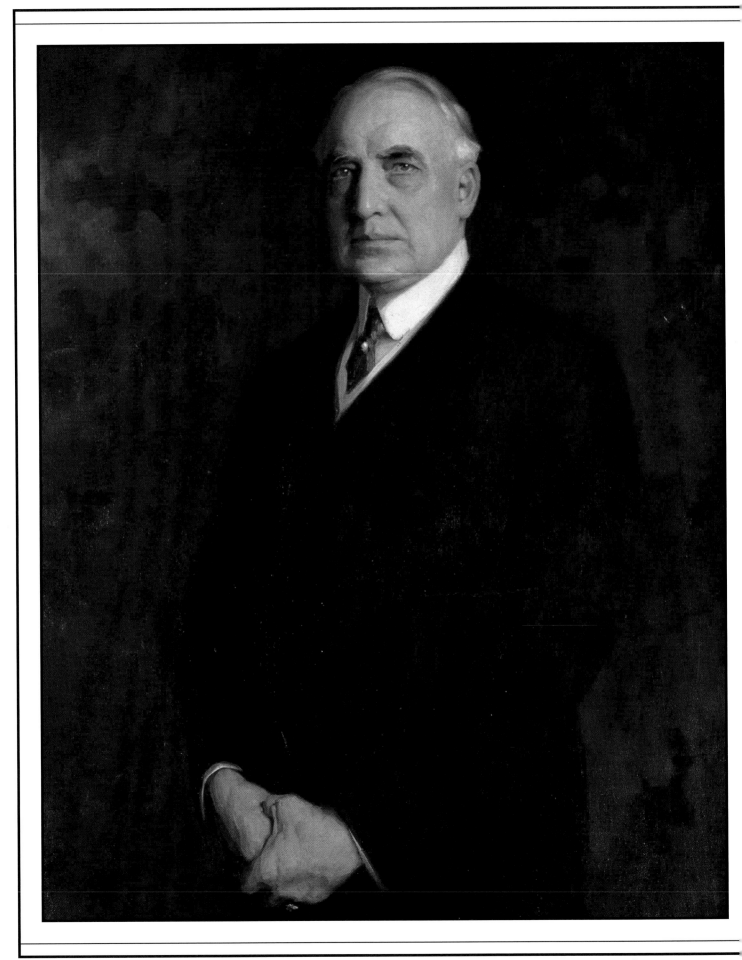

Warren G. Harding

29TH PRESIDENT OF THE UNITED STATES ★ 1921 – 1923

NICKNAME	Wobbly Warren
BORN	Nov. 2, 1865, in Caledonia (now Blooming Grove), Ohio
POLITICAL PARTY	Republican
CHIEF OPPONENT	James Middleton Cox, Democrat (1870–1957)
TERM OF OFFICE	March 4, 1921–Aug. 2, 1923
AGE AT INAUGURATION	55 years old
NUMBER OF TERMS	one (cut short by death)
VICE PRESIDENT	Calvin Coolidge (1872–1933)
FIRST LADY	Florence Kling De Wolfe Harding (1860–1924), wife (married July 8, 1891)
CHILDREN	none
GEOGRAPHIC SCENE	48 states
NEW STATES ADDED	none
DIED	Aug. 2, 1923, in San Francisco, Calif.
AGE AT DEATH	57 years old
SELECTED LANDMARKS	Harding Home and Museum and Harding Memorial (grave), Marion, Ohio

Warren G. Harding delivered his Inaugural Address through a new invention: a megaphone that magnified his voice.

WHEN HE WAS A YOUNG MAN, Warren Gamaliel Harding's friends thought he "looked like a President." Harding's presidential profile helped carry him to the White House, but it did not prepare him for the challenges of the job. Harding became the sixth President to die in office when his health failed him at midterm. His death came just as major scandals about his administration were coming to light.

Harding was born in Ohio. After graduating from Ohio Central College in Iberia, he became a newspaper publisher in the nearby town of Marion. He went on to serve in the state legislature, as lieutenant governor and governor of Ohio, and as a U.S. senator during his climb to prominence in the Republican Party. His habit of changing his mind earned him the nickname "Wobbly Warren." Harding's nomination to the party ticket of 1920 followed much behind-the-scenes, late-night deal making by party leaders, many of whom were heavy smokers. This strategy became known as the "smoke-filled room" approach to politics.

The complex responsibilities of being President began to trouble Harding midway into his term. So did hints of illegal behavior within his administration. In early 1923 an important Harding appointee fled the country because of criminal activity on the job. One of the man's coworkers committed suicide soon after. Then the private secretary of Harding's scandal-plagued attorney general killed himself over a different scheme. Speculation over these events was interrupted when Harding, his health already weakened, began a cross-country trip to visit the U.S. territory of Alaska. He died suddenly during the trip while staying in San Francisco.

Warren G. Harding's Presidency is consistently ranked among the worst in U.S. history because of its widespread corruption. The greatest scandal—the Teapot Dome affair—came to light after his death. Apparently without the President's knowledge, a Harding Cabinet member had granted oil-drilling rights on federal lands like Wyoming's Teapot Dome. The man received sizable illegal payments and even a herd of cattle from oil company officials in exchange.

Warren G. Harding was elected President with the greatest landslide in a century. He earned 60 percent of the popular vote in the first election in which women were able to vote nationwide.

Calvin Coolidge

30TH PRESIDENT OF THE UNITED STATES ★ 1923 – 1929

NICKNAME	Silent Cal
BORN	July 4, 1872, in Plymouth, Vt.
POLITICAL PARTY	Republican
CHIEF OPPONENTS	1st term: none, succeeded Harding; 2nd term: John W. Davis (1873–1955), Democrat and Robert M. La Follette (1855–1925), Progressive
TERM OF OFFICE	Aug. 3, 1923–March 3, 1929
AGE AT INAUGURATION	51 years old
NUMBER OF TERMS	one, plus balance of Warren G. Harding's term
VICE PRESIDENTS	1st term: none; 2nd term: Charles Gates Dawes (1865–1951)
FIRST LADY	Grace Anna Goodhue Coolidge (1879–1957), wife (married Oct. 4, 1905)
CHILDREN	John, Calvin
GEOGRAPHIC SCENE	48 states
NEW STATES ADDED	none
DIED	Jan. 5, 1933, in Northampton, Mass.
AGE AT DEATH	60 years old
SELECTED LANDMARKS	Plymouth, Vt. (birthplace, homestead); Northampton, Mass. (library, homestead); Plymouth Notch Cemetery, Plymouth, Vt.

Vermont-born Calvin Coolidge never lost his fondness for making maple syrup.

CALVIN COOLIDGE'S HIGH STANDARD OF CONDUCT restored trust in the Presidency following the sudden death of his predecessor, Warren G. Harding. Coolidge was a calm, frugal presence in the White House during the extravagance and waste of the Roaring Twenties.

The plain style of Coolidge's Presidency had its roots in his simple New England childhood. His favorite chore, as a red-headed youth in rural Vermont, was making maple syrup. He went on to graduate from Amherst College, become a lawyer, and hold more than a dozen elected posts—including governor of Massachusetts—before rising from Vice President to President in 1923.

Coolidge cooperated with investigations into the Harding scandals. He removed corrupt staff members, and he chose reliable replacements for their posts. He followed a simple strategy: "When things are going along all right, it is a good plan to let them alone." This notion inspired the slogan "Keep Cool With Coolidge" during his successful reelection campaign in 1924.

Coolidge was nicknamed "Red" (for his red hair), "Cal" (short for Calvin), and "Silent Cal" (because he spoke little). His habit of expressing himself with few words was famous. Once a dinner guest told Coolidge she had bet she could get three words of conversation out of him. All he replied was: "You lose." He advised his successor, Herbert Hoover, on how to handle talkative visitors: "If you keep dead still, they will run down in three or four minutes."

Coolidge retired to Massachusetts in 1929. He wrote, served as a trustee for the National Geographic Society, and worked in the insurance industry before his death in 1933. Frugal with words to the end, Silent Cal left behind a will to his estate that was only 23 words long.

Calvin Coolidge was the last President who met with everyone who visited the White House to see its chief resident (above). Several hundred people often called each day. He prided himself on his speed at working through a crowd. Once, he shook hands with 1,900 visitors in only 34 minutes.

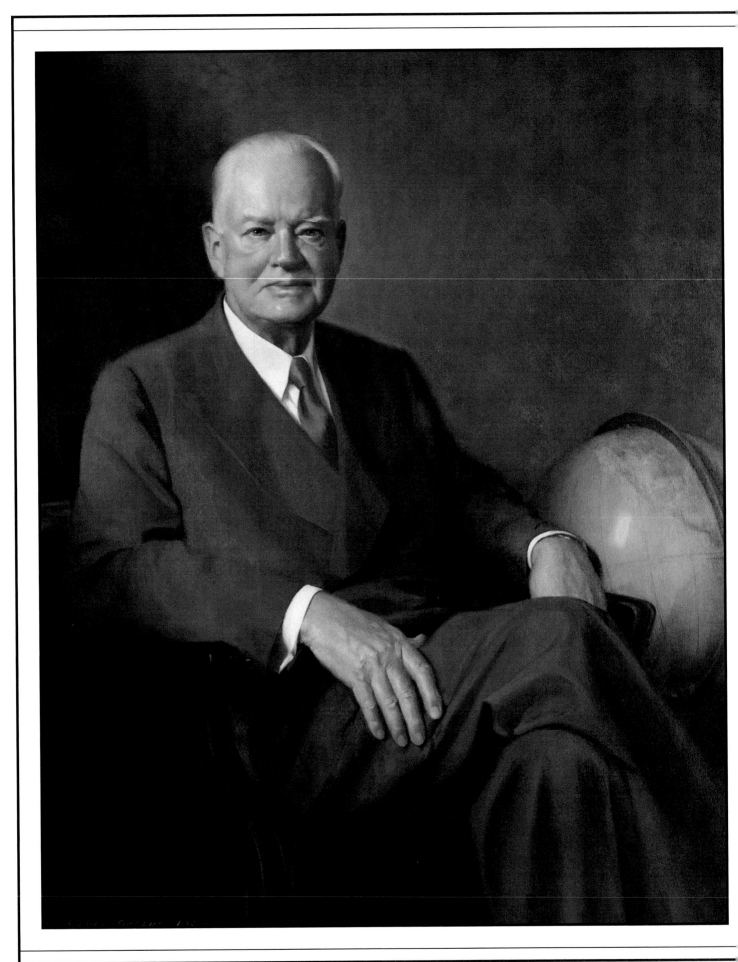

Herbert Hoover

31ST PRESIDENT OF THE UNITED STATES ★ 1929 – 1933

NICKNAME	Chief
BORN	Aug. 10, 1874, in West Branch, Iowa
POLITICAL PARTY	Republican
CHIEF OPPONENT	Alfred Emanuel Smith, Democrat (1873–1944)
TERM OF OFFICE	March 4, 1929–March 3, 1933
AGE AT INAUGURATION	54 years old
NUMBER OF TERMS	one
VICE PRESIDENT	Charles Curtis (1860–1936)
FIRST LADY	Lou Henry Hoover (1874–1944), wife (married Feb. 10, 1899)
CHILDREN	Herbert, Allan
GEOGRAPHIC SCENE	48 states
NEW STATES ADDED	none
DIED	Oct. 20, 1964, in New York, N.Y.
AGE AT DEATH	90 years old
SELECTED LANDMARKS	Newberg, Oreg. (boyhood home); Hoover Institution, Stanford University, Palo Alto, Calif.; Herbert Hoover National Historic Site (including birthplace, presidential library, museum, and grave), West Branch, Iowa

Herbert Hoover directed European relief efforts (above, Poland in 1946) before and after his Presidency. During World War I Finnish citizens used "hoover" as a new verb meaning "to help."

WHEN THE STOCK MARKET CRASHED in October 1929 only a few months after Herbert Clark Hoover had taken office—the President found himself responsible for a different nation from the one he had planned to lead. The Great Depression that followed proved unstoppable and cost him the opportunity for a second term.

Hoover was a successful businessman, scientist, and public servant before becoming President. Born in Iowa and orphaned at age nine, he majored in geology at Stanford University. Hoover then began traveling the globe for the mining industry. While living in London, he received his first public service assignment—evacuating 120,000 Americans from Europe at the start of World War I. Later he helped direct relief efforts for European victims of the war. He went on to serve as secretary of commerce for Warren G. Harding and Calvin Coolidge.

Hoover carried 40 of the 48 states during the 1928 election. Although he had questioned some of the financial policies that led to the stock market crash of 1929, no one anticipated how serious the Great Depression that followed it would become. No economic collapse before or since has been so far-reaching, long lasting, or severe. A desperate public

blamed Hoover for their troubles and, in 1932, turned in large numbers to the Democratic candidate, Franklin D. Roosevelt.

Two U.S. Presidents called Hoover back from retirement to perform national service. He organized post–World War II food relief in Europe for Harry S. Truman, and he evaluated government efficiency for Truman and again for Dwight D. Eisenhower. Hoover lived longer after leaving the White House than any other President—31 years. He died in 1964 at the age of 90.

Herbert Hoover became a multimillionaire during his years as a geologist. He refused to be paid for his public service. Hoover acted more aggressively than any previous President to end hard times after the stock market crashed in 1929 (above). Despite his efforts, suffering continued to spread.

SEEKING STABILITY IN THE ATOMIC AGE

★ *1933 – 1981* ★

1933

Germany revoked the citizenship of physicist Albert Einstein during his 1933 visit to the United States. Among the ideas proposed by this scientific genius was the concept of an atomic bomb.

1945

World War II ended with the explosion of two atomic bombs in Japan, including an attack on Hiroshima on August 6. Nuclear weapons have never again been used in combat.

1946

The first programmable electronic computer weighed 30 tons and used some 18,000 bulky vacuum tubes to transfer information. By 1952 computers were calculating election results.

1957

Racial tensions mounted in Little Rock, Arkansas, after the governor ignored the 1954 Supreme Court ruling, Brown v. Board of Education, *on the integration of public schools.*

The challenges faced by Presidents increased in complexity as the 20th century progressed. Leaders struggled to fight wars, end poverty, preserve democracy, extend equality, survive energy shortages, and heal national wounds. They led citizens through the tragedies of presidential deaths and scandals, too. Much of the era was dominated by the uneasy balance of power between the rivals of the atomic age—the United States and the Soviet Union. Presidents sought to offset the troubles of the times with hopes for a promising future.

1967

Widespread protest of U.S. involvement in the Vietnam War developed during the late 1960s and early 1970s. Young people were among the most visible demonstrators.

1969

On July 20, humans set foot on the moon for the first time. A series of Apollo lunar missions carried 12 U.S. astronauts to the moon six times from 1969 to 1972.

1970s

After the first successful human heart transplant in 1967, scientists tried to perfect the procedure during the 1970s. Medical advances in the 1980s extended the survival rate of patients.

1976

U.S. citizens celebrated the 200th anniversary of the nation's Declaration of Independence with ceremonies, parades, and fireworks.

Franklin D. Roosevelt

32ND PRESIDENT OF THE UNITED STATES ★ 1933 – 1945

NICKNAME	FDR
BORN	Jan. 30, 1882, in Hyde Park, N.Y.
POLITICAL PARTY	Democrat
CHIEF OPPONENTS	1st term: President Herbert Clark Hoover, Republican (1874–1964); 2nd term: Alfred Mossman Landon, Republican (1887–1987); 3rd term: Wendell Lewis Willkie, Republican (1892–1944); 4th term: Thomas Edmund Dewey, Republican (1902–1971)
TERM OF OFFICE	March 4, 1933–April 12, 1945
AGE AT INAUGURATION	51 years old
NUMBER OF TERMS	four (cut short by death)
VICE PRESIDENTS	1st & 2nd terms: John Nance Garner (1868–1967); 3rd term: Henry Agard Wallace (1888–1965); 4th term: Harry S. Truman (1884–1972)
FIRST LADY	Anna Eleanor Roosevelt Roosevelt (1884–1962), wife (married March 17, 1905)
CHILDREN	Anna, James, Elliott, Franklin, John, plus a son died young
GEOGRAPHIC SCENE	48 states
NEW STATES ADDED	none
DIED	April 12, 1945, in Warm Springs, Ga.
AGE AT DEATH	63 years old
SELECTED LANDMARKS	Franklin D. Roosevelt National Historic Site (includes home that was birthplace, childhood, and adult home; presidential library; museum; grave), Hyde Park, N.Y.; Little White House State Historic Site, Warm Springs, Ga.; FDR Memorial, Washington, D.C.

TWO GOOD TERMS DESERVE ANOTHER

NOT SINCE THE DAYS OF ABRAHAM LINCOLN did a President face such challenges as those met by Franklin Delano Roosevelt. During what became the longest Presidency in U.S. history, Roosevelt led the nation out of the Great Depression and saw it safely through the darkest days of World War II. His wife, Eleanor, was an equal partner in his political career.

Franklin D. Roosevelt was the second member of his extended family to become President of the United States. His path to the White House included many of the same political and personal steps taken decades earlier by Theodore Roosevelt, a fifth cousin. Franklin was born at his family's estate in Hyde Park, New York. He called this spot home for most of his life. Roosevelt was his parents' only child. His mother and father took seven weeks to agree upon his name. As was the custom of the era, Roosevelt was clothed in dresses and kilts until age eight. His parents took him on extended trips abroad and had him tutored at home until his teen years.

After graduating from Harvard University in 1904, Roosevelt attended Columbia Law School. He passed the bar exam and took up the practice of law. By then he had already married a distant relative, Anna Eleanor Roosevelt, known as Eleanor. The cousins had met for the first time in 1902, the year Eleanor

Franklin D. Roosevelt was the only person to serve three full terms as U.S. President and be elected to a fourth. He was encouraged during his childhood (top) to pursue public service as an adult. He began courting his distant cousin, Eleanor Roosevelt (above), while a student at Harvard University.

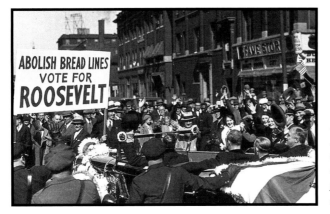

"I pledge you, I pledge myself, to a new deal for the American people."

Franklin D. Roosevelt,
Democratic nomination acceptance speech, July 2, 1932

Franklin D. Roosevelt had the longest Presidency in U.S. history. He took office in 1933 after promising to end the Great Depression (left). When challenges continued at home and started abroad with World War II, voters were reluctant to switch leaders. He died in office in 1945. The 22nd Amendment, which became law in 1951, prohibits anyone from serving more than two terms as President. It was written by lawmakers who were uncomfortable with Roosevelt's extended term of office.

turned 18 and Franklin was 20. At their wedding in 1905 the bride was given away by President Theodore Roosevelt, her uncle.

In 1910 Franklin D. Roosevelt joined the New York Senate. A few years later Woodrow Wilson named him assistant secretary of the Navy. He ran unsuccessfully for the U.S. Senate in 1914 and left the Navy in 1920 to campaign as the running mate of the Democratic presidential nominee, James M. Cox. Illness sidelined his political career in 1921 when he was stricken suddenly with polio. Roosevelt went from being active and

robust one day to being unable to walk two days later. Eleanor encouraged her husband to fight for his recovery. Although he never regained active use of his legs, Roosevelt learned how to stand on leg braces and take limited steps with the assistance of others. Within three years he was practicing law again. Before the decade was out he had become governor of New York.

When Roosevelt ran for President in 1932, the nation was staggering under the burden of the Great Depression—the greatest economic crisis in its history. One-fourth of all workers were unemployed. Countless families had gone broke because of bank failures. More than a million homeless hoboes sought food and work as they roamed the country. Displaced families tacked together shacks in temporary settlements they nicknamed Hoovervilles—after President Herbert Hoover.

The grim national scene prompted voters to flock to Roosevelt and his promise of a "new deal for the American people." He earned 57 percent of the popular vote and won the electoral votes of all but six states. In the three presidential elections that followed, Roosevelt continued his streak of majority victories, earning 61 percent, 55 percent, then 53 percent of the vote.

"While it isn't written in the Constitution, nevertheless it is the inherent duty of the federal government to keep its citizens from starvation," Franklin D. Roosevelt observed. As President he enacted sweeping legislation, including the Social Security Act (being signed at left).

"The only thing we have to fear is fear itself."

Franklin D. Roosevelt,
First Inaugural Address, March 4, 1933

Franklin D. Roosevelt used radio to connect with the American people in the days before television came into widespread use. His series of "fireside chats" (left), delivered in his reassuring voice, united the nation to face the day's challenges. He even used radio to build ties with French citizens. In 1942 he addressed them in their own language to announce the U.S. invasion of occupied French territories in North Africa. Roosevelt became the first President to appear on television, with a 1939 broadcast from the New York World's Fair.

As President, Roosevelt took charge of ending the Depression. Where Hoover had hesitated to interfere, Roosevelt plunged in. The beginning of his Presidency was famous for its rush of legislation and was later referred to as Roosevelt's Hundred Days. During this period, he signed 14 bills in all. Among other things, these new laws restored confidence in the banking industry, employed young men through a Civilian Conservation Corps, launched the construction of dams and power plants in the Tennessee River Valley, aided farmers, established loan programs, and improved working conditions. Later, Roosevelt established the Securities and Exchange Commission to help prevent future financial panics in the stock market. He created the Social Security system, too. This cornerstone program for public welfare assured that senior citizens would have an income during their retirement years and that the unemployed would receive temporary support while they sought new jobs. His programs became known as the New Deal.

In 1932 voters had been asked to "Kick Out Depression With a Democratic Vote." Four years later they agreed overwhelmingly to "Follow Through With Roosevelt." In 1940 they supported Roosevelt's third presidential campaign because he pledged that unless the U.S. was attacked, he would stay out of the war that was spreading around the globe. The next year Japan bombed U.S. naval bases at Pearl Harbor, Hawaii. Roosevelt predicted that the date, December 7, would "live in infamy," and he asked Congress to declare war on Japan. Declarations against Germany and Italy followed. For the rest of his life, the world would be at war.

Franklin D. Roosevelt met with other Allied leaders from World War II in Tehran, Iran, in 1943 (left). Roosevelt befriended "Big Three" ally Joseph Stalin, premier of the Soviet Union (seated at left), by poking fun at their companion Winston Churchill, prime minister of Great Britain (seated at right). He joked about the British, Churchill's cigars, even his moods. Soon the stern-faced Stalin was laughing along, smiling, while Roosevelt playfully called him "Uncle Joe."

Roosevelt's mother was a central figure in his family life along with his wife, Eleanor, and their five children (left). After her husband's death, Eleanor (right) became known as the First Lady of the World for her work with the United Nations. She was part of the first U.S. delegation to that body, chaired its Commission on Human Rights, and helped write its International Declaration of Human Rights. She was the first President's wife to fly abroad.

During World War II Roosevelt took seriously his role as Commander in Chief. He plotted military strategy, appointed key field commanders, and authorized the secret development of the atomic bomb. He formed partnerships with Winston Churchill from Great Britain and, later, with Joseph Stalin of the Soviet Union. The "Big Three" discussed strategies for war and peace, including Roosevelt's idea for starting the United Nations. In 1944, with war raging full tilt, Roosevelt agreed to serve for a fourth term as President. Voters decided not to "change horses in midstream" and returned him to the White House once more.

During the early years of her husband's Presidency, Eleanor Roosevelt tried to broaden the reach of the New Deal to African Americans, working women, children, labor unions, and immigrants. She wrote a daily national newspaper column and met weekly with women reporters. When war took center stage, she shifted her focus to it. Eleanor toured factories, launched battleships, and visited troops around the world. She became her husband's eyes and ears beyond the nation's capital, while he concentrated on military strategy.

In the spring of 1945, Franklin Roosevelt made a visit to the "Little White House," his retreat at Warm Springs, Georgia. Twelve years had passed since his first Inauguration, and it was almost three months since his fourth. (Beginning in 1937, Presidents were inaugurated on January 20 instead of March 4.) Other commitments kept Eleanor from making the trip, but among those joining the

"We look forward to a world founded upon four essential human freedoms
...freedom of speech
...freedom of...worship
...freedom from want
...freedom from fear."

Franklin D. Roosevelt,
State of the Union Address, January 6, 1941

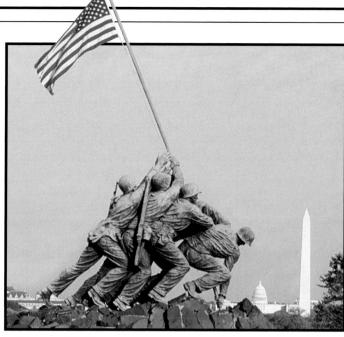

U.S. soldiers fought battles around the globe after the United States joined the fighting of World War II in 1941. U.S. servicemen were part of the Allied forces who stormed the coast of Normandy, France, on D-day, June 6, 1944 (left), in their march to free Europe from German control. Conquest of Pacific islands, including Japan's Iwo Jima in early 1945, helped turn the tide of battle in the Pacific. Later this battle was recalled in a famous public statue (right).

President was Lucy Page Mercer Rutherford. More than 30 years earlier, while she served as Eleanor's secretary, Lucy had fallen in love with Franklin. Although Franklin ended their affair after it was discovered by his wife, he and Lucy secretly renewed their friendship late in his life. During

their visit to Georgia, Roosevelt suddenly fell ill while being sketched for a portrait. He reached for his head and observed: "I have a terrific headache." He was having a stroke. Roosevelt never spoke again and died within hours.

The nation was plunged into grief. Roosevelt was the only President whom many Americans had ever known, and he had helped them survive some of the country's toughest challenges. Roosevelt's combination as "Dr. New Deal" and "Dr. Win the War" had cured the Great Depression. Within months of his death, World War II would end, too. His pattern of federal involvement in national issues became the norm for future leaders. In 1997 Roosevelt became the fourth President ever—and the only 20th-century one—to be recognized with a national monument in Washington, D.C.

The sudden death of Franklin D. Roosevelt in 1945 stunned U.S. citizens. This musician (left) wept over the death of the President. Tears fell as he played at Roosevelt's memorial service. Roosevelt's lasting importance was recognized with the opening of the Franklin Delano Roosevelt Memorial in 1997. Eleanor Roosevelt is recognized at the structure, too. The monument overlooks the cherry-tree-lined Tidal Basin in Washington, D.C. It offers views of the other three presidential memorials. These honor George Washington, Thomas Jefferson, and Abraham Lincoln.

The First Ladies

★ *Partners, Hostesses, and Advocates* ★

So FAR every President of the United States has been a man. However each of these men has partnered with a woman to help him with his duties. Most of the women have been wives of Presidents. Occasionally—either because of poor health or lack of interest—a President's wife has declined to serve as First Lady. If a wife is unavailable, daughters, other female relatives or family friends are asked to step in.

Early on, these presidential partners were addressed with titles such as "Lady," or "Mrs. President." The term "First Lady" became popular by the early 20th century; it recalled the woman's role in the home that is first in importance to the nation.

For more than 100 years the chief duty of the First Lady was to serve as hostess at White House events. However, many of these women, such as Dolley Madison, were more than gracious entertainers; they were shrewd students of politics, too. They knew just how to soothe upset guests and encourage support of their husbands.

Early First Ladies came to the White House with the same background in domestic life as other women of their day. Until the mid-19th

A variety of roles have occupied First Ladies during their partnerships with U.S. Presidents. Louisa Adams (below, right) kept her husband, John Quincy Adams, company in 1828 by winding silk from her own silkworms while he worked nearby. Lucretia Garfield (below, left) helped in the kitchen during 1881. Edith Wilson (far left) stepped in to deal with administrative details in 1919 after a stroke left her husband partially paralyzed. Critics charged that she had become too involved in presidential matters, but her work helped her husband complete his term.

Times change: Martha Washington (top left) concentrated her efforts as "Presidentress" on entertaining; two centuries later First Lady Hillary Rodham Clinton (top right) became the first First Lady to win elected office. In 2000 she campaigned successfully for a seat in the U.S. Senate. Mamie Eisenhower (far left), like other presidential wives, dressed in style for her husband's Inaugural Ball.

century, few had even attended school. Abigail Fillmore was the first President's wife to have held a job of her own (as a school teacher).

When time and interests permit, First Ladies devote attention to national issues and causes. Eleanor Roosevelt expanded the role of the President's wife during her 12 years as First Lady. Because her husband's mobility was limited by polio, she traveled and spoke extensively on his behalf. She pursued her own interests, too—from civil rights to family welfare to benefits for laborers.

In recent decades each First Lady has chosen a program to support. Jacqueline Kennedy established the President's home as a national museum. Lady Bird Johnson supported efforts to beautify the capital city and its monuments. Pat Nixon encouraged national volunteer efforts. Betty Ford spoke out on behalf of handicapped children. Rosalynn Carter took up the cause of the mentally ill, while Nancy Reagan campaigned against illegal drugs, and Barbara Bush promoted the cause of literacy. Hillary Clinton took strong stands on national health care and the welfare of children in this nation and abroad. Laura Bush brought her long-standing interest in literacy to the job of First Lady. Each woman has helped focus national attention on issues that might otherwise have been neglected.

Snapshots (from left to right) show many roles assumed by First Ladies. Eleanor Roosevelt visits with mine workers. Jacqueline Kennedy, who revived interest in White House history, poses in the newly restored residence. Rosalynn Carter greets guests at the President's home. Laura Bush stands shoulder-to-shoulder with members of the armed services in a show of wartime support.

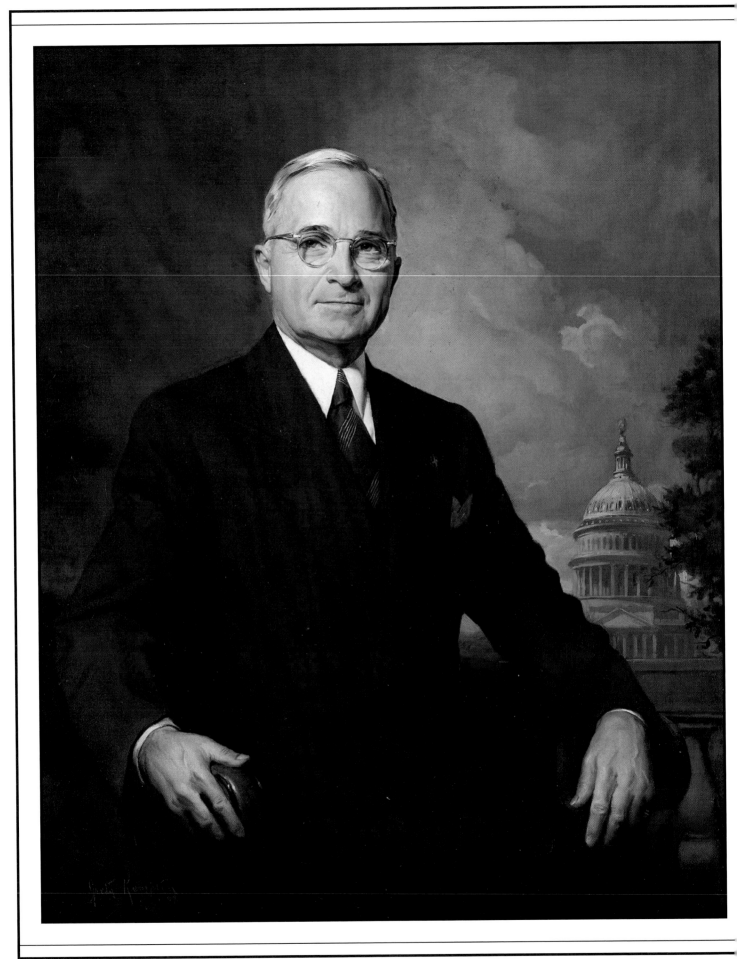

Harry S. Truman

33RD PRESIDENT OF THE UNITED STATES ★ 1945 – 1953

NICKNAME	Give 'Em Hell Harry
BORN	May 10, 1884, in Lamar, Mo.
POLITICAL PARTY	Democrat
CHIEF OPPONENT	1st term: none, succeeded Roosevelt; 2nd term: Thomas Edmund Dewey, Republican (1902–1971)
TERM OF OFFICE	April 12, 1945–Jan. 20, 1953
AGE AT INAUGURATION	60 years old
NUMBER OF TERMS	one, plus balance of Franklin D. Roosevelt's term
VICE PRESIDENTS	1st term: none; 2nd term: Alben William Barkley (1877–1956)
FIRST LADY	Elizabeth (Bess) Virginia Wallace Truman (1885–1982), wife (married June 29, 1919)
CHILDREN	Margaret
GEOGRAPHIC SCENE	48 states
NEW STATES ADDED	none
DIED	Dec. 26, 1972, in Independence, Mo.
AGE AT DEATH	88 years old
SELECTED LANDMARKS	Lamar, Mo. (birthplace); Grandview, Mo. (family farm); Key West Little White House Museum, Key West, Fla.; Harry S. Truman National Historic Site (adult home) and Harry S. Truman Library and Museum (and grave), Independence, Mo.

Harry S. Truman's whistle-stop campaign of 1948

WHEN HARRY S. TRUMAN BECAME PRESIDENT after the sudden death of Franklin D. Roosevelt, he was stunned. "I felt like the moon, the stars, and all the planets had fallen on me," he said. Issues such as the use of atomic weapons, tensions with the Soviet Union, and war in Korea dominated his administration.

Truman was no stranger to challenge when he became President. He grew up on a farm in Missouri, and tight family finances made him the only 20th-century President who did not attend college. Truman's meandering career included work as a railroad timekeeper, a farmer, a World War I artillery captain, and a clothing store owner. He entered politics in 1922 as a local administrator; eventually he spent ten years in the U.S. Senate. In 1944 President Franklin D. Roosevelt persuaded Senator Truman to join his fourth-term reelection ticket.

Only months after becoming Vice President, Truman found himself taking the presidential oath of office because President Roosevelt had died. Soon after that, World War II ended in Europe. Truman decided to use a secret weapon— the atomic bomb—to stop the intense fighting that continued with Japan. He hoped this plan would spare the lives of U.S. troops by ending the war quickly and avoiding the need to invade Japan. Thousands of Japanese died instantly in nuclear attacks at Hiroshima and Nagasaki before Japan agreed to stop fighting. Worldwide casualties by the end of the war topped 10 million people, including more than 400,000 Americans.

International events dominated Truman's Presidency. He

Harry S. Truman married Elizabeth "Bess" Wallace when he was 35 (above); the couple met in Sunday school when he was six. Truman's middle initial did not stand for a middle name; his parents used the letter to honor their own fathers, each of whom had a name that started with "S."

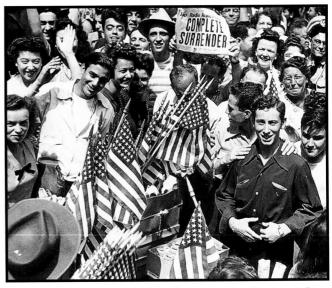

Harry S. Truman met with Allied leaders in July 1945 (left). Celebrations marked the end of World War II (right). The nation enjoyed a postwar boom during Truman's Presidency. Thousands of returning veterans earned free college educations through the G.I. Bill of Rights. Couples who had put off marriage during the war were wed in record numbers and started a "baby boom" of soaring births.

supported the creation of the United Nations and favored the formation of Israel. He used the Marshall Plan to rebuild war-torn Europe and helped form the North Atlantic Treaty Organization (NATO) to fortify the security of western Europe, the U.S., and Canada. In particular, he sought to discourage the expanding influence of the Soviet Union and its political system of communism. Communism—a program of government control over citizens, industries, and finances—was at odds with the U.S. system of democracy, freedom, and market-based capitalism. A Cold War—one with limited fighting but much hostility, mistrust, and stockpiling of nuclear weapons—developed between the United States, the Soviet Union, and their allies.

As tensions grew between the two "blocs" of countries, Truman committed the United States to "support free peoples who are resisting" conquest. When the Soviet Union lowered its so-called Iron Curtain of restricted access to West Berlin, Truman organized a massive airlift of supplies into the city. When war broke out between communist North Korea and independent South Korea in 1950, Truman developed an international army through the United Nations to "contain" the spread of communism. When anticommunist citizens asked for U.S. assistance in Vietnam, Truman sent aid.

A fear of communism at home developed alongside these international worries. U.S. Senator Joseph McCarthy exploited this anxiety by conducting congressional investigations of suspected communists. Among those who eventually joined his efforts was a

Harry S. Truman took delight in an election-eve headline that mistakenly announced the victory of his opponent in 1948. His whistle-stop campaign effort helped clinch his victory. It took him to six million people during a 31,000-mile train journey. "Give 'em hell, Harry!" yelled supporters, when Truman criticized the uncooperative Congress.

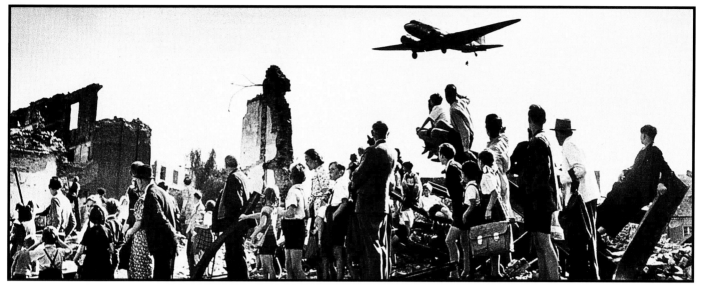

After World War II, Germany and its capital city of Berlin were divided in half; the Soviet Union assumed control over eastern sections, and the U.S., France, and Great Britain oversaw western territories. When the Soviet Union cut off access to West Berlin in June 1948, Western allies delivered necessary supplies to stranded residents (above). Planes landed as often as every few minutes during the Berlin airlift. The Soviet blockade lasted until May 1949.

future President, Senator Richard M. Nixon. McCarthy's Red Scare (named after a symbolic communist color) lasted until 1954, when other senators shut down his hearings.

Truman won election in his own right in 1948. As President he tried to extend Roosevelt's New Deal of federal programs with his own 21-point Fair Deal, but most proposals failed to take hold. His efforts to integrate all races in the armed forces met with both favor and controversy.

"The buck stops here."

A presidential motto on Harry S. Truman's desk

Challenged by so many difficult issues, Truman left the White House with the lowest approval rating for a President up to that time. In later years respect for Truman's handling of tough times increased; since 1962 historians have consistently ranked him among the top ten Presidents.

Truman and his wife retired to Independence, Missouri. Bess Truman lived to age 97—longer than any other First Lady. She died in 1982, ten years after her husband.

Harry S. Truman knew nothing about the development of the atomic bomb until after he became President near the end of World War II. As President he followed the war's progress by visiting the White House war room (left). After the war Truman supported the European recovery plan devised by Secretary of State George C. Marshall (right). The Marshall Plan shared $12 billion over three years with such countries as England, France, and West Germany. It boosted the American economy and helped create democracies throughout Europe. "Peace, freedom, and world trade are indivisible," noted Truman.

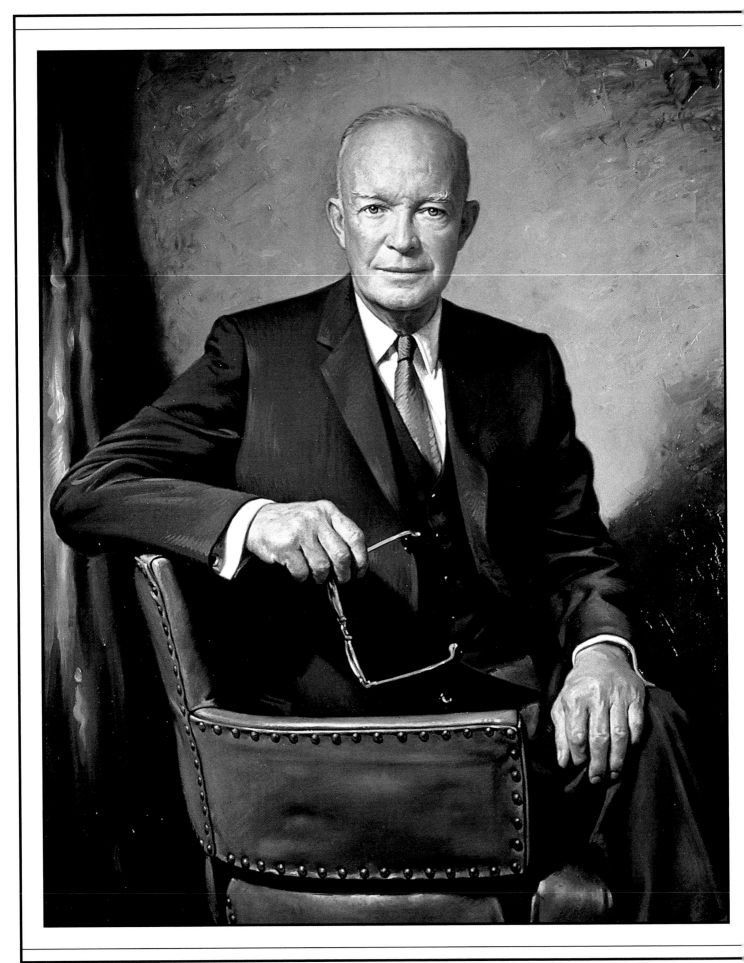

Dwight D. Eisenhower

34TH PRESIDENT OF THE UNITED STATES ★ 1953 – 1961

NICKNAME	Ike
BORN	Oct. 14, 1890, in Denison, Tex.
POLITICAL PARTY	Republican
CHIEF OPPONENT	1st and 2nd terms: Adlai Ewing Stevenson, Democrat (1900–1965)
TERM OF OFFICE	Jan. 20, 1953–Jan. 20, 1961
AGE AT INAUGURATION	62 years old
NUMBER OF TERMS	two
VICE PRESIDENT	Richard M. Nixon (1913–1994)
FIRST LADY	Marie (Mamie) Geneva Doud Eisenhower (1896–1979), wife (married July 1, 1916)
CHILDREN	John, plus a son died young
GEOGRAPHIC SCENE	48 states
NEW STATES ADDED	Alaska, Hawaii (1959)
DIED	March 28, 1969, in Washington, D.C.
AGE AT DEATH	78 years old
SELECTED LANDMARKS	Eisenhower Birthplace State Historical Park, Denison, Tex.; Eisenhower National Historic Site, Gettysburg, Pa. (retirement home); Eisenhower Center (including presidential library, museum, family home, grave), Abilene, Kans.

The Eisenhowers on their wedding day

LIKE GENERALS GEORGE WASHINGTON AND ULYSSES S. GRANT, General Dwight David Eisenhower became President thanks to his popularity as a war hero. Eisenhower—the man who helped bring victory to Europe during World War II—sought to keep peace at home and abroad after becoming President. His moderate political views earned the Republican Party new respect.

Although born in Texas, Eisenhower was raised in Abilene, Kansas, where his father worked in a creamery. He learned lessons about war and peace at an early age while growing up there with five brothers. The boys, all of whom took turns using the nickname "Ike," never hesitated to come to blows among themselves or with others when arguments arose. Even as a youngster, Eisenhower enjoyed studying military history. He went on to graduate from the U.S. Military Academy at West Point and take up a career in the Army. Later that year he met Marie "Mamie" Doud; the couple married soon after.

For the next 26 years, Eisenhower's Army duties took him to bases throughout the United States as well as to the Panama Canal Zone and the Philippines. Along the way he finished first in his class at officer training school and did desk duty at war offices in Washington, D.C. Much to his regret he missed out on World War I combat; he was instead assigned to train others to fight.

His leadership skills and organizational talents were recognized with key military appointments during World War II. Eisenhower was the commander of the combined Allied forces

---

Dwight D. Eisenhower played football at West Point (above) until a knee injury ended his athletic career. His skills as a military leader helped carry him to the White House years later.

> "What counts is not necessarily the size of the dog in the fight—it's the size of the fight in the dog."

Dwight D. Eisenhower, January 31, 1958

Dwight D. Eisenhower served as supreme commander of all Allied forces during the World War II campaigns that liberated North Africa and Europe from German and Italian occupation forces. In June 1944 Eisenhower urged members of the U.S. 101st Airborne Division (left) to accomplish their mission during the impending D-day invasion of France. Later on, Eisenhower toured so many countries as President—27 in all— that his travels were written up in NATIONAL GEOGRAPHIC.

that overran enemy troops in North Africa, Sicily, Italy, and northern Europe. Before the end of the war, he had risen to the Army's highest rank— five-star general. One soldier who spotted the rows of stars on Eisenhower's uniform exclaimed: "Cripes! The whole Milky Way!"

After the war, Eisenhower served as chief of staff for the Army, president of Columbia University, and commander of international troops in Europe. As early as 1943, people had suggested that Eisenhower run for President with either political party. Happy with Army life, he dismissed the idea.

Finally, in 1952, he agreed to run for President as a Republican. Eisenhower faced the same opponent that year and four years later—Adlai Stevenson. Eisenhower's signature grin, victory wave, and record of wartime service encouraged voters to proclaim: "We like Ike!" They proved it by awarding Eisenhower a sizable majority of votes in each election.

Challenges from the Truman administration carried over into Eisenhower's Presidency. Peace talks finally ended the fighting in Korea in 1953. The conflict had killed or wounded more than three million people, including 34,000 Americans. Relations

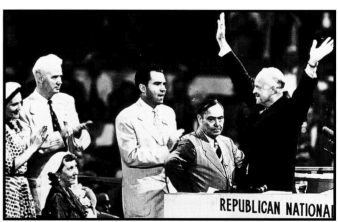

Republicans reclaimed the White House after a 20-year absence thanks to the popular appeal of party nominee Dwight D. Eisenhower (left and right). During his Presidency "Ike" authorized construction of the nation's interstate highway system and collaborated with Canada to create the St. Lawrence Seaway linking the Great Lakes with the Atlantic Ocean. By the end of his administration, citizens could chant: "Ike is nifty, Ike is nifty; started out with 48; ended up with 50," because Alaska and Hawaii had joined the Union.

President-elect Eisenhower visited U.S. troops in Korea during 1952 (left) as part of his efforts to end U.S. military involvement there. Senator Joseph McCarthy continued to inflame U.S. fears of communism at home until his high-profile congressional hearings (right) were shut down in 1954. The domino theory—the idea that communism could spread from one vulnerable country to the next like a row of tumbling dominoes—led the President to develop his Eisenhower Doctrine. This policy fostered increased U.S. assistance of anticommunist efforts in Vietnam during his administration.

with the Soviet Union remained tense. Although Eisenhower urged the Soviets to consider nuclear disarmament, or the reduction of atomic weapons, neither side seemed willing to trust the other. In 1957 the Soviets launched the world's first satellite, Sputnik. Americans feared it might be armed with nuclear weapons. Three years later the Soviets were equally alarmed when they captured a U.S. pilot flying a U-2 spy plane over their country.

At home, Eisenhower worked to make the United States live up to its ideals of freedom and equality. "There must be no second-class citizens in this country," he wrote. The President sent federal troops to Little Rock, Arkansas, to enforce the Supreme Court's *Brown* v. *Board of Education* ruling. This landmark decision called for public schools to be desegregated, or open to children of all races. He also bolstered civil rights by signing new voting laws.

In 1961 Eisenhower and his wife retired to a farm they had purchased in 1950 near Gettysburg, Pennsylvania. Because Eisenhower's career had kept them forever on the go (they moved 28 times during their marriage), this was the first home they ever owned. Although several heart attacks threatened the former President's health, he enjoyed writing his memoirs, playing golf, painting landscapes, and keeping a finger in politics. He died in 1969. Mamie died 10 years later.

Black children and white children in the U.S. were routinely educated in separate schools (left) when Dwight D. Eisenhower became President. Eisenhower favored eliminating such practices. Dwight and Mamie Eisenhower (above) were a popular presidential couple. Mamie acted as a traditional hostess during her years as First Lady. She restored the custom, discontinued during World War II, of holding an annual White House Easter egg roll. Eisenhower changed Franklin D. Roosevelt's name for the presidential retreat in Maryland from Shangri-La to Camp David in honor of their grandson.

John F. Kennedy

35TH PRESIDENT OF THE UNITED STATES ★ 1961 – 1963

NICKNAME	JFK
BORN	May 29, 1917, in Brookline, Mass.
POLITICAL PARTY	Democrat

John F. Kennedy, sits perched on a scooter, with mother Rose, and siblings Eunice, Kathleen, Rosemary, and Joe, Jr.

CHIEF OPPONENT	Richard M. Nixon (1913–1994)
TERM OF OFFICE	Jan. 20, 1961–Nov. 22, 1963
AGE AT INAUGURATION	43 years old
NUMBER OF TERMS	one (cut short by assassination)
VICE PRESIDENT	Lyndon B. Johnson (1908–1973)
FIRST LADY	Jacqueline Lee Bouvier Kennedy (1929–1994), wife (married Sept. 12, 1953)
CHILDREN	Caroline, John, plus a son died young
GEOGRAPHIC SCENE	50 states
DIED	Nov. 22, 1963, in Dallas, Tex.
AGE AT DEATH	46 years old
SELECTED LANDMARKS	Brookline, Mass. (birthplace); Hammersmith Farm, Newport, R.I. (wife's family home, used as a "summer White House"); John F. Kennedy Library and Museum, Boston, Mass.; Arlington National Cemetery, Arlington, Va.

JOHN FITZGERALD KENNEDY WAS ELECTED by the narrowest popular voting margin in history and served as President for only about 1,000 days before he was assassinated. Yet he remains a central figure of the American Presidency. His eloquent calls for peace, justice, and national service inspired action among countless citizens during his lifetime and continue to influence others today.

After his death the Kennedy administration was compared to Camelot, the legendary ancient realm of the fair-minded King Arthur. Kennedy's birth to a privileged family made the perfect place to begin the comparison. His father hoped one of his four sons would become President; eventually three of them campaigned for that office. John (nicknamed Jack) attended prestigious schools and graduated with honors from Harvard University. Although plagued by a string of childhood illnesses, he was athletic, playful, and handsome. A decorated World War II naval officer, Jack took up the family's presidential hopes after his older brother, Joseph, died in combat.

Kennedy met Jacqueline Bouvier during his six years as a U.S. congressman from Massachusetts. Jackie was sophisticated, charming, and beautiful. The pair were married in 1953, soon after Jack became a U.S. senator. Kennedy sought the Democratic presidential nomination in 1960. "We stand today on the edge of a New Frontier,"

John F. Kennedy became a World War II hero after the patrol torpedo boat under his command (left) was destroyed by a Japanese warship (right). Kennedy swam with the surviving crew members to safety several miles away, towing along one injured sailor by clamping the man's life jacket strap in his teeth. When asked later how he became a hero, Kennedy replied: "It was easy—they sank my boat."

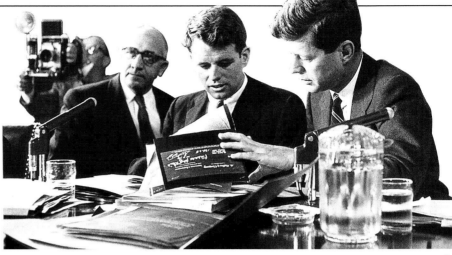

John F. Kennedy's family moved into the White House (left) a few weeks after his Inauguration. His wife, Jacqueline, was an active First Lady while mothering their young children, Caroline and John. Jackie promoted the performing arts and helped foster the Camelot image of the Kennedy Presidency. John F. Kennedy included his brother Bobby among his closest advisers while President (above).

he proclaimed after winning the nomination. Kennedy narrowly defeated Richard Nixon in a tight race. Illegal voting in key states like Texas and Illinois may have helped seal his victory. Kennedy is the only Catholic to be elected President.

Conflicts in the Cold War dominated much of Kennedy's Presidency. First, the U.S. government secretly tried to overthrow Cuba's new communist dictator, Fidel Castro, by helping Cuban exiles invade their homeland at the Bay of Pigs. U.S. involvement proved embarrassing when the mission failed. Then tensions flared when the Soviet Union built a wall dividing East from West Berlin

in Germany. Next the two superpowers narrowly avoided nuclear war during the Cuban missile crisis, a tense standoff resulting from the U.S. discovery of Soviet warheads in Cuba. Secretly Kennedy fought the spread of communism elsewhere by continuing U.S. support of anticommunists in Vietnam. Publicly he urged Americans to win the "space race" against the Soviets by sending astronauts to the moon and back. Cold War tensions eased somewhat in 1963 after the two nations signed a treaty banning most nuclear testing.

Civil rights, including the freedom for all races to vote, was a dominant issue, too. At first Kennedy

Both the Soviet Union and the United States increased their military arsenals (left) during the early years of John F. Kennedy's administration. Cold War tensions were reduced shortly before Kennedy's death when he signed a nuclear-test-ban treaty (right) with the United States, the Soviets, and the United Kingdom, outlawing atomic explosions in the atmosphere, space, and underwater.

John F. Kennedy visited coal miners (left) as part of his presidential campaign in 1960. Near the end of Kennedy's administration more than 200,000 people took part in a March on Washington to commemorate the 100th anniversary of Abraham Lincoln's Emancipation Proclamation. Martin Luther King, Jr., delivered his famous "I have a dream" speech (right) to mark the occasion.

relied on the Justice Department, headed by his younger brother Robert (Bobby), to aid this cause. Later the President publicly supported racial equality. Much of the civil rights legislation Kennedy favored became law in tribute to him after his assassination.

Kennedy was shot and killed on Nov. 22, 1963, while touring Dallas, Texas, in a presidential motorcade. More than a hundred nations sent representatives to his funeral in Washington, D.C. Anyone who could find a television "attended" the event, too. All were moved by the solemn processions, by Jackie's dignity, and by the composure of their children. Hearts broke as three-year-old John-John saluted his father's coffin.

The identity of Kennedy's assassin remains in dispute. Gunman Lee Harvey Oswald was charged with the death but was himself murdered before he could be tried. Repeated investigations have failed to confirm theories that others may have helped Oswald kill the President.

The Camelot image of the Kennedy years endures, even as new facts emerge about the era (such as the extent of the covert, or secret, support his administration gave to anticommunists in Vietnam, and his extramarital affairs while in office). Jack's brother Bobby became a U.S. senator; he was assassinated in 1968 while running for President. His youngest brother, Edward (Teddy), is a U.S. senator; he sought his party's nomination for President in 1980. Jackie remarried five years after her husband's death. She died from cancer in her mid-60s and was buried beside Jack at Arlington National Cemetery.

"Ask not what your country can do for you — ask what you can do for your country."

John F. Kennedy,
Inaugural Address, January 20, 1961

John F. Kennedy was the youngest man ever elected President. (Teddy Roosevelt was the youngest President by succession, not election.) Kennedy was also the youngest one to die, when an assassin shot him in a motorcade (left) just three years after his election. Jacqueline Kennedy modeled her husband's funeral after Abraham Lincoln's. Kennedy's casket even lay in state at the U.S. Capitol on the same platform that was used for Lincoln.

Presidents Who Died in Office

★ The Mysterious Twenty-Year Curse ★

EIGHT OF the nation's Presidents have died before completing their terms of office. Half of these men were victims of illnesses; the others were assassinated. Oddly, seven of these deaths have occurred in a regular pattern. The winner of every five elections from 1840 to 1960 has died before completing his final term. This circumstance has been called the 20-year jinx or the 20-year curse.

The first President to die in office was William Henry Harrison. He died on April 4, 1841, exactly one month after his Inauguration, from complications of a cold. Abraham Lincoln's first term began 20 years after Harrison's. Lincoln died on April 15, 1865,

President Kennedy lies in state, 1963.

within a week of the end of the Civil War, after being shot by a supporter of the defeated South.

Twenty years after Lincoln's first election, James A. Garfield took office. Garfield was shot on July 2, 1881, by a deranged former political supporter. He died two and a half months later.

President William McKinley was shot 20 years afterward. Early in his second term a disgruntled factory worker fired on him in a receiving line. McKinley died eight days later, on Sept. 14, 1901.

The next two sitting Presidents to die five terms apart were victims of natural causes. Warren G. Harding died suddenly on Aug. 2, 1923. Doctors think he may have had a heart attack. Franklin D. Roosevelt was killed by a stroke, a brain injury caused by improper blood flow in the head. He died a few months into his fourth term of office on April 12, 1945.

John F. Kennedy, the last President to die in office, and on a 20-year cycle, was assassinated on Nov. 22, 1963, in Dallas, Texas.

Zachary Taylor was the only President who

The nation mourned the death of Abraham Lincoln after the Civil War by hanging ribbons (far left) in their windows to honor "the late lamented President Lincoln." His body was drawn through the nation's capital in a solemn funeral procession (left) before traveling home to Illinois for burial.

In 1881 Alexander Graham Bell tried to find the bullet lodged in James A. Garfield by an assassin (left). Bell's early metal detector failed, and Garfield died of blood poisoning. Presidential deaths make front-page news (above).

died in office outside of the 20-year death cycle. He died from cholera on July 9, 1850.

Ronald Reagan finally broke the 120-year history of cyclical presidential deaths. Even so, his life was threatened by an assassination attempt in 1981. Prompt modern medical attention saved his life.

Other assassination attempts were made against Presidents Andrew Jackson, Harry S. Truman, and Gerald Ford. An assassin threatened President-elect Franklin D. Roosevelt, too. No Vice Presidents have been assassinated, but seven have died in office.

Often the bodies of fallen Presidents—even those who die after their terms are over—"lie in state." During this honor the coffin of the deceased is temporarily displayed on a platform and visitors file past the casket in tribute. Sometimes the coffin lid is open to show the body inside; other times it is closed and covered with the U.S. flag. Seven Presidents have lain in state in the White House East Room; ten others have rested in the rotunda of the U.S. Capitol. Ronald Reagan received this honor in 2004, the first such tribute to a U.S. President since the death of Lyndon B. Johnson in 1973.

The death of a President brings shock and sorrow to the entire nation, not just to relatives. Mourners bade farewell to William McKinley as his coffin was loaded onto his funeral train (left). John F. Kennedy's family observed his funeral procession (right) while millions of citizens watched via live television broadcast.

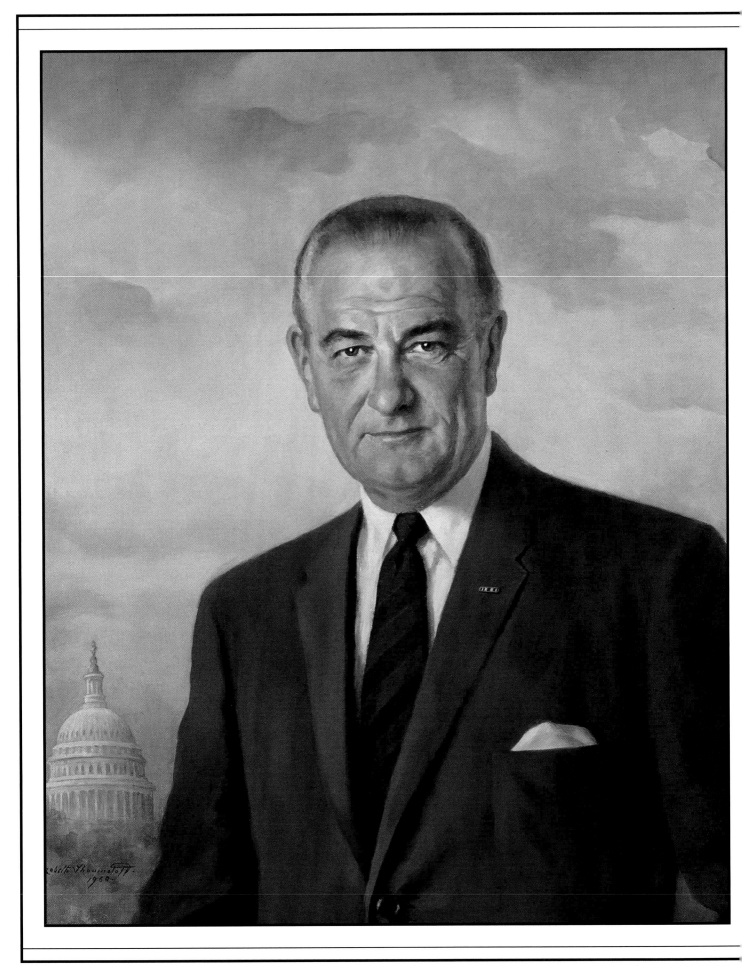

Lyndon B. Johnson

36TH PRESIDENT OF THE UNITED STATES ★ *1963 – 1969*

NICKNAME	LBJ
BORN	Aug. 27, 1908, near Stonewall, Tex.
POLITICAL PARTY	Democrat
CHIEF OPPONENTS	1st term: none, succeeded Kennedy; 2nd term: Barry Morris Goldwater, Republican (1909–1998)
TERM OF OFFICE	Nov. 22, 1963–Jan. 20, 1969
AGE AT INAUGURATION	55 years old
NUMBER OF TERMS	one, plus balance of John F. Kennedy's term
VICE PRESIDENTS	1st term: none; 2nd term: Hubert Horatio Humphrey (1911–1978)
FIRST LADY	Claudia Alta (Lady Bird) Taylor Johnson (1912–present), wife (married Nov. 17, 1934)
CHILDREN	Lynda, Luci
GEOGRAPHIC SCENE	50 states
DIED	Jan. 22, 1973, near San Antonio, Tex.
AGE AT DEATH	64 years old
SELECTED LANDMARKS	Lyndon B. Johnson National Historical Park, Stonewall, Tex., and Johnson City, Tex. (includes visitor center, reconstructed birthplace, school, boyhood home, Johnson Settlement, "Texas White House," LBJ Ranch, and grave); Lyndon Baines Johnson Library and Museum, University of Texas, Austin, Tex.

LBJ and Lady Bird by the U.S. Capitol

LYNDON BAINES JOHNSON CHANNELED ENERGY from the nation's grief over the sudden death of John F. Kennedy into creating a living memorial to the slain leader. Johnson called this legacy the Great Society. He envisioned a nation that offered opportunity, prosperity, and fairness to all citizens. His tireless efforts for this cause brought considerable improvement to the lives of racial minorities and the poor. These accomplishments became overshadowed, however, by increased U.S. involvement in a war in Vietnam.

"No words are sad enough to express our sense of loss," President Johnson observed two days after the funeral of John F. Kennedy. "No words are strong enough to express our determination to continue the forward thrust of America that he began." Johnson, a veteran politician, was uniquely prepared to lead that effort.

The son of a farmer and legislator, Johnson grew up in rural Texas. His childhood mixed hard times with breaks for marble games, endless chores with a memorable visit to the Alamo. After finishing high school, he drifted around California for two years doing odd jobs. Later he enrolled at Southwest Texas State Teachers College; he graduated in 1930. Johnson met his future wife, Claudia "Lady Bird" Taylor, while working for a U.S.

Lyndon B. Johnson became the only U.S. President to take the oath of office on an airplane when he was sworn in aboard Air Force One (above) two hours after the assassination of John F. Kennedy. The plane was preparing to take him back to Washington, D.C., along with Kennedy's body. Johnson was flanked by his wife on one side and Kennedy's widow (at right) on the other. Jacqueline Kennedy still wore the clothes stained during the shooting of her husband.

Lyndon B. Johnson gathered to celebrate his Inauguration in 1965 with family and his new Vice President, Hubert H. Humphrey. The Cold War had figured prominently in his reelection. Voters were troubled when Johnson's opponent spoke about the reasonableness of using nuclear weapons in a war. Democrats attacked this "hawkish," or warlike, position with a television commercial that shifted from the scene of a child playing with a daisy to the exploding mushroom cloud of a nuclear bomb.

congressman. Her nickname gave the couple the same initials after they were married. In future years, their daughters, their Texas ranch, and even a family dog bore names that yielded the trademark L.B.J. initials.

Johnson was elected to the House of Representatives six consecutive times beginning in 1937. He received a Silver Star for World War II service while on leave from Congress. He earned the nickname "Landslide Lyndon" in 1948 when he won his first U.S. Senate seat by nothing like a landslide—just 87 votes. He was reelected overwhelmingly six years later. In 1960 Kennedy asked the influential senator to be his running mate. (He had just defeated Johnson in a spirited contest for their party's presidential nomination.) Johnson's southern background helped secure their victory that fall.

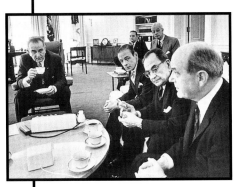

As President, Lyndon B. Johnson (above, at left) declared a "war on poverty." He worked two shifts a day, sleeping a few hours at night and napping in his pajamas between shifts during the day. Johnson was famous for giving "the treatment"—intense verbal and physical communication—to anyone whose support he needed. "You really felt as if a St. Bernard had licked your face for an hour, had pawed you all over," explained one recipient. Few could resist his pitch.

After Kennedy was assassinated three years later, Johnson suggested the nation create an improved Great Society as a way of commemorating the slain President. Using skills from his years as a powerful U.S. senator, Johnson influenced Congress to pass sweeping laws. Among other things, this legislation secured fair voting rights for minorities, funded education programs, battled poverty and crime, encouraged fair housing practices, strengthened access to health care, aided environmental cleanup and conservation, and established federal services such as the Public Broadcasting Service. No President has ever been more successful at ushering legislation through Congress.

Johnson won outright election to the Presidency in the midst of this burst of legislation. Voters agreed to go "All the Way With LBJ" in 1964. He truly was "Landslide Lyndon" by then, earning 16 million more votes than his opponent. This edge gave him 61 percent of the popular vote.

The Vietnam War undercut Johnson's domestic triumphs. Before his administration was over, the United States had dropped more tons of bombs over the divided countries of North and

"Let this session of Congress be known as the session which did more for civil rights than the last hundred sessions combined."

Lyndon B. Johnson, State of the Union Address, January 8, 1964

Race relations and civil rights were a dominant issue during the Presidency of Lyndon B. Johnson. Johnson sought to end practices of discrimination such as segregated schools and waiting rooms (left) by signing new legislation to protect human rights regardless of race (center). He appointed the first African American to the Supreme Court in 1967—Thurgood Marshall (right). His emphasis on Civil Rights kindled a shift in the South to the Republican Party.

South Vietnam than it had used in Europe during all of World War II. Yet, despite these efforts, North Vietnamese communists were more committed than ever in the fight to reunite North with South. Widespread opposition developed to the war among U.S. citizens, particularly as the growing level of their nation's involvement became fully known.

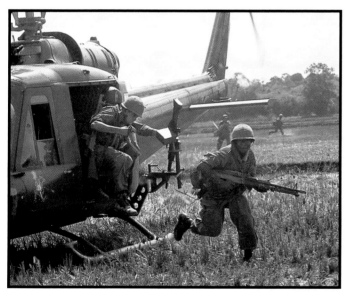

Sticking with the Cold War instincts of earlier Presidents, Lyndon B. Johnson insisted that the Vietnam War had to be won to prevent the spread of communism throughout Southeast Asia. Secretly he sent more and more aid to anticommunist South Vietnam until, by the end of his Presidency, more than half a million U.S. soldiers were on duty there.

Public protests about the Vietnam War forced Johnson to abandon thoughts of running for reelection in 1968. Instead, he pledged to seek peace between the North and South Vietnamese. His efforts were unsuccessful; the two sides had difficulty even agreeing what shape to make their negotiating table.

In 1969 Johnson retired with Lady Bird to the LBJ Ranch near Johnson City, Texas. He wrote his memoirs, managed his farm, and regretted the bitter end of his Presidency. Johnson had had a severe heart attack years earlier while a U.S. senator; he suffered two more during his retirement. The last one proved fatal. After lying in state at the U.S. Capitol, President Johnson's body was buried at his family ranch. Lady Bird Johnson continues to live in Texas.

The Johnsons enjoyed the beauty of the hill country in their native Texas (above). During their years together in the White House, Lady Bird promoted legislation to limit unsightly billboards along highways. She encouraged better landscaping of public areas in the nation's capital and elsewhere, too. Today, she promotes the study and cultivation of wildflowers around the country.

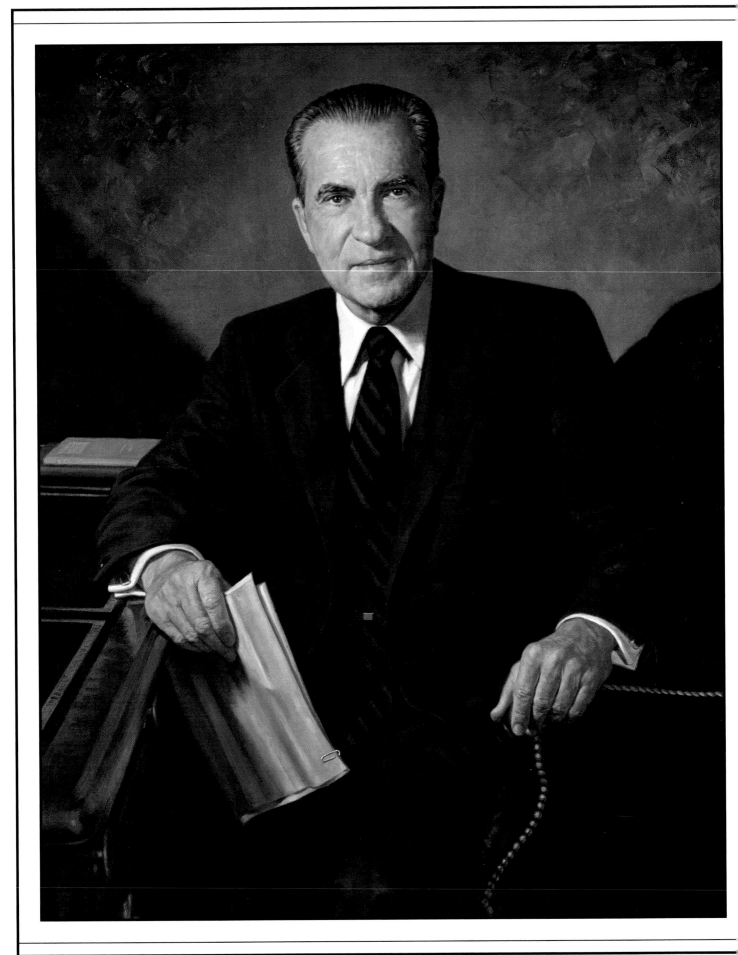

Richard M. Nixon

37TH PRESIDENT OF THE UNITED STATES ★ 1969 – 1974

NICKNAME	Tricky Dick
BORN	Jan. 9, 1913, in Yorba Linda, Calif.
POLITICAL PARTY	Republican
CHIEF OPPONENTS	1st term: Hubert Horatio Humphrey, Democrat (1911–1978) and George Corley Wallace, American Independent (1919–1998); 2nd term: George Stanley McGovern, Democrat (1922–present)
TERM OF OFFICE	Jan. 20, 1969–Aug. 9, 1974
AGE AT INAUGURATION	56 years old
NUMBER OF TERMS	two (cut short by resignation)
VICE PRESIDENTS	1st term and 2nd term (partial): Spiro Theodore Agnew (1918–1996); 2nd term (balance): Gerald R. Ford (1913–present)
FIRST LADY	Thelma Catherine (Pat) Ryan Nixon (1912–1993), wife (married June 21, 1940)
CHILDREN	Patricia, Julie
GEOGRAPHIC SCENE	50 states
DIED	April 22, 1994, in New York, N.Y.
AGE AT DEATH	81 years old
SELECTED LANDMARKS	Richard Nixon Library and Birthplace (includes museum and grave), Yorba Linda, Calif.

Richard M. Nixon vacationed in Florida with his wife, daughters, and future son-in-law before embarking on his 1968 presidential campaign.

RICHARD MILHOUS NIXON WAS FORCED TO RESIGN from office after the public learned how he had encouraged the use of illegal activity to support his administration. He is the only U.S. President to resign, and the only one to leave office alive without completing his term. The importance of Nixon's official accomplishments in office are diminished by his serious abuses of presidential power.

Throughout his long political career, Nixon made much of his humble origins. He grew up in Southern California where his family struggled against threats of poverty and ill health. Two of his four brothers died by the time he was 20. Nixon paid for his education at nearby Whittier College by working long hours as manager of the vegetable section in his father's grocery store. Later he graduated from Duke University Law School in North Carolina and opened a law practice back home. He met his future wife, Thelma "Pat" Ryan, when they acted together in a local play. He served as a noncombat naval officer in the Pacific during World War II.

Nixon won seats in the U.S. House in 1946 and the U.S. Senate in 1950. By then, people were calling him "Tricky Dick" because of "dirty tricks" (including illegal campaign funding and sensational character attacks) he used to get elected. He won notice for his part in Senator Joseph McCarthy's "Red Scare" search for communists. Then Nixon became Dwight D. Eisenhower's Vice President. He lost the 1960 presidential race to John F. Kennedy and the 1962 California governor's race before being elected President in 1968.

Richard M. Nixon, who served in the U.S. Navy during World War II (above), contributed to a growing public mistrust of government during his Presidency. The more often he used his trademark phrase, "Let me make one thing perfectly clear," the less sure citizens became that they were hearing the truth. This "credibility gap" had begun after World War II as the public realized government actions did not always match government claims.

Richard M. Nixon spoke with astronauts in space (left) after their successful landing on the moon, July 20, 1969. "That's one small step for a man, one giant leap for mankind," observed Neil Armstrong as he left the first human footprints in space. Nixon toured the country with enthusiasm whether he was campaigning or appearing as President (right). During his administration the nation's voting age was lowered from 21 to 18 by Constitutional amendment.

In the White House at last, Nixon was eager to mark his place in history. At home he tried to improve welfare, protect the environment, and reduce crime. He fought double-digit inflation caused by large military budgets and energy shortages. He often ignored or stretched laws that met with his disapproval (from those that regulated wiretapping procedures to those that funded Native American education programs). Federal courts often overruled him.

Abroad Nixon improved relations between the United States and the communist nations of China and the Soviet Union. He made celebrated trips to each country, and he signed new agreements limiting the spread of nuclear weapons. Although Nixon entered the White House with a pledge to end the Vietnam War, the task proved difficult. Even as more troops came home, fighting spread to nearby countries. North Vietnam took control of South Vietnam in 1975, two years after the nations made "peace" and U.S. troops had withdrawn. Many Americans were bitter about the war's costs: 58,000 U.S. lives and $110 billion.

Nixon expanded on his use of "dirty tricks" while President. He and other staff members broke laws in their efforts to discover embarrassing information about his rivals and enemies (a list of more than 40,000 names). They hired people to commit burglaries and tap phones in their search for "dirt."

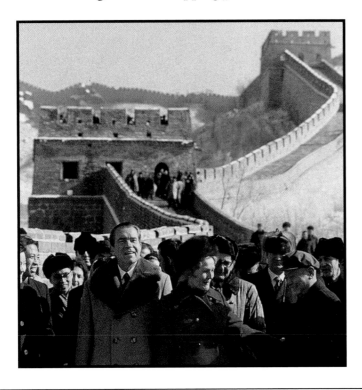

In 1972 Richard M. Nixon became the first U.S. President to visit China. Nixon helped dissolve hostilities between the two nations by meeting with communist leaders and visiting landmarks like the Great Wall (left). Three months later he met with communist leaders in the Soviet Union.

They silenced their helpers with "hush money," spent federal campaign funds improperly, made illegal use of government records, and filed false income tax reports.

In 1972 Nixon's associates hired men to burglarize Democratic Party offices at the Watergate building in Washington, D.C. (They hoped to gain insider information there that would help Nixon be reelected later that year.) The Watergate scandal that ended Nixon's Presidency began after the burglars were caught. The investigation of the break-in did not progress quickly enough, though, to prevent Nixon's landslide reelection in 1972.

For more than two years Nixon and others tried to hide their involvement in the crime. They denied that Nixon was involved in planning the caper or its cover-up. Newspaper reporters and members of Congress led increasingly intense investigations into possible crimes. Eventually the Supreme Court forced Nixon to release secret tape recordings he had made of his White House conversations. The tapes confirmed that Nixon had lied about his innocence in

"Pat" Nixon earned her nickname for being born near St. Patrick's Day. She traveled widely as First Lady and promoted volunteer work. Daughters Julie (left) and Tricia were married after their father's election.

planning illegal activities and covering them up.

On August 9, 1974, Nixon resigned from office. Otherwise he faced the likelihood of impeachment by the House of Representatives and removal from office through a trial in the U.S. Senate. More than 20 other people, including top White House staff members, a former attorney general, and a former secretary of commerce were found guilty of crimes, fined, and/or sent to jail. Nixon's first Vice President, Spiro Agnew, had resigned from office in an earlier scandal involving bribery and income tax evasion. After Agnew's successor, Gerald Ford, became President, he spared Nixon from prosecution by pardoning him for any crimes he may have committed.

Nixon lived another two decades. He and his wife eventually settled in the New York City area. He died in 1994. Historians have rated Nixon's Presidency as one of the worst in U.S. history. As classified documents from his administration continue to be made public, scholars will further evaluate his reputation and legacy.

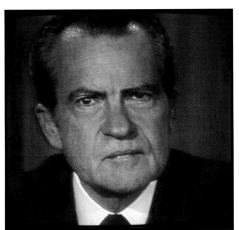

"Those who hate you don't win unless you hate them. And then you destroy yourself."

Richard M. Nixon, parting speech, August 9, 1974

Richard M. Nixon announced his plans to resign from office during a televised address in August 1974 (left). Scandals resulting from the bungled burglary two years earlier of offices in the Watergate building (right) had led citizens to call for his removal from office (center). Nixon had defused an earlier scandal with another emotional television appearance. In 1952 he preserved his spot as Vice President on Dwight D. Eisenhower's ticket by denying, during a televised speech, his illegal use of campaign funds. His remarks became known as the "Checkers speech" because he admitted that the family dog, Checkers, had been a political gift.

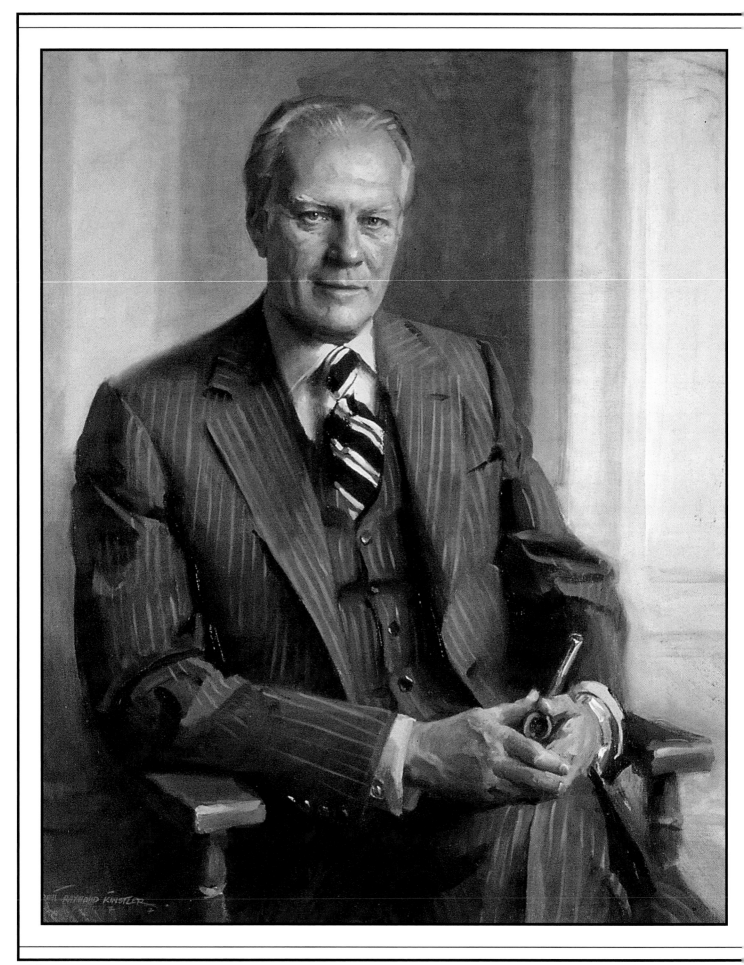

Gerald R. Ford

38TH PRESIDENT OF THE UNITED STATES ★ *1974 – 1977*

NICKNAME	Jerry
BORN	July 14, 1913, in Omaha, Nebr.
POLITICAL PARTY	Republican
CHIEF OPPONENT	none, succeeded Nixon
TERM OF OFFICE	Aug. 9, 1974–Jan. 20, 1977
AGE AT INAUGURATION	61 years old
NUMBER OF TERMS	one (partial)
VICE PRESIDENT	Nelson Aldrich Rockefeller (1908–1979)
FIRST LADY	Elizabeth (Betty) Bloomer Warren Ford (1918–present), wife (married Oct. 15, 1948)
CHILDREN	Michael, John, Steven, Susan
GEOGRAPHIC SCENE	50 states
SELECTED LANDMARKS	Omaha, Nebr. (birthplace); Gerald R. Ford Library, Ann Arbor, Mich.; Gerald R. Ford Museum, Grand Rapids, Mich.

Gerald R. Ford rejected offers to play professional football after college and went to law school instead. Years later, Lyndon B. Johnson joked that Ford had "played football too long without a helmet." Ford replied by showing up at a public event with an old helmet that no longer fit. "Heads tend to swell in Washington," he joked.

GERALD RUDOLPH FORD IS THE ONLY PRESIDENT never elected to the offices of President or Vice President. He was promoted to both roles during the turbulent political changes of the early 1970s. In the wake of President Richard M. Nixon's resignation, Ford worked to restore the confidence of citizens in their Chief Executive.

Ford came to the Presidency after serving 25 years as one of Michigan's representatives to Congress. A native of Nebraska, he was a graduate of the University of Michigan and Yale University Law School. During World War II, he earned ten battle stars for combat duty in the Navy. He married Elizabeth "Betty" Bloomer Warren, a former professional dancer, in 1948.

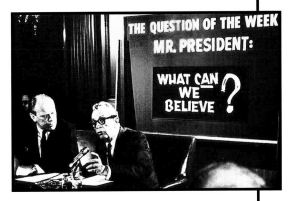

Ford, who joined Congress in 1949, became Vice President in 1973. He was appointed to the post by then President Nixon after Vice President Spiro T. Agnew was forced by scandals to resign from office. When the scandal-plagued Nixon himself resigned in disgrace some eight months later, Ford became President. "This is an hour of history that troubles our minds and hurts our hearts," Ford noted. Yet he praised the soundness of the nation for its successful transfer of power from Nixon to himself. "Our Constitution works; our great Republic is a government of laws and not of men. Here the people rule," he said.

With words like these and with honest behavior, Ford began restoring citizen trust in the government. His efforts to resolve other challenges—such as double-digit inflation, high unemployment, and economic recession—were less successful. Ford drew criticism, too, for granting Nixon a full pardon for crimes committed while President. In a close contest in 1976, Ford lost his chance to gain outright election to the White House and retired to California.

Public distrust of the Presidency (above) carried over from Nixon's term in office to Ford's. The U.S. celebrated the 200th anniversary of the signing of the Declaration of Independence during Ford's Presidency.

The Electoral College

★ Gatekeepers of the Presidency ★

IN MOST COUNTRIES, national elections are straightforward affairs. Eligible voters have the opportunity at a specified time to mark their preference on a ballot of various choices. Victors are declared based on the tabulated results.

Citizens of the United States participate in a more complex, two-step process. The outcome of the Presidency rests not, as is often thought, with the votes cast on Election Day. In fact these votes only determine the membership of an electoral college that is charged by the U.S. Constitution with selecting the President and Vice President of the United States.

Each state has as many members in the electoral college as it has U.S. Senators and Representatives (*see map*). The first electoral college had 69 members. Today there are 538. In order to become President, a candidate

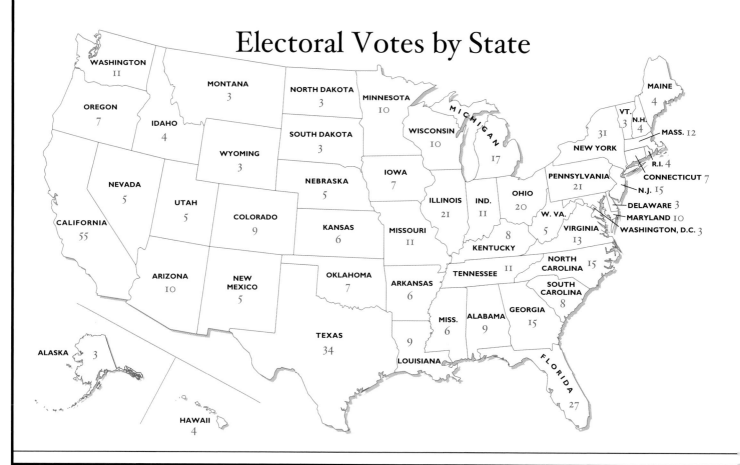

Electoral Votes by State

WASHINGTON 11

OREGON 7

MONTANA 3

IDAHO 4

NEVADA 5

CALIFORNIA 55

UTAH 5

WYOMING 3

NORTH DAKOTA 3

SOUTH DAKOTA 3

NEBRASKA 5

COLORADO 9

KANSAS 6

MINNESOTA 10

WISCONSIN 10

IOWA 7

MICHIGAN 17

ILLINOIS 21

IND. 11

OHIO 20

MISSOURI 11

W. VA. 5

KENTUCKY 11

MAINE 4

VT. 3

N.H. 4

MASS. 12

NEW YORK 31

R.I. 4

CONNECTICUT 7

PENNSYLVANIA 21

N.J. 15

DELAWARE 3

MARYLAND 10

WASHINGTON, D.C. 3

VIRGINIA 13

NORTH CAROLINA 15

ARIZONA 10

NEW MEXICO 5

OKLAHOMA 7

ARKANSAS 6

TENNESSEE 11

SOUTH CAROLINA 8

MISS. 6

ALABAMA 9

GEORGIA 15

TEXAS 34

LOUISIANA 9

FLORIDA 27

ALASKA 3

HAWAII 4

The accompanying map shows the latest allocation of the nation's 538 electoral college votes. The states' share of the total is reevaluated every ten years based on changes in the U.S. census of state populations. Over the years the electoral college has been the subject of more proposed amendments than any other topic. The controversial election of 2000 (right) revived this debate, but no national reforms have been made.

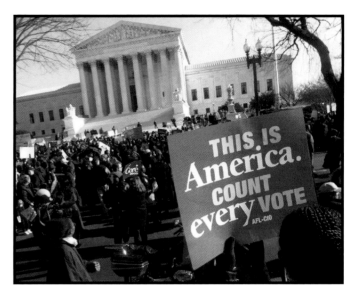

must win a majority, at least one more than half, of all electoral votes, or 270.

The founding fathers established the electoral college to assure that the President and Vice President would be selected by an elite group of learned and well-qualified individuals, fairly distributed among the states. At the time, few people had the right to vote, and members of the electoral college were either appointed by governors or selected by state legislatures. The earliest members of the electoral college voted independently, based on their individual judgements.

During the 1820s, as voting rights began to expand, states started to entrust citizens with the selection of electors. Then as now, voters expressed preferences for their state's electors (who usually go unnamed) by their selection of a presidential candidate. Victory within each state goes to the electors who represent the political party of the victorious candidate. This "winner-take-all" formula is used today by most states and the District of Columbia. Maine and Nebraska allocate electoral votes in proportion to the the support received by various candidates.

Members of the electoral college vote during separately held state meetings on an appointed day in December, and their votes are tabulated in front of a joint session of Congress in early January. If controversies arise, members of Congress are empowered to intervene. Otherwise the selection process for President and Vice President is complete.

Thus every presidential election has two sets of results, the popular vote and the elec-toral college vote. In most cases, the winner of the popular vote is victorious in the electoral college, as well. However four of the nation's 55 presidential elections have brought victory to men who failed to win the popular vote.

Three of these elections occurred during the 19th century. Inconclusive voting by the electoral college in 1824 prompted the House of Representatives to award the Presidency to John Quincy Adams. Rutherford B. Hayes became President following the election of 1876 when disputes over the selection of electors forced Congress to refer the decision to a special commission. In 1888 Benjamin Harrison defeated Grover Cleveland without dispute in the electoral college yet failed to win a majority of popular votes.

The long absence of further discrepancies between popular and electoral voting led many to view the electoral college as a largely ceremonial body. In the election of 2000, though, ballot irregularities in Florida left the choice of that state's electors in doubt. Five weeks of debate followed. Action by the U.S. Supreme Court led Florida's electoral votes to fall by default to George W. Bush. He became President despite having lost the popular election by more than 500,000 votes.

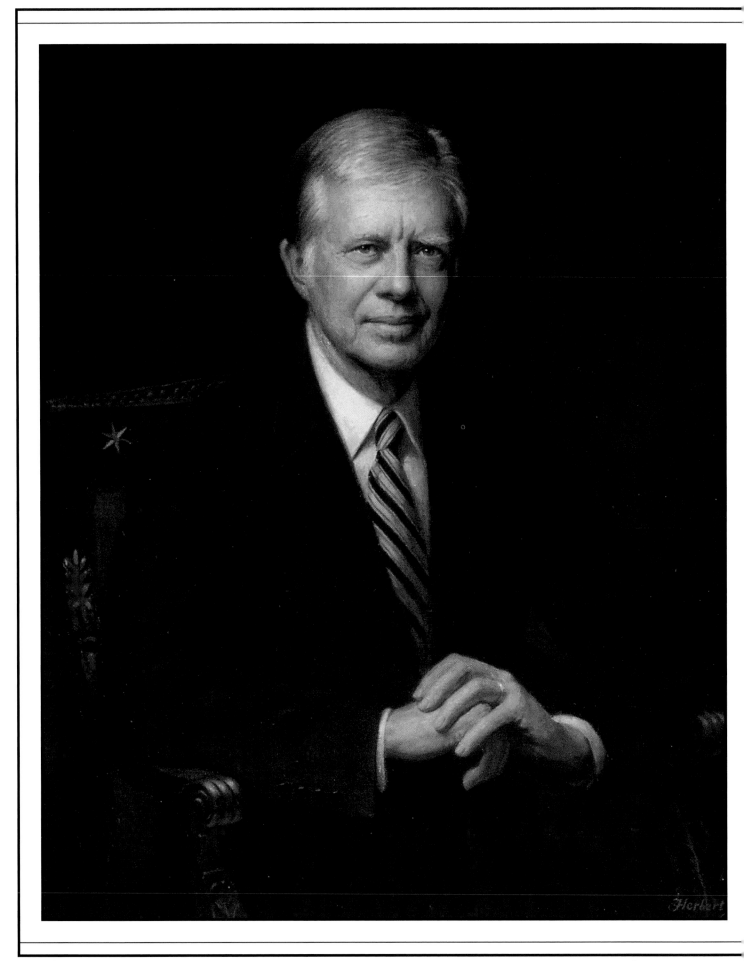

Jimmy Carter

39TH PRESIDENT OF THE UNITED STATES ★ *1977 – 1981*

NICKNAME	Jimmy
BORN	Oct. 1, 1924, in Plains, Ga.
POLITICAL PARTY	Democrat
CHIEF OPPONENT	President Gerald R. Ford, Republican (1913–present)
TERM OF OFFICE	Jan. 20, 1977–Jan. 20, 1981
AGE AT INAUGURATION	52 years old
NUMBER OF TERMS	one
VICE PRESIDENT	Walter Frederick (Fritz) Mondale (1928–present)

The Carters on their wedding day

FIRST LADY	Rosalynn Smith Carter (1927–present), wife (married July 7, 1946)
CHILDREN	John, James, Donnel, Amy
GEOGRAPHIC SCENE	50 states
SELECTED LANDMARKS	Plains Nursing Center, Inc., Plains, Ga. (birthplace); Jimmy Carter National Historic Site, Plains, Ga.; The Carter Center and the Jimmy Carter Library, Atlanta, Ga. (includes a museum)

JAMES EARL CARTER, JR., WAS THE FIRST PERSON elected President from the Deep South since Zachary Taylor in 1848. Economic troubles at home combined with other challenges from abroad (including citizens being taken hostage in Iran) cost him his bid for a second term of office. Carter returned to the world stage after his Presidency ended, serving as an advocate for international peace. In 2002 he became the third U.S. President to win a Nobel Peace Prize.

Carter liked his nickname, "Jimmy," so much that he was sworn in as President by that name. As a child growing up in the Deep South, Carter had been known by another nickname, too: "Hot," short for "Hot Shot." Carter helped with chores on his father's sizable peanut farm, attended schools segregated by race, and played with children both black and white. He graduated 59th out of the 820 students in his class at the U.S. Naval Academy at Annapolis. He married the best friend of one of his sisters and took up a career in the U.S. Navy.

After his father's sudden death in 1953, Carter left the Navy and his post as a nuclear submarine engineer to manage the family farm.

Jimmy Carter (above) was nicknamed "Jimmy Cardigan" after he wore a sweater instead of a suit when he addressed the nation during a televised fireside chat in 1977. Carter dispensed with other formal precedents, too. Bands stopped playing "Hail to the Chief" for his public entrances. He sent his daughter, Amy, to public schools. Sometimes he even carried his own suitcase and stayed at private homes when he traveled.

"Let us create together a new national spirit of unity and trust."

Jimmy Carter, Inaugural Address, January 20, 1977

Jimmy Carter broke with precedent during his Inaugural Parade in 1977. Instead of riding in a motorcade, he walked from the U.S. Capitol toward the White House with his daughter, Amy; his wife, Rosalynn; and other family members. As First Lady, Rosalynn sat in on Cabinet meetings, represented the nation abroad, and spoke out in favor of mental health care.

Carter was elected, in part, because voters liked the fact that he was an "outsider"—someone who was not part of national politics and the recent Watergate scandals. Being an "outsider" turned into a drawback after Carter became President. Because he ignored the political strategies of Congress, legislators on Capitol Hill regularly refused to pass his bills. The economy did not cooperate either. Years of extravagant government spending and a new wave of energy shortages sent price inflation higher than ever. Citizens were literally stranded at empty gas pumps in their search for gasoline.

Although these issues proved troublesome to solve, Carter took other significant action. He pardoned citizens who had illegally avoided fighting in the Vietnam War, appointed people from diverse backgrounds to key posts, reduced the rules that governed national transportation systems, increased protection of the environment, and promoted research about alternative forms of energy. He also established a Department of Energy and a separate Department of Education.

Later he served in the Georgia Senate. As governor of the state during the early 1970s, Carter criticized racial discrimination, the practice of favoring whites over blacks and other races. Carter entered the presidential race of 1976 almost completely unknown to the rest of the country. His tireless campaigning won him the Democratic Party nomination and, in what became a tight race, the Presidency.

Carter emphasized respect for human rights in his relations with other nations. He withheld U.S. foreign aid from countries with unjust governments. Carter arranged for Panama to assume control of the canal that the United States had built through its territory years before. He expanded relations with China. He tried to further limit the spread of nuclear weapons. He organized international protests, including a controversial boycott of the 1980 summer Olympics in Moscow, after the Soviet Union invaded nearby Afghanistan.

The popularity of nuclear energy suffered during the Carter Presidency after a serious accident occurred in 1979 at the Three Mile Island nuclear power plant near Harrisburg, Pennsylvania (left). Jimmy Carter encouraged scientists to develop new forms of energy using such renewable resources as the sun and the wind.

Jimmy Carter helped negotiate important treaties between Egyptian President Anwar Sadat and Israel's Prime Minister Menachem Begin in 1978 (left). Their Camp David Accords were reached with Carter's help at the presidential retreat in Maryland. These agreements renewed hopes for peace in the Middle East, a region that had been torn apart by wars and terrorism. The most difficult challenge Carter faced in his Presidency was the Iranian hostage crisis. Fifty-two Americans were held prisoner by Iranian militants (right) for 444 days. They were finally set free after Carter left office in January 1981.

Carter's greatest foreign policy challenge began in 1979 when angry Iranians stormed the U.S. Embassy in Tehran and captured its occupants. They held 52 Americans as hostages for the rest of Carter's Presidency. All efforts to free the prisoners were unsuccessful.

As President, Carter's popularity ranged from very high to very low. It shifted depending on the state of the economy, the status of the hostage crisis, and his success at restoring confidence in government. He lost his reelection bid by a wide margin.

Just 56 years old when he left office, Carter began an active retirement life that continues today. Carter writes best-selling books. He teaches at Emory University in Atlanta, Georgia. He and his wife, Rosalynn, help build homes for the needy with Habitat for Humanity. In addition, the couple founded the Carter Center in Atlanta, Georgia. From that base Carter helps negotiate peace agreements between nations, works with others to verify that countries have fair elections, and directs efforts to improve health in developing lands. These and his other efforts to increase world peace earned him the Nobel Peace Prize in 2002. Only two other Presidents—Theodore Roosevelt and Woodrow Wilson—have been so honored.

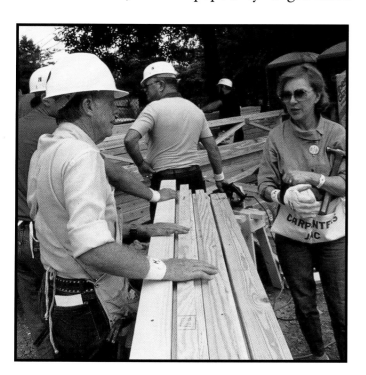

Former President Jimmy Carter and his wife, Rosalynn, volunteer each year as construction workers with Habitat for Humanity. This organization builds houses for poor people in the United States and abroad. "Now is the best time of all," Carter says about his retirement years. Writing, teaching, peacemaking, engaging in community service, and being a grandparent keep him challenged and fulfilled.

FOOTPRINTS ON THE GLOBAL FRONTIER

★ *1981 – Present* ★

1986

U.S. space shuttle missions were halted for more than two years after the Challenger *blew apart on January 28. All seven crew members died.*

1989

Berlin citizens marked the end of the Cold War by tearing down the wall that had divided their city into separate zones. East united with West to embrace democracy.

1990

South African officials released Nelson Mandela from his 27-year imprisonment. When they ended apartheid—a system that oppressed the black majority—Mandela was elected president soon after.

1991

Iraq's invasion of Kuwait led to the Persian Gulf War. Fires at sabotaged oil wells burned long after the fighting was done.

The Cold War gave way near the end of the 20th century to a new frontier of shifting global alliances. The Soviet Union dissolved. The European Union expanded. Trade, population, even disease became more mobile. Although some nations moved closer to peace, old hatreds erupted elsewhere—often fueled by religious differences. Threat of terrorism began to rise among angry groups of outsiders. The United States and United Nations have sought to balance their roles in the changing scene, at times as collaborators and sometimes not.

1995

The bombing of the Murrah Federal Building in Oklahoma City on April 19 shocked the nation. Two American members of the anti-government militia movement were responsible.

1997

Scientists announced they had successfully cloned the first mammal: Their sheep named Dolly was genetically identical to its parent. Nations have discouraged efforts to clone humans.

2001

On September 11 members of the Al Qaeda terror network crashed hijacked jets into the World Trade Center in New York City and other targets. The towers were destroyed and over 2,700 people died.

2004

The U.S.-led invasion of Iraq in 2003 resulted in the capture of Saddam Hussein that December. By the next year the former dictator was being tried on charges of human rights abuse.

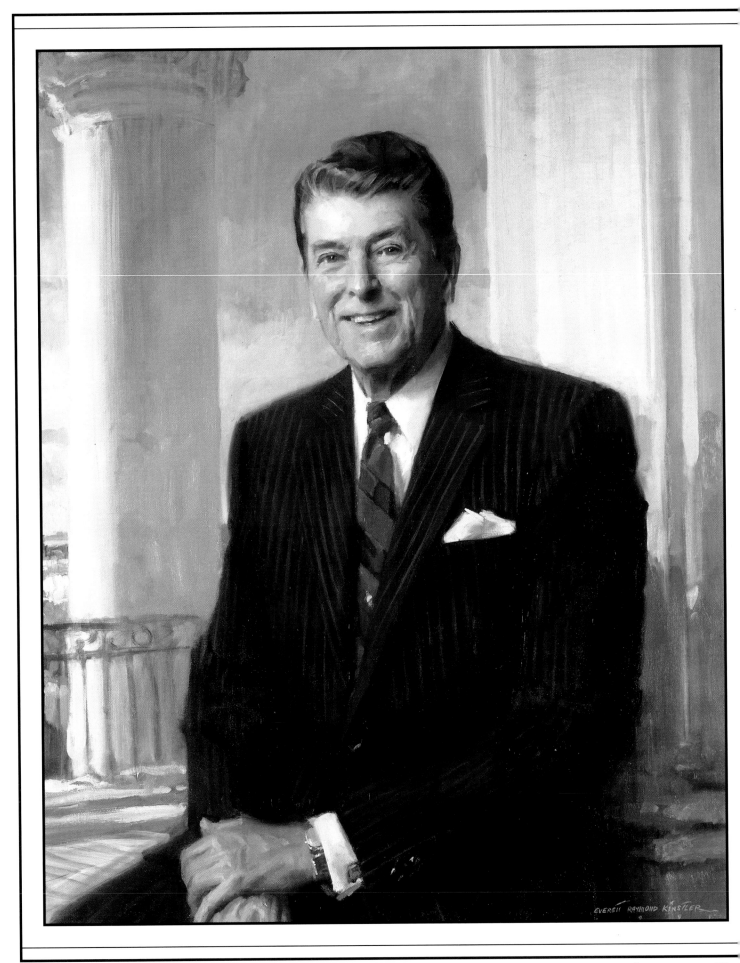

Ronald Reagan

40TH PRESIDENT OF THE UNITED STATES ★ *1981 – 1989*

Nancy Davis and Ronald Reagan starred together in Hellcats of the Navy, *the last movie either of them made.*

RONALD WILSON REAGAN WAS THE OLDEST person to become President, at age 69, and lived the longest, to age 93. Yet this former Hollywood actor and governor of California brought a youthful optimism to his work. The "Great Communicator" strengthened support for the Republican Party and filled federal courts with conservative judges. He helped force the end of the Cold War, too, though at an economic cost that haunted future Presidents.

Reagan ended his presidential career near the end of the 20th century, but he was born during a simpler era when the century was just beginning. He grew up in small towns in northern Illinois, particularly Dixon. His family called him "Dutch," short for "fat little Dutchman." He enjoyed playing sports and was a popular actor at the public schools he attended and at Eureka College in Eureka, Illinois.

After graduation he worked as a radio sports announcer in the Midwest. In 1937 Reagan moved to Hollywood. He made 53 movies and hosted two television shows during the next three decades. Even his World War II service involved making training films for the armed forces. Reagan "lived" so many lives through the parts he played in movies that he sometimes got them mixed up later on with his own story. (He recalled combat scenes from movies, for example, as if they were events from of his own service during World War II.) Reagan married two Hollywood actresses. He is the only President who had a marriage (his first one) end in divorce.

Reagan's experiences as a union labor leader in Hollywood, public speaker, and political volunteer helped interest him in running for office. Although he had grown up loyal to the Democratic Party, he began supporting Republicans during the Eisenhower era. He officially joined the Republican Party in 1962. In

Nancy Davis met her future husband, Ronald Reagan, when both of them were acting in Hollywood. They married three years later (above). Nancy Reagan appeared in a total of 11 films. As First Lady she encouraged children to "Just Say No" to illegal drugs.

In 1983 the United States entered into combat for the first time since the Vietnam War by invading the Caribbean island of Grenada (left). Ronald Reagan ordered the invasion after American residents there seemed threatened by an unexpected change of national leadership. The Reagan administration drew criticism because of the Iran-contra scandal: secret foreign policy dealings by high-level government officials, including Lieutenant Colonel Oliver North (above) that contradicted official policy.

1966 Californians elected him to the first of two terms as governor. Reagan sought his party's presidential nomination twice (in 1968 and 1976) before earning it in 1980. Citizens voted "yes" to elect Reagan as President because they generally answered "no" to his query about their lives during the Carter Presidency: "Are you better off than you were four years ago?" He was reelected four years later.

In an effort to improve the economy, Reagan cut taxes, reduced federal spending in some areas, and increased government spending on defense by $1.5 trillion over seven years. He proposed the first trillion-dollar federal budget. His economic program came to be known as "Reaganomics." It suggested that if economic benefits such as tax cuts were made to the wealthy, these savings would "trickle down" and help less affluent citizens. This vision of "supply-side economics" became a cornerstone of the modern Republican Party. Although

Challenges of the job: Ronald Reagan fired 13,000 air traffic controllers in 1981 when they went out on strike (left). An assassin attempted to shoot the President a few months after he took office (right). Reagan reassured those around him with his good humor. "If I had had this much attention in Hollywood, I'd have stayed there," he joked to the hospital staff. Prompt emergency care saved his life.

Like all Presidents, Ronald Reagan appointed officials (left), federal judges, and Supreme Court judges. He put new judges in half of the nation's federal court seats, and he placed three new judges on the nation's highest court, including its first woman judge, Sandra Day O'Connor. By being able to select so many judges, Reagan was able to shape the opinions of the federal courts to reflect his own vision for the judiciary system. Ronald Reagan's plan of increased spending on national defense put a strain on the U.S. economy and added to the national debt. His program was even tougher on the Soviet Union. America's old Cold War foe simply could not afford to keep up in the military arms race anymore. Mikhail Gorbachev, a new, more moderate Soviet leader, sought to limit the use of nuclear weapons. The two leaders (right) signed an agreement in 1987 that reduced stockpiles of nuclear missiles for the first time.

inflation and unemployment eventually improved during his administration, new problems developed. The collapse of the savings and loan industry, sizable annual budget deficits, and a growing national debt, for example, became costly concerns that would take years for future Presidents to solve.

The Reagan administration bred its share of scandals. The greatest one, the Iran-contra scandal, involved illegal sales of arms to the Middle Eastern nation of Iran. Profits from the sales were secretly diverted to support rebel forces in Nicaragua, a country in Central America. Upper level administrators encouraged the activity. Other charges of illegal behavior forced the resignations of Reagan's secretary of labor, the attorney general, and senior staff members at the Environmental Protection Agency, the Central Intelligence Agency, the Defense Department, and the Department of Housing and Urban Development.

Reagan remained popular despite the scandals and criticisms of his Presidency. Some credited this success to his Hollywood looks and his skill as the "Great Communicator." Others called him the "Teflon President," because, just like the non-stick pan surface, nothing bad ever "stuck" to his image.

Reagan was 77 years old when he retired with his wife, Nancy, to Los Angeles. In 1994 he was diagnosed with Alzheimer's disease, an illness that affects memory, and he led an increasingly secluded life. His death ten years later prompted tributes on both coasts. After lying in state at the U.S. Capitol and receiving the honor of a state funeral, his body was flown home to California for a sunset burial.

"What I'd really like to do is go down in history as the President who made Americans believe in themselves again."

Ronald Reagan, 1981

Ronald Reagan's death in 2004 brought the nation its first presidential state funeral in more than 20 years. At one point during the week-long series of events, his casket was moved by horse-drawn caisson (left) to the U.S. Capitol for public viewing. Burial took place on the grounds of Reagan's presidential library in Simi Valley, California.

George Bush

41ST PRESIDENT OF THE UNITED STATES ★ *1989 – 1993*

NICKNAME	Poppy
BORN	June 12, 1924, in Milton, Mass.
POLITICAL PARTY	Republican
CHIEF OPPONENT	Michael Stanley Dukakis, Democrat (1933–present)
TERM OF OFFICE	Jan. 20, 1989–Jan. 20, 1993
AGE AT INAUGURATION	64 years old
NUMBER OF TERMS	one
VICE PRESIDENT	James Danforth (Dan) Quayle, III (1947–present)
FIRST LADY	Barbara Pierce Bush (1925–present), wife (married Jan. 6, 1945)
CHILDREN	George, Robin (died young), John, Neil, Marvin, Dorothy
GEOGRAPHIC SCENE	50 states
SELECTED LANDMARKS	George Bush Presidential Library, Texas A&M University, College Station, Tex.

George Bush played baseball for Yale University. He was named after a grandfather, George Herbert Walker, who was known as "Pop." Bush was called "Little Pop" or "Poppy" into his adulthood.

GEORGE HERBERT WALKER BUSH presided over a continued shift in Republican Party thinking towards conservative viewpoints. U.S. armed forces took part in two military actions, including the Persian Gulf War, during a Presidency that witnessed the collapse of the Soviet Union. A sagging economy undercut Bush's war-time popularity by the time of his reelection bid.

Bush brought years of varied government experience and a distinguished personal background with him to the White House. The son of a wealthy U.S. senator, Bush attended elite private schools. He enlisted in the military after high school and became the Navy's youngest pilot. Bush earned a Distinguished Flying Cross as a Navy bombing pilot in the Pacific during World War II. After the war he graduated with honors from Yale University.

Bush worked in the oil business in Texas for 18 years before seeking his first public office. He lost a 1964 U.S. Senate bid, but he gained a seat in the U.S. House of Representatives two years later. After two terms he made a second unsuccessful run for the Senate. For the next ten years he was appointed by Republican Presidents Richard M. Nixon and Gerald R. Ford to a series of prominent posts: U.S. ambassador to the United Nations, chairman of the Republican National Committee, top U.S. diplomat in China, and director of the Central Intelligence Agency.

Bush eyed the Vice Presidency in 1968 and 1974, and he sought the Republican presidential nomination in 1980. Instead, he earned eight years of experience as Ronald Reagan's Vice President before gaining the Presidency himself in 1988.

George Bush married Barbara Pierce (above) while on leave from World War II service. The couple had met two years before during an earlier shore leave. Both claim to have fallen in love at first sight.

"Out of these troubled times...
a new world order can emerge:
a new era, freer from the
threat of terror, stronger in
the pursuit of justice, and more
secure in the quest for peace."

George Bush, September 12, 1990

Soldiers donned special suits to protect themselves from chemical and biological weapons during the Persian Gulf War of 1991. National pride over U.S. success in combat pushed approval ratings of the President to a record-breaking 89 percent. However, concerns about the economy undercut George Bush's support by the time he sought reelection in 1992.

Bush inherited from Reagan a national and world scene that was in transition. Most notable was the rapid transformation of the Soviet Union from a Cold War superpower into a splintered collection of former communist states. First Poland, then East Germany, Czechoslovakia, Hungary, Yugoslavia, Bulgaria, Albania, and, finally, the Soviet Union

In 1989 the Exxon Valdez *oil tanker ran aground off the shore of Alaska. The accident resulted in the largest oil spill in the nation's history. Almost 11 million gallons of oil polluted more than 1,000 miles of shoreline and killed hundreds of thousands of animals. The cost of Exxon's cleanup (above) and fines totaled more than $3 billion.*

itself, turned against the Communist form of government. The Soviet Union dissolved, and Russia emerged as its most powerful descendant. Most of the momentum for these changes came from within the region itself, but the Bush administration supported these moves toward democracy. The only remaining strongholds of communism by the end of the Bush Presidency were China, Cuba, Laos, North Korea, and Vietnam.

In 1989 Bush ordered U.S. troops to invade Panama. Their mission was to seize Manuel Noriega, the country's military leader, and bring him to the United States so he could stand trial on charges of drug trafficking. He was captured four days later. (Eventually he was tried, convicted, and imprisoned for his illegal activity.) The invasion

The hair of Barbara Bush turned to a distinctive silver at an unexpectedly early age following the death of her three-year-old daughter to leukemia. She and her husband lived in more than two dozen homes in 17 cities before moving into the White House. As First Lady, Barbara Bush promoted literacy and other education programs. Entertainers were among those attending the third national literacy awards she hosted at the White House (above).

George Bush poses with his four sons (left, from left to right: Neil, John, George W., and Marvin). Two sons followed their father into politics. John, called "Jeb," became the governor of Florida in 1998. Jeb's older brother, George W., was elected governor of Texas in 1994 and put the Republican Party back in the White House in the tight presidential race of 2000. Commander in Chief George Bush reviews a ceremonial guard in 1989 (right).

caused significant property damage, left 500 Panamanians dead, and cost the lives of 23 Americans.

A year later the U.S. took part in combat again. Iraq's 1989 invasion of neighboring Kuwait, a tiny oil-rich nation on the Persian Gulf, provoked worldwide outrage. The United States led an international fight in the region several months later that liberated Kuwait and severely damaged Iraq's military defenses. Iraq's leader, Saddam Hussein, remained in command of his nation, but other governments agreed to enforce sanctions, or restrictions, on Iraq until the nation could prove it no longer possessed weapons of mass destruction. The war, which lasted only a few months, cost more than $60 billion, a sum that many nations helped pay. The United States lost 148 lives during the war; Iraqi deaths may have been as high as 100,000.

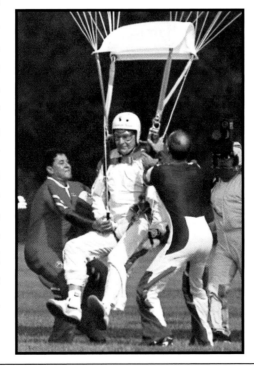

These international events often overshadowed domestic policy during the Bush administration. Nonetheless, the President worked to rescue the bankrupt savings and loan industry, fought rising unemployment, signed a new Clean Air Act, and agreed to legislation that promoted equal rights of access for the disabled. Enormous budget deficits continued to swell the national debt. They forced Bush to break his 1988 campaign promise—"Read my lips: No new taxes." This change and a worsening economy cost Bush his reelection bid in 1992. Voters gave him the lowest support at the polls earned by any sitting President since William Howard Taft. This loss was tempered by the election of Bush's son, George W., in 2000. Many administrators from the first Bush Presidency returned to serve under the son.

Four years after retiring to Texas, George Bush made news by making his first parachute jump since World War II. This time it was just for fun.

In the President's Shadow

★ *Security, the Media, and Presidential Perks* ★

Today's Presidents may share the same residence as their predecessors, but their work and lifestyles are vastly different. The first Presidents handled much of their own paperwork, for example. They met freely with citizens who dropped by the White House, too. As the nation and its government grew in size, so did the complexity of the job for its Presidents.

Now Presidents travel by jet and limousine, not horse and buggy. The size of their staffs has grown from a handful to the hundreds. The cost of running the White House has kept a parallel pace. The risks and realities of presidential assassinations have tightened the Presidents' freedom of movement. Gone are the days when John Quincy Adams could walk alone from the White House to the Potomac River and swim there in the nude.

Now more than two dozen secret service agents take turns guarding the President and his family members around the clock. Other staff members help manage the President's busy calendar, write many of his speeches, and advise the President on everything from foreign policy to party politics.

As a result, today's Presidents are more isolated than ever before from ordinary life. William Henry Harrison once strolled beyond the White House gates to do a little grocery shopping. Ulysses S. Grant took off by himself

Secret service agents began guarding the life of the U.S. President following the assassination of William McKinley in 1901. Since then they've done everything from protecting the presidential limousine (above left) to supervising ordinary movements of the President and family members (above right). Whether the Chief Executive wants to buy flowers for the First Lady, browse through a music store, or go for a jog, secret service agents assure that the outing is safe and sound.

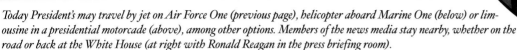

Today President's may travel by jet on Air Force One (previous page), helicopter aboard Marine One (below) or limousine in a presidential motorcade (above), among other options. Members of the news media stay nearby, whether on the road or back at the White House (at right with Ronald Reagan in the press briefing room).

on speeding buggy rides. But no President sets foot beyond the grounds of the White House today just on a whim or all alone.

However, even as the lives of Presidents have become more controlled, their activities have grown in national visibility. Expanding media coverage by newspapers, radio, television, and the Internet assures that the public knows more than ever about what a President says and does. All major news outlets assign one or more people to cover the President's activities. There are some 2,000 members of this presidential press corps.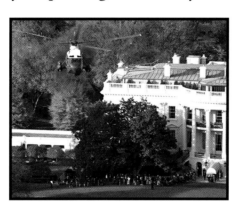

This many reporters could not possibly follow every single move of the President. Instead small groups of them—a few dozen or so at a time—take turns with the work. They are called the press pool because they pool, or collect their reports, then share them with everyone in the press corps.

One representative of each day's press pool writes an eyewitness summary of the day's events. These reports are filled with colorful details so that other reporters will be able to visualize and write vivid news accounts.

Additional members of the pool make still photos, video footage, and audio recordings to share with the press corps. The reports of the press pool form the basis for the hundreds of news stories seen by the public.

Today's Presidents balance the demands and scrutiny of their jobs with many impressive perks, or benefits. For starters, they receive an annual salary of $400,000. (George Washington earned $25,000 a year.) They have free housing at the White House as well as at the presidential retreat of Camp David in nearby Maryland.

These homes offer many luxuries that cushion the impact of their isolation. Presidents may enjoy swimming, bowling, horseback riding, skeet shooting, and woodland walks without ever leaving home. They can screen movies in a private theater and read the latest books in a private library, too.

When it's time to travel, Presidents may choose between a fleet of limousines, a jet named Air Force One, a helicopter, a yacht, even a bullet-proof train car. Yet at the end of the day, they tread the same stairs to bed as have all the Presidents since John Adams.

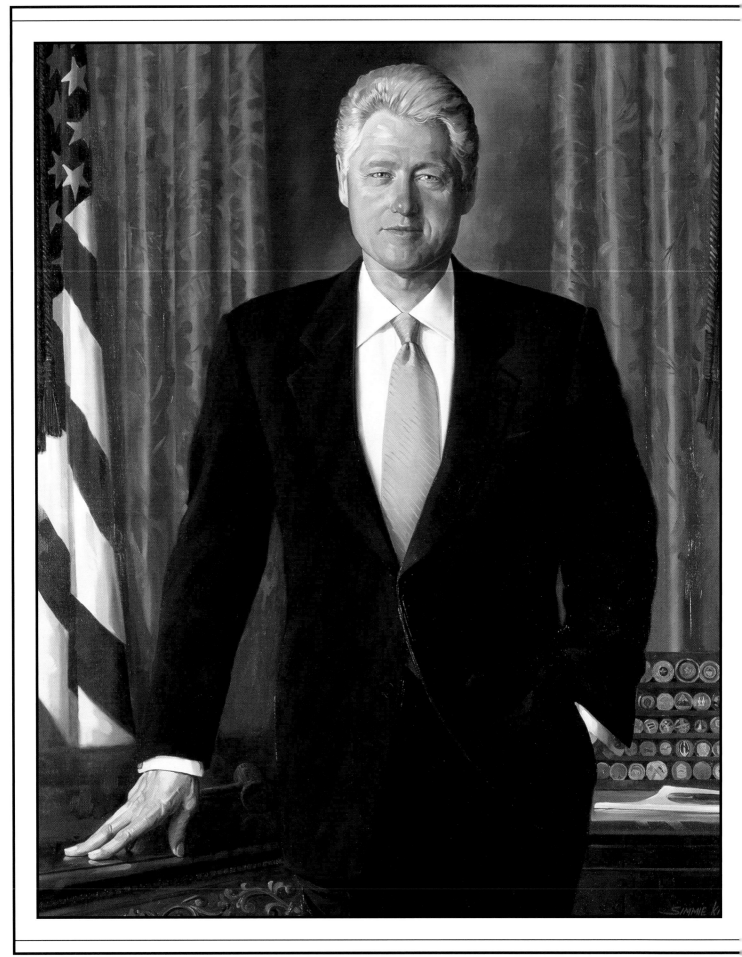

William Jefferson Clinton

42ND PRESIDENT OF THE UNITED STATES ★ 1993 – 2001

NICKNAME	Comeback Kid
BORN	Aug. 19, 1946, in Hope, Ark.
POLITICAL PARTY	Democrat
CHIEF OPPONENTS	1st term: President George Bush, Republican (1924–present) and Henry Ross Perot, Independent (1930–present); 2nd term: Robert Joseph Dole, Republican (1923–present) and Henry Ross Perot, Reform (1930–present)
TERM OF OFFICE	Jan. 20, 1993–Jan. 20, 2001
AGE AT INAUGURATION	46 years old
NUMBER OF TERMS	two
VICE PRESIDENT	Albert Gore, Jr. (1948–present)
FIRST LADY	Hillary Diane Rodham Clinton (1947–present), wife (married Oct. 11, 1975)
CHILDREN	Chelsea
GEOGRAPHIC SCENE	50 states
SELECTED LANDMARKS	Presidential Library, Little Rock, Ark.

WILLIAM JEFFERSON CLINTON BROUGHT THE DEMOCRATIC PARTY its first two-term Presidency since the era of Franklin Delano Roosevelt. Clinton earned respect internationally for his leadership and work for world peace. At home he balanced the federal budget for the first time in decades and reduced the national debt. These professional successes were undercut by bitter partisan political fighting over real and alleged scandals. Impeached by the House of Representatives on charges of misconduct, Clinton was tried and acquitted by the U.S. Senate.

Clinton was the first U.S. President born after World War II. He grew up in Hot Springs, Arkansas, where he did well in school. As a youth, Clinton joined the Boy Scouts, sang in the church choir, and raced to complete crossword puzzles. Later he graduated from Georgetown University in Washington, D.C., and studied as a prestigious Rhodes Scholar at England's Oxford University before turning his attention to law. He met his future wife, Hillary Rodham, while the two of them were law students at Yale University.

After graduating, Clinton taught law at the University of Arkansas and took up politics. By 1978, at age 32, he had become the

Bill Clinton's 1963 handshake with President John F. Kennedy helped cement his childhood ambition to be President. Clinton was known until age 16 by the birth name he shared with his natural father, William Jefferson Blythe, who died before Bill was born. Later, he adopted his stepfather's last name.

During his youth Bill Clinton played the saxophone in a jazz trio called The Three Blind Mice; sunglasses completed the musicians' attire. During presidential elections he performed twice on nationally televised talk shows. Clinton jammed with other musicians at a White House jazz festival (above).

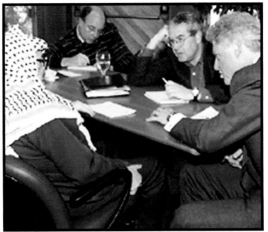

Bill Clinton,
State of the Union Address, 1996

Throughout his Presidency Bill Clinton tried to foster peaceful relations in the Middle East. In meetings with Israeli and Palestinian leaders (left), Clinton sought to improve understanding between people of different religions with conflicting interests in the same territory.

nation's youngest governor. Although unseated in the next election, Clinton became known as the "Comeback Kid" after he regained his post in 1982. He went on to serve four consecutive terms as governor of Arkansas. As a presidential candidate in 1992, Clinton portrayed himself as a moderate Democrat, one who understood the perspective of a majority of Americans. Clinton and his vice presidential nominee, Al Gore, became the youngest national ticket ever elected; they were the first all-Southern ticket since the Jackson administration of 1828. The two men were reelected four years later, making Clinton one of only five Presidents in the century to complete two terms of office.

As President, Clinton (helped by a booming economy) began balancing the federal budget for the first time in four decades. He created free trade between the United States, Canada, and Mexico

with the North American Free Trade Agreement (NAFTA), and he normalized U. S. trade relations with China. As his Presidency progressed, Clinton wielded increasing influence over efforts to end hostilities at trouble spots in the Middle East, Europe, and elsewhere.

Clinton lived up to his image as the "Comeback Kid" during a Presidency that was challenged by party politics, international instability, and personal scandal. He battled with Congress over how to manage the budget, taxes, health care, and trade while he labored to define the role of the United States as a peacemaker in a post–Cold War world. Frequently Clinton found himself trying to focus attention on the nation's business even as investigators probed into his handling of administrative and personal matters.

In 1998 Kenneth Starr, an independent prosecutor, accused Clinton of breaking laws to conceal a romantic relationship with a White House intern. The House of Representatives considered Starr's charges and voted to impeach the President, or recommend that he be tried by the Senate and removed from office. They accused Clinton of lying under oath and using illegal means to keep his

During the last six years of Bill Clinton's administration, Kenneth Starr (near left) led a series of investigations into possible illegal behavior by the President (far left) and associates. These proceedings became ensnared in bitter partisan, or political party, disputes. Republicans accused Democrats of hiding the truth, while Democrats accused Republicans of trying to undermine the Clinton Presidency with false charges.

Bill Clinton worked with world leaders (left), including Boris Yeltsin of Russia (right), to reduce arms and improve international relations during his Presidency. In addition to his efforts to increase peace in the Middle East, Clinton encouraged an end to violence between Catholics and Protestants in Northern Ireland. He defended human rights in Haiti, Bosnia, Kosovo, and other war-torn regions, too, using U.S. troops when necessary.

affair a secret. Clinton was acquitted by the U.S. Senate during the trial that followed in 1999. He and Andrew Johnson are the only two Presidents to be impeached and tried by Congress.

Clinton succeeded at broadening the Democratic Party base of support during his Presidency. Many past supporters of the Republican Party, particularly a wide variety of voters from middle-income levels, sided with the Democrats instead. However the taint of personal scandal surrounding Clinton by the end of his administration limited

how effectively he could support the presidential bid of his own Vice President in 2000.

Hillary Clinton assumed a broader range of responsibilities as First Lady than any other President's wife since Eleanor Roosevelt. She headed an effort to reform the nation's health care system, traveled extensively on behalf of her husband, promoted children's rights, and wrote a weekly newspaper column. She protected the privacy of her teenage daughter, Chelsea, and supported her husband during the scandals that plagued his Presidency. She became the first First Lady to seek and win elected office by running for the U.S. Senate during the final year of her husband's Presidency. The Clintons make their home in New York State.

"There is nothing wrong with America that cannot be cured by what is right with America."

Bill Clinton,
First Inaugural Address, January 20, 1993

Bill Clinton shared the spotlight during the celebration of his Inauguration in 1997 with his daughter, Chelsea, and wife, Hillary. During his second term, opinion polls showed that most citizens supported Clinton's performance as President even though the House of Representatives was recommending he be removed from office.

Election Day

★ Landslides, Upsets, and Contested Results ★

PRESIDENTIAL ELECTIONS take place every four years in November on the first Tuesday after the first Monday in the month. The nation's 55 elections have produced a number of memorable contests, whether because of close finishes, landslide victories, surprise endings, or controversial results.

Often Presidents are chosen with a clear majority of popular support, that is by winning more than half of all votes cast. About a third of the time, though, candidates have become President by winning only a plurality of votes, or at least one more than anyone else but not more than half of all votes. Such victors include Abraham Lincoln (his first election), Woodrow Wilson (both elections), and Bill Clinton (both elections).

Some election finishes are dramatically close. In the controversial 1960 election John F. Kennedy defeated Richard M. Nixon by not quite 120,000 votes out of more than 68 million votes cast, or a fraction of one percent of the total. Similarly close results occurred during the victories of James A. Garfield in 1880, Grover Cleveland in 1884, and Richard M. Nixon in 1968.

Other elections feature surprise outcomes. So many analysts had predicted Harry S. Truman's defeat in 1948 that the first edition of the Chicago Tribune actually reported the wrong election outcome. Instead of "Dewey Beats Truman," it turned out that Truman had won with an election upset margin of just over two million votes.

Some elections bring controversy, such as the debate in the U.S. Congress (above) over who should win the 1876 contest between Rutherford B. Hayes and Samuel J. Tilden. Others offer surprises: Harry S. Truman (left, voting in the Missouri primary) defied predictions and won his 1948 reelection bid. A few are marked by milestones. The passage of the Voting Rights Act of 1965, for example, brought increased access to the polls for African Americans in Alabama (far left) and other Southern states.

In 2000 a controversial Supreme Court ruling ended the recounting of hard-to-read ballots in Florida (above, left). As a result George W. Bush became the first President since 1888 to enter the White House with a victory in the electoral college but not in the popular vote. Four years later he triumphed in both tallies (above, right) despite losing ground to his opponent, Massachusetts Senator John Kerry, during a series of nationally televised presidential debates (above, center). In the end Bush earned a majority of votes cast (51 percent), the first president to do so since his father did in 1988. His tally of nearly 60 million votes is greater than that of any other presidential candidate.

In contrast, the election of 1936, which many people expected to end in a close finish or even an upset, instead brought a landslide reelection victory for Franklin D. Roosevelt. Roosevelt buried his challenger by earning 60 percent (versus 36 percent) of the popular vote and all but eight electoral college votes.

In 1964 Lyndon B. Johnson earned the greatest election landslide victory ever by defeating his chief opponent in the popular voting 61 to 38 percent. Other notable landslides occurred in 1920 for Warren G. Harding (with 60 percent of the vote), for Richard M. Nixon in 1972 (60 percent), and in 1984 with Ronald Reagan (59 percent).

U.S. citizens 18 or older, regardless of race, creed, color, or gender, may register to vote. Voter turnout, that is the number of people who actually vote on Election Day, can be a critical factor in a candidate's success or defeat. More potential voters turned out for the elections of the 19th century than they have since the year 1900 (when 73 percent voted). Now voter participation rarely rises much beyond the 50 percent mark. That is, only about half of all eligible voters typically cast ballots. Not since 1968 have at least 60 percent of eligible

voters gone to the polls, although turnout was nearly that high in 2004. Participation dipped below 50 percent as recently as 1996.

Usually the outcome of elections is known within hours after the closing of polls. Winning candidates celebrate with victory speeches, while the losers concede, or admit defeat, in concession speeches.

Occasionally, though, election results are unclear or become controversial, especially when the outcome of the popular vote triggers uncertainty about electoral college vote tallies. The 1876 election prompted the longest such delay—four months—before Rutherford B. Hayes was named President. His selection came just three days before the scheduled presidential Inauguration. Other lengthy delays occurred with the 1824 choice of John Quincy Adams (three months), and, most recently, for George W. Bush in 2000 (five weeks).

A President's level of support during an election is seen as a measure of national confidence in that person. Someone who wins by a wide margin is said to hold a mandate, or the sign of widespread national support. Presidents elected with a mandate bring considerable political influence to their work.

George W. Bush

43RD PRESIDENT OF THE UNITED STATES ★ *2001 – present*

NICKNAME	Dubya (W.)
BORN	July 6, 1946, in New Haven, Conn.
POLITICAL PARTY	Republican
CHIEF OPPONENTS	1st term: Albert Arnold Gore, Jr., Democrat (1948–present) Ralph Nader, Green (1934–present); 2nd term: John Kerry, Democrat (1943–present); Ralph Nader, Green (1934–present)
TERM OF OFFICE	Jan. 20, 2001–present
AGE AT INAUGURATION	54 years old
NUMBER OF TERMS	ongoing
VICE PRESIDENT	Richard Bruce Cheney (1941–present)
FIRST LADY	Laura Welch Bush (1946–present), wife (married November 5, 1977)
CHILDREN	Jenna, Barbara (twins)
GEOGRAPHIC SCENE	50 states

Two future Presidents were captured in this family snapshot from 1955. George Bush, the nation's 41st Chief Executive, holds his young son, George W. Bush, who became the nation's 43rd President in 2001. Wife, mother, and future First Lady Barbara Bush looks on. During the son's Presidency, the similar names of the men were distinguished by the use of the son's middle initial, W., a letter which had become his nickname, as well. Some people referred to them by the number of their administrations, too, that is as #41 and #43.

A FIVE-VOTE MARGIN OF VICTORY in electoral college voting propelled George Walker Bush into the Presidency in 2000 despite his second-place finish in the popular vote. Only three 19th-century presidents—John Quincy Adams, Rutherford B. Hayes, and Benjamin Harrison—shared this circumstance. Unlike these men, Bush, who was the son of a President, earned a second term in the White House. He and his father, the nation's 41st President, are the second father-son pair of Chief Executives.

A family tradition of elected public service began while George W. Bush was growing up in Texas. He was six years old when his grandfather became a U.S. senator. Twelve years later his father made his first bid for elected office. As a child George W. Bush played baseball and dreamed of becoming a star athlete. However, he shadowed his father's rise to political life by attending the same private high school as his father and the same college, Yale University. He graduated in 1968 with a major in history. Bush served in the Air Force National Guard during the Vietnam War and learned how to fly an F-102 fighter jet. Later he earned a degree from Harvard Business School.

In 1975 Bush returned to Texas and, like his father, found work in the oil industry. He married Laura Welch in 1977, just three months after they had met. The next year Bush made an unsuccessful bid for election to the U.S. House of Representatives. Later he became an owner and manager of the Texas Rangers baseball team. He was elected governor of Texas in 1994 and was reelected four years later.

Bush campaigned for the Presidency in 2000 against the Vice President, Al Gore. Their contest ended with a hotly disputed debate over the bungled counting of election returns in Florida, a

During the Vietnam War, George W. Bush joined the Air Force National Guard (above). Questions over unfinished service requirements became a campaign issue during his presidential bids.

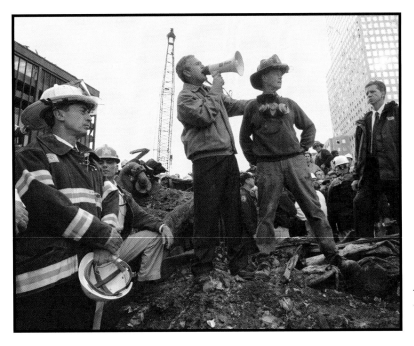

"America was targeted for attack because we're the brightest beacon for freedom and opportunity in the world. And no one will keep that light from shining."

George W. Bush,
September 11, 2001

The terrorist attacks of September 11, 2001 became a rallying point for the administration of George W. Bush. His leadership drew praise at first, particularly after his dramatic visit to Ground Zero at the site of the collapsed twin towers from New York's World Trade Center. Public opinion grew more divided later on.

state governed by Bush's brother. Neither candidate could earn the required electoral college support without a Florida victory. Counts certified by the state's Republican leaders showed Bush defeating Gore by 537 votes, but with an unusually large number of disqualified ballots. Intervention by the U.S. Supreme Court ended vote recounts, effectively making Bush President even though he trailed Gore nationally by more than 500,000 popular votes.

In a nationally televised victory address on December 13, Bush promised to lead the country with a program of "compassionate conservatism." He took office with the narrowest of political margins in Congress and the first-ever equally divided U.S. Senate. The nation's economy, already in a slowdown, dropped into recession soon after, and unemployment began to rise. In an effort to stimulate the economy, Bush pushed through sweeping tax cuts and reforms. These reforms were later blamed for creating a large federal budget deficit.

The catastrophic series of terrorist attacks that took place on September 11, 2001, brought an international focus to Bush's Presidency and created a huge surge in his popularity. Bush sought to strengthen national defense through the creation of a Department of Homeland Security. He authorized the U.S. invasion of Afghanistan in order to

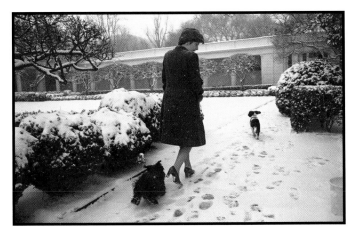

George W. Bush, the father of twin girls (above left), brought a strong commitment to faith and family to the White House that was shared by his wife, Laura (above right). The First Lady, a former teacher and librarian, promoted childhood literacy. She walks (at right) through a wintry White House Rose Garden.

Scenes from a presidency dominated by foreign policy: Meeting with Vice President Richard Cheney and other senior advisers in the Oval Office planning for the Iraq War (above left) and walking through White House during a state visit by Russian leader Vladimir Putin (above, right). Bush, who learned how to fly fighter jets as a member of the National Guard, piloted onto the deck of the U.S.S. Abraham Lincoln *for a dramatic visit (below) in May of 2003 with troops from the Iraq War. His declaration of "Mission Accomplished" proved premature. Armed resistance mushroomed into renewed fighting soon after and persisted into his second term of office.*

capture those responsible for the U.S. attacks, including Al Qaeda terrorist leader Osama bin Laden.

Subsequently Bush and his advisors advocated for an invasion of nearby Iraq, the focus of the Persian Gulf War during his father's Presidency. They claimed the country harbored terrorists and potential chemical or nuclear weapons of mass destruction under the untrustworthy control of long-time ruler, Saddam Hussein. Despite considerable international disapproval, U.S. forces attacked the country in March of 2002. In a matter of weeks they overwhelmed Iraq's army. However, disagreement and chaos quickly enveloped much of the country, making it difficult for occupying forces to secure the region.

Public support for the Iraq War declined with the region's growing instability, mounting costs, continued casualties, and the failure to find stockpiles of weapons of mass destruction. Public opinion fell further after news emerged of the widespread abuse by U.S. soldiers of Iraqi prisoners of war.

The war and the President's handling of the threat of terrorism drew increasing scrutiny during the 2004 presidential election, particularly after the contest settled into a two-man race between Bush and Massachusetts Senator John Kerry, a decorated Vietnam War veteran. Other election issues included the continued sluggish performance of the economy, the rising U.S. budget deficit, the net loss of more than a million U.S. jobs, rising health care costs, and an increase in the number of uninsured citizens.

Despite these concerns, voters chose to stay the course, favoring Bush's background on national security and his commitment to conservative social issues. This time Bush won in both the popular and electoral college voting. Thus he became the first President to win reelection after first failing to earn a majority of the popular votes. He was also the first to retake the White House despite the fact that fewer than half of his countrymen, according to political polls, approved of his job performance.

Former Presidents

★ *Serving as Elder Statesmen* ★

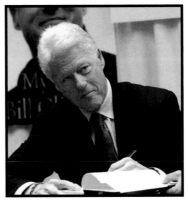

For U.S. Presidents, it's only a matter of time before their jobs come to an end. No matter how popular they may be or how much they relish their work, four to eight years after taking office, they're out of work.

Presidents have completed their administrations when they were as young as 50 (Theodore Roosevelt) and as old as 77 (Ronald Reagan). Some have enjoyed lengthy retirements. Herbert Hoover's lasted 31 years. Others, as in the case of James K. Polk, are very brief. (He died fewer than four months into his retirement.)

Usually the nation has at least one living former President at any given time, but on five occasions there have been none. Richard M. Nixon was President during the last such period. There have never been more than five former Presidents alive at once.

Some former Presidents have continued in public service after leaving the White House. John Quincy Adams and Andrew Johnson joined the U.S. Congress. William Howard Taft was appointed Chief Justice of the U.S. Supreme Court. Others, like Herbert Hoover and Jimmy Carter, have played less formal roles but have assisted in government studies, peacemaking, or international humanitarian efforts. Carter earned a Nobel Peace Prize for his postpresidential work.

Other former Presidents have kept busy by writing and speaking about their lives, by teaching, with travel, or by just having fun. In recent decades former Presidents have spent considerable time helping to establish their presidential libraries, too.

In a show of respect, Chief Executives continue to be addressed as Mr. President even after they leave office. The earliest ones departed the White House with little more

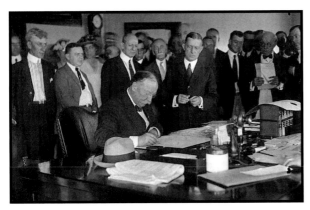

Two years after his presidential retirement, John Quincy Adams won election to the U.S. House of Representatives. He served there for 17 years (above) until his death at age 80. William Howard Taft, who had always wanted to serve on the Supreme Court, earned that distinction (far left) eight years after leaving the White House. Bill Clinton, like many former Chief Executives, wrote his autobiography in the years following his Presidency. It became a bestseller during Clinton's 2004 book-signing tour (left).

than this title. Not until 1958 did Congress begin appropriating money for presidential retirement funds. Harry S. Truman received the first such pension; it totaled $25,000 a year. Presidential widows were granted pensions of $10,000; later this sum was increased to $20,000.

Today Presidents earn an annual retirement salary of over $170,000. In addition they receive office support, health care benefits, some paid travel expenses, access to free U.S. postage, and assistance with their presidential libraries. All former Presidents through Bill Clinton receive lifetime protection for themselves and their wives by members of the Secret Service. Subsequent retired Chief Executives are covered for ten years only.

Although Presidents have no formal role in the government after leaving the White House, they are usually viewed as important elder statesmen. Sitting Presidents may seek their advice. Former Presidents and First Ladies gather for important events, such as state funerals. Occasionally they may publicly voice their opinions about government, especially in a show of support for the current President. Only rarely do they openly criticize a sitting President, and in such cases their views are treated seriously and with respect.

Jimmy Carter, who was only 56 years old at the end of his Presidency, went on to distinguish himself in the decades that followed as a peacemaker and moderator of democratic elections. His career of retirement service earned him the Nobel Peace Prize in 2002 at age 78, the only former President to win this honor.

They may offer their endorsement of new candidates for President, too.

Former Presidents often find that their popularity fluctuates with time. Even those who may not have been well regarded on leaving office can gain public support later on, as did Jimmy Carter, for example. Reputations continue to evolve and shift, even after the Presidents' deaths.

The death of a former President starts off a period of national mourning and recognition. U.S. flags fly at half mast for 30 days. Some Presidents or family members may plan simple burial ceremonies. Others request elaborate state funerals. The death of Ronald Reagan in 2004, for example, prompted a week-long series of services on both U.S. coasts. Planning for the elaborate events began years before his death.

Often the death of a former President brings together his surviving peers. Four former Presidents, George Bush, Jimmy Carter, Gerald R. Ford, and Bill Clinton, (clockwise from second row with their wives) joined President George W. Bush and his Vice President to mourn the passing in 2004 of Ronald Reagan.

CHART OF

Presidential Election Results

1789 – present

ELECTION YEAR	NUMBER OF PRESIDENCY	NAME OF PRESIDENT, YEARS OF OFFICE, AND CHIEF OPPONENTS	NAME OF POLITICAL PARTY	NAME OF VICE PRESIDENT	PERCENTAGE OF POPULAR VOTE	ELECTORAL VOTE
1789	1	George Washington, 1789–1797	Federalist	John Adams	Popular	69
		John Adams	Federalist		voting	34
		Others			began in	35
1792		George Washington, 1789–1797	Federalist	John Adams	1824.	132
		John Adams	Federalist			77
		George Clinton	Federalist			50
		Others				5
1796	2	John Adams, 1797–1801	Federalist	Thomas Jefferson		71
		Thomas Jefferson	Democratic-Republican			68
		Thomas Pinckney	Federalist			59
		Aaron Burr	Democratic-Republican			30
		Others				48
1800	3	Thomas Jefferson, 1801–1809	Democratic-Republican	Aaron Burr		73
		Aaron Burr	Democratic-Republican			73
		John Adams	Federalist			65
		Charles C. Pinckney	Federalist			64
		John Jay	Federalist			1
1804		Thomas Jefferson, 1801–1809	Democratic-Republican	George Clinton		162
		Charles C. Pinckney	Federalist			14
1808	4	James Madison, 1809–1817	Democratic-Republican	George Clinton		122
		Charles C. Pinckney	Federalist			47
		George Clinton	Democratic-Republican			6
1812		James Madison, 1809–1817	Democratic-Republican	Elbridge Gerry		128
		DeWitt Clinton	Federalist			89
1816	5	James Monroe, 1817–1825	Democratic-Republican	Daniel D. Tompkins		183
		Rufus King	Federalist			34
1820		James Monroe, 1817–1825	Democratic-Republican	Daniel D. Tompkins		231
		John Quincy Adams	Democratic-Republican			1
1824	6	John Quincy Adams, 1825–1829	Democratic-Republican	John C. Calhoun	30.5%	84
		Andrew Jackson	Democratic-Republican		43.1%	99
		William Crawford	Democratic-Republican		13.1%	41
		Henry Clay	Democratic-Republican		13.2%	37
1828	7	Andrew Jackson, 1829–1837	Democratic	John C. Calhoun	56.0%	178
		John Quincy Adams	National Republican		44.0%	83
1832		Andrew Jackson, 1829–1837	Democrat	Martin Van Buren	54.9%	219
		Henry Clay	National Republican		42.4%	49
		Others			2.6%	18

ELECTION YEAR	NUMBER OF PRESIDENCY	NAME OF PRESIDENT, YEARS OF OFFICE, AND CHIEF OPPONENTS	NAME OF POLITICAL PARTY	NAME OF VICE PRESIDENT	PERCENTAGE OF POPULAR VOTE	ELECTORAL VOTE
1836	8	Martin Van Buren, 1837–1841	Democrat	Richard M. Johnson	50.9%	170
		William Henry Harrison	Whig		36.6%	73
		Others			12.4%	51
1840	9	William Henry Harrison, 1841	Whig	John Tyler	52.8%	234
		Martin Van Buren	Democrat		46.8%	60
		James G. Birney	Liberty		0.3%	0
	10	John Tyler, 1841–1845	Whig	None		
1844	11	James K. Polk, 1845–1849	Democrat	George M. Dallas	49.6%	170
		Henry Clay	Whig		48.1%	105
		James G. Birney	Liberty		2.3%	0
1848	12	Zachary Taylor, 1849–1850	Whig	Millard Fillmore	47.4%	163
		Lewis Cass	Democrat		42.5%	127
		Martin Van Buren	Free-Soil		10.1%	0
	13	Millard Fillmore, 1850–1853	Whig	None		
1852	14	Franklin Pierce, 1853–1857	Democrat	William R. D. King	50.9%	254
		Winfield Scott	Whig		44.1%	42
		John P. Hale	Free-Soil		5.0%	0
1856	15	James Buchanan, 1857–1861	Democrat	John C. Breckinridge	45.3%	174
		John C. Frémont	Republican		33.1%	114
		Millard Fillmore	Know-Nothing		21.6%	8
1860	16	Abraham Lincoln, 1861–1865	Republican	Hannibal Hamlin	39.8%	180
		Stephen A. Douglas	Democrat		29.5%	12
		John C. Breckinridge	Democrat		18.1%	72
		John Bell	Constitutional Union		12.6%	39
1864		Abraham Lincoln, 1861–1865	Republican	Andrew Johnson	55.0%	212
		George B. McClellan	Democrat		45.0%	21
	17	Andrew Johnson, 1865–1869	Democrat	None		
1868	18	Ulysses S. Grant, 1869–1877	Republican	Schuyler Colfax	52.7%	214
		Horatio Seymour	Democrat		47.3%	80
1872		Ulysses S. Grant, 1869–1877	Republican	Henry Wilson	55.6%	286
		Horace Greeley	Democrat		43.9%	
1876	19	Rutherford B. Hayes, 1877–1881	Republican	William A. Wheeler	48.0%	185
		Samuel J. Tilden	Democrat		51.0%	184
1880	20	James A. Garfield, 1881	Republican	Chester A. Arthur	48.5%	214
		Winfield S. Hancock	Democrat		48.1%	155
		James B. Weaver	Greenback-Labor		3.4%	0
	21	Chester A. Arthur, 1881–1885	Republican	None		
1884	22	Grover Cleveland, 1885–1889	Democrat	Thomas A. Hendricks	48.5%	219
		James G. Blaine	Republican		48.2%	182
		Benjamin F. Butler	Greenback-Labor		1.8%	0
		John P. St. John	Prohibition		1.5%	0
1888	23	Benjamin Harrison, 1889–1893	Republican	Levi P. Morton	47.9%	233
		Grover Cleveland	Democrat		48.6%	168
		Clinton B. Fisk	Prohibition		2.2%	0
		Anson J. Streeter	Union Labor		1.3%	0

ELECTION YEAR	NUMBER OF PRESIDENCY	NAME OF PRESIDENT, YEARS OF OFFICE, AND CHIEF OPPONENTS	NAME OF POLITICAL PARTY	NAME OF VICE PRESIDENT	PERCENTAGE OF POPULAR VOTE	ELECTORAL VOTE
1892	24	Grover Cleveland, 1893–1897	Democrat	Adlai E. Stevenson	46.1%	277
		Benjamin Harrison	Republican		43.0%	145
		James Weaver	Populist		8.5%	22
		John Bidwell	Prohibition		2.2%	0
1896	25	William McKinley, 1897–1901	Republican	Garret A. Hobart	51.1%	271
		William J. Bryan	Democrat		47.7%	176
1900		William McKinley	Republican	Theodore Roosevelt	51.7%	292
		William J. Bryan	Democrat/Populist		45.5%	155
		John C. Woolley	Prohibition		1.5%	0
	26	Theodore Roosevelt, 1901–1909	Republican	None		
1904		Theodore Roosevelt, 1901–1909	Republican	Charles W. Fairbanks	56.4%	336
		Alton B. Parker	Democrat		37.6%	140
		Eugene V. Debs	Socialist		3.0%	0
		Silas C. Swallow	Prohibition		1.9%	0
1908	27	William Howard Taft, 1909–1913	Republican	James S. Sherman	51.6%	321
		William J. Bryan	Democrat		43.1%	162
		Eugene V. Debs	Socialist		2.8%	0
		Eugene W. Chafin	Prohibition		1.7%	0
1912	28	Woodrow Wilson, 1913–1921	Democrat	Thomas R. Marshall	41.9%	435
		Theodore Roosevelt	Progressive		27.4%	88
		William H. Taft	Republican		23.2%	8
		Eugene V. Debs	Socialist		6.0%	0
		Eugene W. Chafin	Prohibition		1.5%	0
1916		Woodrow Wilson, 1913–1921	Democrat	Thomas R. Marshall	49.4%	277
		Charles E. Hughes	Republican		46.2%	254
		A.L. Benson	Socialist		3.2%	0
		J. Frank Hanly	Prohibition		1.2%	0
1920	29	Warren G. Harding, 1921–1923	Republican	Calvin Coolidge	60.4%	404
		James M. Cox	Democrat		34.2%	127
		Eugene V. Debs	Socialist		3.4%	0
		P. P. Christensen	Farmer–Labor		1.0%	0
	30	Calvin Coolidge, 1923–1929	Republican	None		
1924		Calvin Coolidge, 1923–1929	Republican	Charles G. Dawes	54.0%	382
		John W. Davis	Democrat		28.8%	136
		Robert M. La Follette	Progressive		16.6%	13
1928	31	Herbert Hoover, 1929–1933	Republican	Charles Curtis	58.2%	444
		Alfred E. Smith	Democrat		40.9%	87
1932	32	Franklin D. Roosevelt, 1933–1945	Democrat	John N. Garner	57.4%	472
		Herbert Hoover	Republican		39.7%	59
		Norman Thomas	Socialist		2.2%	0
1936		Franklin D. Roosevelt, 1933–1945	Democrat	John N. Garner	60.8%	523
		Alfred M. Landon	Republican		36.5%	8
		William Lemke	Union		1.9%	0
1940		Franklin D. Roosevelt, 1933–1945	Democrat	Henry A. Wallace	54.8%	449
		Wendell Willkie	Republican		44.8%	82

ELECTION YEAR	NUMBER OF PRESIDENCY	NAME OF PRESIDENT, YEARS OF OFFICE, AND CHIEF OPPONENTS	NAME OF POLITICAL PARTY	NAME OF VICE PRESIDENT	PERCENTAGE OF POPULAR VOTE	ELECTORAL VOTE
1944		Franklin D. Roosevelt, 1933–1945	Democrat	Harry S. Truman	53.5%	432
		Thomas E. Dewey	Republican		46.0%	99
	33	Harry S. Truman, 1945–1953	Democrat	None		
1948		Harry S. Truman, 1945–1953	Democrat	Alben W. Barkley	50%	303
		Thomas E. Dewey	Republican		49.9%	189
		J. Strom Thurmond	States' Rights		2.4%	39
		Henry A. Wallace	Progressive		2.4%	0
1952	34	Dwight D. Eisenhower, 1953–1961	Republican	Richard M. Nixon	55.1%	442
		Adlai E. Stevenson	Democrat		44.4%	89
1956		Dwight D. Eisenhower, 1953–1961	Republican	Richard M. Nixon	57.6%	457
		Adlai E. Stevenson	Democrat		42.1%	73
1960	35	John F. Kennedy, 1961–1963	Democrat	Lyndon B. Johnson	49.9%	303
		Richard M. Nixon	Republican		49.6%	219
	36	Lyndon B. Johnson, 1963–1969	Democrat	None		
1964		Lyndon B. Johnson, 1963–1969	Democrat	Hubert H. Humphrey	61.1%	486
		Barry M. Goldwater	Republican		38.5%	52
1968	37	Richard M. Nixon, 1969–1974	Republican	Spiro T. Agnew	43.4%	301
		Hubert H. Humphrey	Democrat		42.7%	191
		George C. Wallace	American Independent		13.5%	46
1972		Richard M. Nixon, 1969–1974	Republican	Spiro T. Agnew Gerald R. Ford	60.6%	520
		George S. McGovern	Democrat		37.5%	17
	38	Gerald R. Ford, 1974–1977	Republican	Nelson A. Rockefeller		
1976	39	Jimmy Carter, 1977–1981	Democrat	Walter F. Mondale	50.1%	297
		Gerald R. Ford	Republican		47.9%	240
1980	40	Ronald Reagan, 1981–1989	Republican	George Bush	50.9%	489
		Jimmy Carter	Democrat		41.2%	49
		John B. Anderson	Independent		7.9%	0
1984		Ronald Reagan, 1981–1989	Republican	George Bush	59.0%	525
		Walter F. Mondale	Democratic		41.0%	13
1988	41	George Bush, 1989–1993	Republican	Dan Quayle	53.4%	426
		Michael S. Dukakis	Democrat		45.6%	111
1992	42	William Jefferson Clinton, 1993–2001	Democrat	Al Gore	43.0%	370
		George Bush	Republican		37.0%	168
		H. Ross Perot	Independent		19.0%	0
1996		William Jefferson Clinton, 1993–2001	Democrat	Al Gore	49.0%	379
		Robert J. Dole	Republican		41.0%	159
		H. Ross Perot	Reform		8.0%	0
2000	43	George W. Bush, 2001–present	Republican	Richard B. Cheney	48.0%	271
		Al Gore	Democrat		48.5%	266
		Ralph Nader	Green		2.7%	0
		Others			0.8%	0
		Abstained				1
2004		George W. Bush, 2001–present	Republican	Richard B. Cheney	51.0%	274
		John Kerry	Democrat		48.0%	252
		Ralph Nader	Independent		1%	0

Index

Boldface indicates illustrations.

★ A ★
Adams, Abigail **22**, 23
Adams, John 8, **20–23**, 24, 27, 28, **37**, 85, 103, 126
   family 43, 116
   Vice Presidency **8**, 18, 22, 58, 59
Adams, John Quincy **42–43**, 47, 126, **142**, 184, 196, **196**
   birthplace **21**
   elections 40, 46, 169, 191, 193
Adams, Louisa **142**
Afghanistan
   invasion by United States 194–195
African Americans
   civil rights 151, 154–155, **155**, 172
   desegregation **134**, 151, **151**, **161**
   voting rights 88, **88**, **190**
   see also Slavery
Agnew, Spiro T. **59**, 165
Alamo, Battle of **13**
Al Qaeda 175, 195
Anthony, Susan B. **75**
Arkansas
   Presidents 103, **186–189**
Arlington National Cemetery, Virginia 121, 155
Armstrong, Neil **164**
Arthur, Chester Alan **96–97**
   administration 119
   children **97**
Articles of Confederation 17–18
Atomic bombs 127, **134**, 145, 151, 179

★ B ★
Barney (dog) **117**
Begin, Menachem **173**
Bell, Alexander Graham 91, **157**
Berlin Airlift 146, **147**
Berlin Wall 154, **174**
Bicentennial celebrations **135**, 167
bin Laden, Osama 195
Blaine, James 99
Booth, John Wilkes 81, **81**
Bryan, William Jennings 110, 111
Buchanan, James **72–73**

Burr, Aaron 27, **28**, 29, **58**
Bush, Barbara 143, **181**, **182**, **193**, **197**
Bush, George **180–183**, 193, **193**, **197**
   children 182, **183**
Bush, George W. 7, 43, 127, **127**, **183**, **192–195**, **197**
   administration **58**, 183, **195**
   children **194**
   elections 169, 191, **191**
   salary 102
Bush, John "Jeb" **183**
Bush, Laura 143, **143**, **191**, 193, **194**, **197**

★ C ★
Calhoun, John C. 59
California
   Presidents 103, **162–165**
   statehood 69
Camp David Accords **173**
Campaign slogans 55, 62, 71, 99, 124, 131, **137**, 139, 150, 160
Carter, Jimmy 102, 127, **170–173**, 196, 197, **197**
   administration 59
   children 117, 171, **172**
Carter, Rosalynn 143, **143**, **171**, **172**, 173, **173**, **197**
Castro, Fidel 154
Challenger (space shuttle) **174**
Cheney, Richard **58**, **195**
Chicago, Illinois 74
China, People's Republic of 164, **164**, 172
Churchill, Winston **139**, 140
Civil rights 151, 154–155, **155**, 161
Civil War 49, 53, 57, **74**, 78–79, 123, **126**, 127
   casualties **80**
   military service of Presidents **87**, 87–88, 91, **105**, 109, 126
   Reconstruction 74, 80, 83
Clark, William 12, 30
Clay, Henry 62
Cleveland, Frances 100, **100**, **101**
Cleveland, Grover **98–101**, 102, 105, 126, 169, 190
   children 100, **101**, 116
Clinton, Hillary Rodham 143, **143**, 187, 189,

189, **197**
Clinton, William J. **58**, 103, 126, **186–189**, 190, **196**, 197, **197**
   children 117, **117**, 189, **189**
Cloning **175**
Coins **12**
Cold War 146, 150–151, 154, 177, 182
Communism 146–147, 151, 154, 182
Computers **134**
Confederate States of America 78
Connecticut
   Presidents 7, 103, **192–195**
Constellation (ship) **23**
Constitution, U.S. **12**, 18, 33–34, 35, 36
   amendments 59, 79, 88, 89, 107, 120, 138, 164
   Bill of Rights 33
   Presidency 13, 23, 29, 36, 57, 89, 168
   and slavery 79
   Vice Presidency 23, 29, 57, 58, 59, 168
   wartime restrictions 127
Constitutional Convention 12, **17**, 18, 33, **33**, 35
Continental Congress 16, 21, 28
Coolidge, Calvin 103, **130–131**
   administration 133
Cox, James M. 138
Cuba 110, 154

★ D ★
Declaration of Independence 22, 23, **27**, 28, 55
   Bicentennial celebrations **135**, 167
Democratic Party 62, 71, 84–85, 189
   campaigns 84, 85
   conventions **65**
   donkey symbol **84**
Desegregation **134**, 151
Dickinson, Susanna **13**
Douglas, Stephen 77
Douglass, Frederick **48**, 88
Duryea brothers 75

★ E ★
Earthquakes **106**
Economy 53, 172, 178–179, 183, 194

financial crisis 51, 52, 101, **107**, 133, 138
Edison, Thomas **74**, 91
Einstein, Albert **134**
Eisenhower, Dwight D. 127, 133, **148–151**
   administration 163
   library 93
   supporter **65**
Eisenhower, Mamie **143**, 149, **149**, 151, **151**
Electoral college 18, 29, 40, 43, 58, 91, 100, 105, 168–169
   map showing votes by state 168
Enola Gay (airplane) **127**

★ F ★
Federalist Party 19, 29, 30, 84, 85
Fillmore, Abigail **69**, 143
Fillmore, Millard **67**, **68–69**, 85
First Ladies 142–143
Ford, Betty **85**, 143, 167, **197**
Ford, Gerald R. **85**, **103**, 157, 165, **166–167**, 197
   administration 181
Franklin, Benjamin 22, **27**, 28

★ G ★
Garfield, James A. **94–95**, 156, **157**, 190
   children 117
Garfield, Lucretia **142**
Georgia
   Presidents 103, **170–173**
Gettysburg Address 78, **81**
Gold Rush **48**
Gorbachev, Mikhail **179**
Gore, Albert, Jr. **58**, 188, 193–194
Grand Old Party (GOP) 84
Grant, Julia 89
Grant, Ulysses S. 63, 79, 80, **86–89**, 127, 184–185
   administration 119
Great Depression **107**, 133, 138, **138**, 139
Great Society 159, 160
Green Party 85
Grenada
   invasion by United States **178**

★ H ★

Habitat for Humanity 173
Hamilton, Alexander **18, 28,
58**
Hamlin, Hannibal **79**
Harding, Warren G. **64, 102,**
121, **128–129,** 131, 156,
191
administration 133
Harrison, Benjamin 41, 55,
104–105, 109
administration 113
election 99, 100, 169, 193
grandchildren **117**
Harrison, William Henry **34,
52,** 53, **54–55,** 85, 105,
184
death 58–59, 102, 156
Hayes, Lucy **91**
Hayes, Rutherford B. **90–91,**
109, 169, **190,** 191, 193
Heart transplants **135**
Hemings, Sally 31
Hiroshima, Japan **134,** 145
Hoban, James **24**
Hoover, Herbert 103, **132–133,**
138, 196
library 93
Humphrey, Hubert H. **58, 160**
Hussein, Saddam **175,** 183, 195

★ I ★

Illinois
Presidents **76–81,** 103,
176–179
Immigration 75
Inaugural addresses 55, 57,
78–79, **100, 129**
Inaugurations **8,** 19, **39, 45,**
46–47, 69, **88,** 110,
121, 160, 172, **189**
Inventions **13, 29, 30, 31,** 74,
75, 91, 106, 111, **129,
134**
Iowa
Presidents 103, **132–133**
Iran-Contra scandal **178,** 179
Iranian hostage crisis 173, **173**
Iraq
invasion of Kuwait **174,** 183
Iraq War **127,** 175, 195, **195**

★ J ★

Jackson, Andrew **44–47,** 52, 61,
62, 84, **85,** 127, 157
administration 51, 52,
59, 73
Jackson, Rachel 46
Japan
arrival of Matthew C.
Perry **49**
nuclear bomb attacks
127, 134, 145
Jefferson, Martha **31**
Jefferson, Thomas 12, **18,** 19,
24, **26–31,** 39, 41, 84

administration 34, 40, 43,
58
death 23, 103
grandchildren 116
landmarks **30,** 31, **31**
Vice Presidency 23
Johnson, Andrew 78, **82–83,**
196
impeachment 102, **102**
Johnson, Lady Bird 143, **159,**
159–160, **160,** 161, **161**
Johnson, Lyndon B. 127,
158–161, 167, 191
administration **58**

★ K ★

Kansas
Presidents **148–151**
slavery debate 71, **71**
Kennedy, Edward 155
Kennedy, Jacqueline 143, **143,**
153, **154,** 155, **155,** 159
burial 121
Kennedy, John F. **64,** 103, **117,
152–155,** 159, 160, **187,**
190
death 121, 156, **156, 157**
family 117, **117, 153, 154,** 155,
157
Kennedy, Robert F. **154,** 155
Kentucky
Presidents **76–81,** 103
Kerry, John **191,** 195
Key, Francis Scott 13, **35**
King, Martin Luther, Jr. **58,**
155
Knox, Henry **18**
Korean War 146, 150, **151**
Kuwait
invasion by Iraq **174,** 183

★ L ★

Lafayette, Marquis de **18**
League of Nations 123, 124, 125
Lee, Robert E. **79,** 123
Lewis, Meriwether 12, 30
Lewis and Clark Expedition
12, 30, 31
Lincoln, Abraham **76–81,** 84,
103, 126, 190
children 79–80, **80,** 116
Civil War 88, **126,** 127
death 80–81, **81,** 155, 156,
156
landmarks 92, **92,** 93
Lincoln, Mary Todd **77,** 79, 80,
80
Little Rock, Arkansas **134,** 151
Louisiana Purchase 12, 27, 28,
30, 40

★ M ★

Madison, Dolley **33,** 34, 35, **35,**
142
Madison, James **32–35,** 40, 126,
127

administration 43
Maine
electoral votes 169
statehood 41
Maine (ship) **110**
Mandela, Nelson **174**
Manifest Destiny 62, **62**
Marshall, George C. **147**
Marshall, John **13,** 23
Marshall, Thurgood **161**
Marshall Plan 146, 147
Massachusetts
Presidents **20–23, 42–43,**
102, 103, **152–155,**
180–183
McCarthy, Joseph 146–147,
151, 163
McKinley, Ida **109**
McKinley, William **108–111,**
119, 156, **157,** 184
administration 114
Mexican War **48,** 63
Michigan
Presidents **166–167**
Missouri
Presidents 103, **144–147**
statehood 41
Missouri Compromise 41, 71
Mondale, Walter 59
Money **12,** 17, 101
Monroe, Elizabeth 41, **41**
Monroe, James 33, **38–41,** 103
administration 43
children 117
Monroe Doctrine 41
Monticello, Virginia **30,** 31, **31**
Moon landing **135, 164**
Mount Vernon, Virginia 16, **18,**
19

★ N ★

Nagasaki, Japan 145
National Geographic Society
trustees 121, 131
Native Americans **12,** 34, 46,
47, 53, **53, 78**
Nebraska
electoral votes 169
Presidents 103, **166–167**
New Deal 139, 140, 147
New Hampshire
Presidents **70–71,** 103
New Jersey
Presidents **98–101,** 103
New Orleans, Louisiana **12,**
28, 30, **47**
New York
Presidents **50–53, 68–69,**
98–103, 112–115,
136–141
Vice Presidents 59
Nixon, Pat 143, 163, **163, 165**
Nixon, Richard M. **64,** 102,
102, 103, 127, 154,
162–165, 167, 190, 191,
196

administration 59, 181
family 117, **163, 165**
Nobel Peace Prize 114, 115,
115, 124, 171, 173,
196, **197**
Noriega, Manuel 182
North, Oliver **178**
North Carolina
Presidents **44–47, 60–63,**
82–83, 103
Nuclear power plants 172
Nuclear weapons 127, **134,** 145,
151, 172, 179

★ O ★

O'Connor, Sandra Day 179
Ohio
Presidents **86–91, 94–95,**
102, 103, **104–105,**
108–111, 118–121,
128–129
Oil spills **182**
Oklahoma
new settlers **75**
Oklahoma City bombing
175
Oregon Trail **48,** 62
Oswald, Lee Harvey 155

★ P ★

Panama
invasion by United States
182–183
Panama Canal 111, **115,** 119,
120, 172
Pennsylvania
Presidents **72–73,** 103
Perry, Matthew C. **49**
Persian Gulf War **174, 182,** 183
Philadelphia, Pennsylvania
18, 19
Philadelphia (ship) **23**
Philippine Islands 110–111, 119,
120
Pierce, Franklin **70–71**
administration 73
family **71**
Pinckney, Charles 34
Political campaigns 62, **64–65,**
84–85, 105, 110, 111,
114, 119, **145, 155**
banners **84, 100, 109**
Political cartoons **52,** 62, **73,**
89, 111
Political conventions 65, **65**
Political parties 19, 23, 51–52,
84–85, 189
map showing Presidents'
affiliations 103
Polk, James K. 47, **60–63,**
103, 196
administration 73
tomb **92**
Polk, Sarah 63, **63**
Pony Express 49
Postage stamps **18,** 61

Presidents
assassinations 80–81, 95, 109, 111, 155, 156, 184
attempted assassinations 46, 113, 157, **178**
as elder statesmen **196–197**
elections **190–191**, 198–201
facts and statistics 102–103
impeachment 83, 165, 187, 188–189
landmarks **92**, 92–93
map showing birthplaces 103
map showing landmarks 93
military service 126–127
oath of office 8
pets 116, 117, **117**
press corps 111, 185, **185**
qualifications 8
religions 103
salary 102, 185, 197
security 184–185
transportation **184**, 185, **185**
Putin, Vladimir **195**

★ R ★

Railroads **49**
Randolph, Edmund **18**
Reagan, Nancy 143, **177**, 179
Reagan, Ronald 102, 103, 157, **176–179**, **185**, 191, 196
administration **36**, 181
funeral **179**, 197, **197**
Religious freedom 28–29
Republican Party 84–85, 95, 101, 189
birthplace **85**
elephant symbol **84**
Revolutionary War **16**, 16–17, 22, 45, **45**
Roaring Twenties **107**, 131
Roosevelt, Edith **114**
Roosevelt, Eleanor **127**, **137**, 137–138, 140, **140**, 143, **143**
Roosevelt, Franklin D. **64**, 102, 126, 127, 133, **136–141**, 191
administration 145
campaign banner **84**
children **140**
death 156, 157
library 93
memorial **92**, 141
Roosevelt, Theodore **85**, 102, **112–115**, 119, 124, 137, 138, 196
children 115, 116, **116**, 117
military service 110, 114, **114**, 127
Vice Presidency 111
White House 24
Rutherford, Lucy Page Mercer 141

★ S ★

Sacagawea **12**
Sadat, Anwar **173**
Scandals 89, **89**, 129, 131, 164–165, 179, 188–189
Scott, Dred 73, **73**
Secret Service 117, 184, **184**, 197
Segregation **151**, **161**
Slavery **13**, **30**, 31
and Civil War **49**, 78, **79**
Dred Scott case 73, **73**
Emancipation Proclamation 78, **81**
opposition 29, 35, 43, 48, 69
and statehood 41, 53, 61, 62–63, 67, 69, 71
Smithsonian Institution, Washington, D.C. 115
South Carolina
Presidents 44–47, 103
Soviet Union 146, 147, 150–151, 154, 164, 179, 182
Spanish-American War 110–111, 114, **114**
Spoils system 52, 97
Stalin, Joseph **139**, 140
Starr, Kenneth 188, **188**
Statue of Liberty, New York Harbor, New York **75**
Stevenson, Adlai 150
Stock market crash 133, **133**
Supreme Court, U.S. 121
2000 election 169, 191, 194
Brown v. Board of Education **134**, 151
justices **13**, 19, 23, 119, 121, **161**, 179, 196, **196**
on slavery 73

★ T ★

Taft, Helen 119, 121, **121**
Taft, William Howard 85, 102, **118–121**, 124, 196, **196**
Taylor, Zachary **66–67**, 69, 85, 156–157
Teapot Dome affair 129
Tennessee
Presidents **82–83**
Terrorism
Oklahoma City bombing **175**
September 11, 2001 attacks 127, **175**, **194**, 194–195
Texas **13**, 48, 52–53, 57
Presidents 103, **148–151**, **158–161**, **192–195**
statehood 62, 63
Three Mile Island nuclear power plant, Middletown, Pennsylvania 172
Tilden, Samuel J.
election controversy **190**

Timelines 12–13, 48–49, 74–75, 106–107, 134–135, 174–175
Titanic (ship) **106**
Tripolitan War **28**
Truman, Bess **145**, 147
Truman, Harry S. 24, 103, 127, 133, **144–147**, 157, 190, **190**, 197
Trust busting 114, 119
Tyler, John **56–57**, 85, 103
Vice Presidency 58–59
Tyler, Julia **57**

★ U ★

United Nations 124, 140, 146
University of Virginia **29**, 31, 35
U.S. Capital
New York, New York 19
Philadelphia, Pennsylvania 19
U.S. Capitol building, Washington, D.C. **18**, 34, 43, 46, **100**, 179
U.S. Congress 36, **37**, 43, 83, **190**, 196, **196**
U.S. Government
branches 36–37
Cabinet 19, **36**, 47, 172, 194
checks and balances 36
U.S. Navy **23**
U.S. Senate 120

★ V ★

Valley Forge, Pennsylvania **16**
Van Buren, Hannah **53**
Van Buren, Martin 47, **50–53**, 62
Vermont
Presidents **96–97**, 103, **130–131**
Vice Presidency 22, 58–59
residence 58, 59
Vietnam War 146, 151, 154, 155, 160–161, **161**, 164, 172
military service of Presidents 126, 193, **193**
opposition 127, **127**, **135**, 161
Virginia
Presidents **14–19**, **26–35**, **38–41**, **54–57**, **66–67**, 102, 103, **122–125**
Voting and voting rights 75, 88, **88**, **107**, **190**, 191

★ W ★

War of 1812 **13**, **25**, 29, **34–35**, 46, **47**, 126, 127
Wars 126–127
see also specific wars by name
Washington, George 8, **14–19**, 34, 39, 85, 126, **126**, 127
administration **36**, 40, 43

false teeth **102**
home 16, **18**, **19**
inauguration **8**
landmarks **92**
salary 102, 185
White House 24, **24**
Washington, Martha 16, **18**, 19, **143**
Watergate building, Washington, D.C. **165**
Watergate scandal 165
Westward expansion 41, **48**, 61, 62, **62**, **75**
Whig Party 57, 69, 85
Whiskey Rebellion 126, **126**
White House, Washington, D.C. 8, **22**, **24–25**, 185
bathtub **120**
burning **25**, 34
children 115, **116–117**
cutaway view **25**
improvements 24, **40**, 69, 71, **120**
Oval Office **6**, 24, **117**, **195**
Rose Garden **194**
visitors 30, 46–47, **131**
war room **147**
weddings **100**, **117**, 124–125
Whitney, Eli **13**
Wilson, Edith 125, **125**, **142**
Wilson, Ellen 124–125
Wilson, Woodrow **37**, **121**, **122–125**, 126, **126**, 190
administration 138
Women's rights **22**, 75, 88, **107**
Woodhull, Victoria Claflin 88
World Trade Center, New York, New York
September 11, 2001 attack 127, **175**, **194**, 194–195
World War I **107**, 123, **123**, 124, **124**, **125**, **126**, 133
relief efforts **133**
World War II 127, 139–140, **141**, 145, **146**, **147**
atomic bombs 127, **134**, 145
military service of Presidents 149–150, **150**, **153**, **177**, 181
relief efforts 133
Wright, Orville and Wilbur **106**

★ Y ★

Yellowstone National Park, U.S. 88, **97**
Yeltsin, Boris **189**
Yorktown, Virginia **16**, 17

Resource Guide

BOOKS

Allen, Thomas B. *George Washington, Spymaster: How the Americans Outspied the British and Won the Revolutionary War.* Washington, D.C.: National Geographic, 2004.

Bausum, Ann. *With Courage and Cloth: Winning the Fight for a Woman's Right to Vote.* Washington, D.C.: National Geographic, 2004.

Bunch, Lonnie G. et al. *The American Presidency: A Glorious Burden.* Washington, D.C.: Smithsonian Institution Press, 2000.

Ethier, Eric. *Wit and Wisdom of the Presidents.* Lincolnwood, Ill.: Publications International, 1998.

Harness, Cheryl. *Abe Lincoln Goes to Washington, 1837–1865.* Washington, D.C.: National Geographic, 1997.

_____. *George Washington.* Washington, D.C.: National Geographic, 2000.

_____. *Thomas Jefferson.* Washington, D.C.: National Geographic, 2004.

_____. *The Revolutionary John Adams.* Washington, D.C.: National Geographic, 2003.

_____. *Young Abe Lincoln: The Frontier Days, 1809–1837.* Washington, D.C.: National Geographic, 1996.

_____. *Young Teddy Roosevelt.* Washington, D.C.: National Geographic, 1998.

Johnston, Robert D. *The Making of America: The History of the United States from 1492 to the Present.* Washington, D.C.: National Geographic, 2002.

Klapthor, Margaret Brown. *The First Ladies.* Washington, D.C.: White House Historical Association with the cooperation of National Geographic, 1995.

Friedel, Frank. *The Presidents of the United States.* Washington, D.C.: White House Historical Association with the cooperation of National Geographic, 1994.

Kunhardt, Jr, Philip B., Philip B. Kunhardt III, and Peter W. Kunhardt. *The American President.* New York: Riverhead Books, Penguin Putnam Inc., 1999.

McPherson, James M., general editor. *"To the Best of My Ability": The American Presidents.* New York: Dorling Kindersley, 2001 (revised edition).

Provensen, Alice. *The Buck Stops Here.* New York: Browndeer Press, Harcourt Brace & Company, 1997.

Sandler, Martin W. *Presidents, A Library of Congress Book.* New York: HarperCollins Publishers, 1995.

Schanzer, Rosalyn. *George vs. George: The American Revolution as Seen from Both Sides.* Washington, D.C.: National Geographic, 2004.

St. George, Judith. *In the Line of Fire– Presidents' Lives at Stake.* New York: Holiday House, 1999.

Walker, Diana. *Public & Private: Twenty Years Photographing the Presidency.* Washington, D.C.: National Geographic, 2002.

VIDEOS AND TELEVISION PROGRAMS

1600 Pennsylvania Avenue: The White House. National Geographic Educational Film and Video, 1997.

Air Force One. National Geographic Television Special and Video, 1996.

The American President (listed as a book) is also a film series distributed by PBS.

Inside the U.S. Secret Service. National Geographic Channel, 2004.

Inside the White House. National Geographic Television Video, 2001.

The Presidents. The American Experience, Public Broadcasting Service. http://www.pbs.org/wgbh/amex/presidents/intro.html

PLACES TO VISIT

"The American Presidency," permanent exhibit, National Museum of American History, Smithsonian Institution, Washington, D.C.

The White House, Washington D.C.

See also pages 92–93 and each President's fact box.

WEB SITES

About Government, Dirksen Congressional Center http://www.aboutgovernment.org/print_usgov_exec_presidents.htm

American Museum of the Moving Image http://livingroomcandidate.movingimage.us/index.php

National Archives and Records Administration Electoral College http://www.archives.gov/federal_register/electoral_college/

PRESIDENTIAL LIBRARIES
http://www.archives.gov/presidential_libraries/addresses/addresses.html

PRESIDENTIAL SPEECHES
http://www.geocities.com/americanpresidencynet/archive.htm

Bibliography

Aikman, Lonnelle. *The Living White House.* Washington, D.C.: White House Historical Association and National Geographic Society, 1996 (tenth edition).

_____. *We, the People: The Story of the United States Capitol—Its Past and Its Promise.* Washington, D.C.: The United States Capitol Historical Society and National Geographic Society, 1991 (fourteenth edition).

Boller, Paul F., Jr. *Presidential Anecdotes.* New York: Oxford University Press, 1981.

_____. *Presidential Wives.* New York: Oxford University Press, 1988.

Brinkley, Alan and Davis Dyer; editors. *The Reader's Companion to the American Presidency.* Boston: Houghton Mifflin Company, 2004.

Caroli, Betty Boyd. *First Ladies.* New York: Oxford University Press, 1995 (expanded edition).

DeGregorio, William A. *The Complete Book of U.S. Presidents.* New York: Wings Books, Random House, 2003 (fifth edition, revised).

Freidel, Frank. *The Presidents of the United States of America.* Washington, D.C.: White House Historical Association and National Geographic Society, 1995 (fourteenth edition).

Graff, Henry F., editor. *The Presidents, A Reference History.* New York: Charles Scribner's Sons, 1996 (second edition).

Hamilton, Alexander. *James Madison and John Jay. The Federalist Papers.* New York: New American Library, 1961.

Kane, Joseph Nathan. *Facts about the Presidents: A Compilation of Biographical and Historical Information.* New York: The H.W. Wilson Company, 2001 (seventh edition), with new co-authors: Janet Podell and Steven Anzovin.

Keyssar, Alexander. *The Right to Vote: The Contested History of Democracy in the United States.* New York, New York: Basic Books, 2000.

Klapthor, Margaret Brown. *The First Ladies.* Washington, D.C.: White House Historical Association and National Geographic Society, 1999 (ninth edition).

Kruh, David and Louis Kruh; *Presidential Landmarks.* New York: Hippocrene Books, Inc., 1992.

Pearce, Lorraine. *The White House: An Historic Guide.* Washington, D.C.: White House Historical Association and National Geographic Society, 1999 (twentieth edition).

Purcell, L. Edward, editor. *Vice Presidents: A Biographical Dictionary.* New York: Checkmark Books, Facts On File, 2001.

Shaefer, Peggy. *The Ideals Guide to Presidential Homes and Libraries.* Nashville: Ideals Press, 2002.

The World Almanac and Book of Facts. New York: World Almanac Books, 2004.

Additional resources were consulted for individual essays, including presidential biographies, newspaper articles, and Internet sites.

★ ★ ★

Ann Bausum has written two other books for National Geographic: *With Courage and Cloth: Winning the Fight for a Woman's Right to Vote,* and *Dragon Bones and Dinosaur Eggs: A Photobiography of Explorer Roy Chapman Andrews.* The daughter of a history professor, she grew up with a love of research and American history. She tackled each presidency as its own assignment, immersing herself in reference volumes, historical documents, and period anecdotes. Finding the facts she knows kids will love is her favorite part of research. A graduate of Beloit College, she lives in Wisconsin with her husband and two sons.

Consultant **William B. Bushong** is currently the White House Historical Association's Staff Historian specializing in history of the executive mansion. He is a frequent contributor to *White House History,* and his publications include *Uncle Sam's Architects: Builders of the Capitol,* and *The North Carolina Executive Mansion: The First One Hundred Years.* He also administers the Association's Web site: www.whha.org.

Credits

Abbreviations:
LC = The Library of Congress
WHHA (WHC) = White House Historical Association
(White House Collection)
t = top, b = bottom, c = center, l = left, r = right

Cover: All images courtesy White House Historical Association with the exception of George W. Bush, courtesy of the White House, and flags, CORBIS.

1, Joe Sohm/Visions of America; 2-3, Getty Images News Services; 6, photo by BW, WHHA; 7, WHHA; 8, Stock Montage.

THE PRESIDENCY AND HOW IT GREW
12 (t, l-r), WHHA (WHC); 12 (b, l-r), National Archives; Chase Manhattan Bank Money Museum; Chicago Historical Society; Doris S. Clymer; 13 (b, l-r) Getty Images News Services; The New York Public Library, Stokes Collection/Art Resource; The Granger Collection, NY; courtesy Alamo Museum; 14, WHHA (WHC); 15 (l), courtesy LC; 15 (r), courtesy LC; 16 (t, l), courtesy LC; 16 (t, r), Fraunces Tavern Museum; 16 (b), James E. Russell; 17 (t), Colonial Williamsburg Foundation; 17 (b), Virginia Museum of Fine Arts, Richmond. Gift of Edgar & Bernice Chrysler Garbisch. Photo: Ron Jennings; 18 (t, l), courtesy Acacia Mutual Life Ins. Company; (t, r), Continental Insurance Companies; (b, l), Metropolitan Museum of Art, bequest of William Nelson, 1903; (b, r), courtesy LC; 19, courtesy LC; 20, WHHA (WHC); 21 (l), Adams National Historical Site/NPS/Bob Allnut; (r), courtesy University of Texas at Austin; 22 (t), Joseph H. Bailey/courtesy Adams National Historic Site; (b), Lisa Biganzoli/NGS Image Collection; 23 (l), The New York Public Library/Art Resource; (r), Collection of The New York Historical Society; 24 (t), WHHA; (b), WHHA (WHC); 25 (t), WHHA; (b), WHHA (WHC); 26, WHHA (WHC); 27 (l), courtesy LC; (r), Andrew J. Wilhelm; 28 (t, l), Collection of The New York Historical Society; (t, r), courtesy of the Rhode Island Historical Society; (b), Louisiana Historical Society; 29 (t), Marie-Louise Brimberg/NG Image Collection; (b), University of Virginia Special Collections Library; 30 (t), Arthur Lidov/NG Image Collection; (b), Vlad Kharitonov, NG Image Collection; 31 (t), Linda Bartlett/NG Image Collection; (c), Thomas Jefferson Foundation, Monticello; (b), WHHA; 32, WHHA (WHC); 33 (l), WHHA (WHC); (r), Eastern National Park & Monument; 34 (t, l), New York Historical Society; (t, r), CULVER PICTURES; (b), New Haven Colony Historical Society; 35 (t, l), Collection of The New York Historical Society; (t, r), WHHA (WHC); (b), Newman Galleries; 36 (t), The White House, Michael Evans; (b, l), The Granger Collection, NY; (b, r), The Ronald Reagan Presidential Library & Museum; 37 (background), Vlad Kharitonov, NG Image Collection; (b, l), Collection of The New York Historical Society; (b, c), CULVER PICTURES; (b, r), CORBIS, 38, WHHA (WHC); 39 (l), Emory Kristof, NG Image Collection; (r), Pierre Mion; 40 (t), The New York Public Library/Art Resource; (c), courtesy LC; (b), Crown Publishers; 41 (t), James Russell, NG Image Collection; (b), WHHA (WHC); 42, WHHA (WHC); 43, courtesy LC; 44, WHHA (WHC); 45 (l), Joseph H. Bailey , NG Image Collection; (r), Chicago Historical Society; 46 (t, l), Collection of The New York Historical Society; (t, r), courtesy LC; (b), Chicago Historical Society; 47 (t), Yale University Art Gallery/Ken Heinen; (b. l), David S. Boyer; (b, r), CULVER PICTURES.

FROM SEA TO SHINING SEA
48 (t, l-r), WHHA (WHC); 48 (b, l-r), Bettmann/CORBIS; WHHA; courtesy LC; Bettmann/CORBIS; 49 (b, l-r), Association of American Railroads, DC; Painting by William Heine from Mrs. Mary C. Owens/George Mobley, NG Historical Picture Services; CULVER PICTURES; Thomas Gilcrease Institute; 50, WHHA (WHC); 51 (l), courtesy LC; (r), Stock Montage; 52 (t), Bettmann/CORBIS; (b), CULVER PICTURES; 53 (t), Woolaroc Museum; (b), Columbia County Historical Society; 54, WHHA (WHC); 55 (l), CULVER PICTURES; (r), courtesy LC; 56, WHHA (WHC); 57 (l), Benjamin Perley Poore; (r), Pierre Mion; 58 (t), The White House; 58 (b, l-r), North Wind Picture Archives; Bettmann/CORBIS; Getty Images News Services; The White House; 59, Bettmann/CORBIS; 60, WHHA (WHC); 61 (l-r), Bettmann/CORBIS; Bettmann/CORBIS; 62 (t, l-r), Bettmann/CORBIS; CULVER PICTURES; (b), courtesy LC; 63 (l-r), CULVER PICTURES; CULVER PICTURES; 64 (t), CORBIS; 64 (b, l-r), Dean Conger, NG Image Collection; CORBIS; 65, (t) CORBIS; (b), Bettmann/ CORBIS; 66, WHHA (WHC); 67 (l-r), courtesy LC; CULVER PICTURES;

68, WHHA (WHC); 69 (l-r), CULVER PICTURES; CULVER PICTURES; 70, WHHA (WHC); 71 (l-r), New Hampshire Historical Society; CULVER PICTURES; 72, WHHA (WHC); 73 (l-r), Bettmann/CORBIS; Missouri Historical Society, St. Louis.

A NEW BIRTH OF FREEDOM
74 (t, l-r), WHHA (WHC); 74 (b, l-r), Loudermilk Print Shop; Joe Bailey, NGS; CORBIS; Bettmann/CORBIS; 75 (b, l-r), courtesy LC; Western History Collection, University of Oklahoma Library; Corcoran Gallery of Art; courtesy The American Automobile Manufacturers Association; 76, WHHA (WHC); 77 (l-r), Lloyd Ostenforf; K & G Unlimited; 78 (t), Chicago Historical Society; (b), courtesy LC; 79 (t), Bettmann/Corbis; (b), courtesy LC; 80 (t, l-r), courtesy LC; courtesy LC; (b, l-r), Collection of The New York Historical Society; 81 (t, l-r), courtesy LC; Victor Boswell, NG Image Collection; (b, l-r), courtesy National Park Service, Museum Management Program; Museum of the City of New York; 82, WHHA (WHC); 83 (t), courtesy LC; courtesy LC; 84 (t), courtesy Franklin D. Roosevelt Library; 84 (b, l-r), Vlad Kharitonov, NG Image Collection; Vlad Kharitonov, NG Image Collection; 85 (t, l-r), Ripon Commonwealth Press; courtesy Gerald R. Ford Library; 85 (b, l-r), CORBIS; Brown Brothers; Brown Brothers; 86, WHHA (WHC); 87 (t), courtesy LC; 87 (b, l-r), Chicago Historical Society; courtesy LC; 88 (t, l-r), courtesy LC; courtesy LC; 88 (b), Bettmann/Corbis; 89 (t, l-r), Bettmann/Corbis; courtesy LC; 89 (b), WHHA (WHC); 91, courtesy Rutherford B. Hayes Presidential Center; 92 (t), Johnny Thompson; 92 (b, l-r), courtesy LC; CORBIS; courtesy Abraham Lincoln Presidential Library & Museum; 94, WHHA (WHC); 95, Engraving, 1861 courtesy Kiplinger Washington Collection; 96, WHHA (WHC); 97 (l-r), courtesy LC; US National Park Service; 98, WHHA (WHC); 99, Bettmann/Corbis; 100 (t, l-r), courtesy LC; CORBIS; (b, l-r), courtesy LC; CORBIS; 101 (t), CULVER PICTURES; (b), Bettmann/CORBIS; 102 (t, l-r), Smithsonian Institution; National Photo; 102. (b. l-r), courtesy Gerald R. Ford Library; Bettmann / CORBIS; 103 courtesy Gerald R. Ford Library; 104, WHHA (WHC); 105 (l-r), courtesy LC; CORBIS.

AMERICA TAKES CENTER STAGE
106 (t, l-r), WHHA (WHC); 106 (b. l-r), courtesy LC; courtesy LC; The LeBaron Collection; Ken Marschall; 107 (b, l-r), Bettmann/CORBIS; courtesy LC; Archive Photo/Getty Images; Getty Images News Services; 108, WHHA (WHC); 109 (l-r), courtesy LC; CULVER PICTURES; 110 (t), Chicago Historical Society; (b), courtesy LC; 111 (t), courtesy LC; (b), Bettmann/CORBIS; 112, WHHA (WHC); 113 (l-r), Robert Oakes, NG Image Collection; courtesy LC; 114 (t), CULVER PICTURES; (b, l-r), CULVER PICTURES; Getty Images News Services; 115 (t, l-r), Brown Brothers; courtesy LC; (b), Theodore Roosevelt Collection, Harvard College Library; 116, courtesy LC; 117 (t, l-r), WHHA; courtesy LC; courtesy LC; National Archives; (b, l-r), CORBIS; Liaison/Getty Images; The White House; 118, WHHA (WHC); 119 (l-r), courtesy LC; Emory Kristof, NG Image Collection; 120 (t, l-r), courtesy LC; CULVER PICTURES; (b), CULVER PICTURES; 121 (t, l-r), courtesy LC; courtesy LC; (b, l-r), courtesy LC; WHHA (WHC); 122, WHHA (WHC); 123 (l-r), Punch Publications; courtesy LC; 124 (t, l-r), UPI/CORBIS; CULVER PICTURES; UPI/CORBIS; (b), courtesy LC; 125 (t), Brown Brothers; (b), courtesy LC; 126 (t), Mort Kunstler; 126 (b, l-r), Getty Images News Services; Getty Images News Services; 127 (t), CORBIS; 127 (b, l-r), Gustav LeGray/The J. Paul Getty Museum; Wally McNamee/CORBIS; Anja Niedringhaus/Pool/CORBIS; 128, WHHA (WHC); 129, courtesy LC; 130, WHHA (WHC); 131 (l-r), Bettmann/CORBIS; Stock Montage; 132, WHHA (WHC); 133 (l-r), courtesy National Archives; courtesy LC.

SEEKING STABILITY IN THE ATOMIC AGE
134 (t, l-r), WHHA (WHC); 134 (b, l-r), Bettmann/CORBIS; courtesy National Archives; courtesy IBM; UPI/CORBIS; 135 (b, l-r), Bernie Boston; NASA; Scott Shapiro/Index Stock; Wally McNamee/CORBIS; 136, WHHA (WHC); 137 (t, r), courtesy Franklin D. Roosevelt Library;137 (b, l-r), Robert Calafiore, Hartford University American Political Life Collection; courtesy Franklin D. Roosevelt Library; 138 (t), Bettmann/Corbis; (c), courtesy Social Security Administration; (b), AP/Wide World Photos; 139 (t), Getty Images News Services; Robert Calafiore, Hartford University American Political Life Collection; (b), AP/Wide World Photos; 140 (l-r), Bettmann/Corbis; Getty Images News Services; 141 (t, l-r), Bettmann/Corbis; Sandra Baker/Index

Stock; (b), Getty Images News Services; 142 (l-r), WHHA (WHC); Bettmann/Corbis; WHHA (WHC); 143 (t, l-r), Joe Bailey, NG Image Collection; Liaison/Getty Images; (c), WHHA (WHC); (b, l-r), UPI/CORBIS; courtesy LC; Steve Raymer, NG Image Collection; CORBIS; 144, WHHA (WHC); 145 (l-r), CORBIS; courtesy Harry S. Truman Library; 146 (t, l-r), US Army; Getty Images News Services; (b), CORBIS; 147 (t), Getty Images News Services; (b, l-r), Arthur Shilstone, NG mage Collection; AP/Wide World Photos; 148, WHHA (WHC); 149 (l-r), courtesy Dwight D. Eisenhower Library; courtesy Dwight D. Eisenhower Library; 150 (t), courtesy Dwight D. Eisenhower Library; (b, l-r), courtesy Dwight D. Eisenhower Library; courtesy Dwight D. Eisenhower Library; 151 (t, l-r), AP/Wide World Photos; UPI/CORBIS; 151 (b, l-r), AP/Wide World Photos; courtesy Dwight D. Eisenhower Library; 152, WHHA (WHC); 153 (t), courtesy John F. Kennedy Library; (b, l-r), courtesy John F. Kennedy Library; courtesy John F. Kennedy Library; 154 (t, l-r), AP/Wide World Photos; courtesy LC; (b, l-r), Liaison/Getty Images; courtesy John F. Kennedy Library; 155 (t, l-r), Getty Images News Services; (b, l-r), Archive Photo/Getty Images; (b), Liaison/Getty Images; 156 (t), James P. Blair, NG Image Collection; (b, l-r), James P. Blair, NG Image Collection; courtesy LC; 157 (t, l-r), courtesy LC; Bettmann/Corbis; courtesy Franklin D. Roosevelt Library; 157 (b, l-r), Archive Photo/Getty Images; Arlan Wiker, NG Image Collection; 158, WHHA (WHC); 159 (l-r), courtesy Lyndon B. Johnson Library and Museum; AP/Wide World Photos; 160 (t), George F. Mobley, NG Image Collection; (b), LBJ Library and Museum; 161 (t, l-r), courtesy LC; courtesy Lyndon B. Johnson Library and Museum; Dennis Brack/BLACK STAR; 161 (b, l-r), Albert Chang; courtesy Lyndon B. Johnson Library and Museum; 162, WHHA (WHC); 163 (l-r), courtesy National Archives/Nixon Archives; courtesy National Archives/Nixon Archives; 164 (t, l-r), Kenneth Garrett; James L. Stanfield, NG Image Collection; 164 (b), courtesy National Archives/Nixon Archives; 165 (t), courtesy National Archives/Nixon Archives; 165 (b, l-r), Joseph H. Bailey, NG Image Collection; Dennis Brack/BLACK STAR; Stephen St. John, NG Image Collection; 166, WHHA (WHC); 167 (l-r), courtesy Gerald R. Ford Library; courtesy Gerald R. Ford Library; 169, CORBIS; 170, WHHA (WHC); 171 (l-r), courtesy Jimmy Carter Library & Museum; Grace-Sygma/CORBIS; 172 (t), Wilbur E. Garrett, NG Image Collection; (b), Liaison/Getty Images; 173 (t, l-r), D.B. Owen/BLACK STAR; Liaison/Getty Images; (b), BLACK STAR.

FOOTPRINTS ON THE GLOBAL FRONTIER
174 (t, l-r), WHHA (WHC); WHHA (WHC); WHHA (WHC); The White House; 174 (b, l-r), Anthony Suau/Getty Images; Getty Images News Services; Steve McCurry/MAGNUM; Steve McCurry/MAGNUM; 175 (b, l-r), Reuters/Getty Images; Reuters/Getty Images; Getty Images News Services; Getty Images News Services; 176, WHHA (WHC); 177 (l-r), courtesy National Archives; courtesy National Archives; 178 (t, l-r), David Alan Harvey, NGS; Consolidated News Pictures/Getty Images; (b, l-r), BLACK STAR; Archive Photo/Getty Images; 179 (l-r), Larry Downing/Woodfin Camp & Associates; Liaison/Getty Images; (b), Getty Images News Services; 180, WHHA (WHC); 181 (l-r), courtesy George Bush Presidential Library; courtesy George Bush Presidential Library; 182 (t), Archive/Getty Images; (c), Natalie Fobes; (b), Mike Theiler/Archive Photos/Getty Images; 183 (t, l-r), Newsmakers/Liaison/Getty Images; Brad Markel/Liaison/Getty Images; (b), Adees A. Latif/Archive Photos / CORBIS; 184 (t), courtesy Clinton Presidential Library;(b, l-r), Bettmann/ CORBIS; Getty Images News Services; 185 (t, l-r), Getty Images News Services; The White House; (b), The White House; 186, WHHA (WHC); 187 (l-r), Archive Photos/Getty Images; Sygma/CORBIS; 188 (t, l-r), Sygma/CORBIS; Sygma/CORBIS; (b, l-r), Joe Sohm/Visions of America; Arnie Sachs/Archive Photos/Getty Images; 189 (t, l-r), Richard Ellis/CORBIS; Mark Reinsteiun/Index Stock; (b), Sygma/CORBIS; 190 (t) Northwind Picture Archives (b, l-r), Flip Schulke/CORBIS; Bettmann/CORBIS; 191 (l-r), Reuters/ CORBIS; Getty Images News Services; (b, l-r), Bettmann/CORBIS; 192, The White House; 193 (l-r), Newsmakers/Liaison/Getty Images; Texas National Guard/CORB IS; 194 (t), The White House; (b, l-r) Getty Images News Services; The White House; The White House; 195 (t, l-r), The White House; The White House; (b), Reuters/ CORBIS; 196 (t), North Wind Picture Archives; (b, l-r), Bettmann/CORBIS; Chip East/CORBIS; 197 (t), Getty Images News Services; (b), Getty Images News Services.

For Sam and Jake
— AB

★ ★ ★

Acknowledgments: The publisher gratefully acknowledges the kind assistance of Michael Beschloss, Presidential Historian, who reviewed the first edition in page proof form; Harmony Haskins and the White House Historical Association for their generous support of the project; Katie McCormick-Lelyveld from the Kerry/Edwards 2004 Campaign; Lynden Steele from the White House; Anne Heiligenstein from the Texas Governor's office; Jeanette Larson, Texas librarian; Beloit College Library; Beloit Public Library; Lyle Rosbotham; and Betty Behnke and Vlad Kharitonov of the National Geographic Image Collection. Special thanks go to Robert D. Johnston, Ph.D. of the University of Illinois at Chicago for reviewing and commenting on the updated and new material in the second edition.

The type for this book is set in Hoefler Text.
Design by Bea Jackson

Printed in the United States of America

Library of Congress Cataloging-in-Publication Data
Bausum, Ann
    Our country's presidents / by Ann Bausum
       p. cm.
    First Edition ISBN 0–7922–7226–9 (published 2001)
    2nd Trade Edition ISBN 0–7922–9329–0
    Library Edition ISBN 0–7922–9330–4
    1. Presidents—United States—Biography—Juvenile Literature. [1. Presidents.] I. Title.
E176.1.B28 2000
973'.09'—dc21
[B]   00-042164

Front cover: (from left to right) Presidents George Washington, Thomas Jefferson, Abraham Lincoln, Franklin Delano Roosevelt, John F. Kennedy, and George W. Bush. the document showing The Presidential Oath of Office was created digitally by placing Dearest script on top of parchment paper.

Back cover: The seal of the President of the United States. This seal was redesigned by President Truman in 1945.

Half title page: A detail from the original seal of the President of the United States, where the eagle's head faced the arrows clenched in its talons. The eagle now faces the olive branch.

Title page: The faces of Presidents George Washington, Thomas Jefferson, Theodore Roosevelt, and Abraham Lincoln are carved in stone at Mount Rushmore in South Dakota.

Foreword page: The Oval Office in 2004.

Although titled "Reception at Mount Vernon," this painting likely portrays a scene similar to the ones that took place during Martha Washington's years as the first First Lady, too. She stands (at right) to receive the latest visitors to her home.

★ OUR COUNTRY'S ★

FIRST LADIES

A special supplement to
Our Country's Presidents *that includes*
profiles and portraits of the nation's First Ladies
from Martha Washington to Laura Bush

Ann Bausum

WITH A FOREWORD BY
FIRST LADY LAURA BUSH

NATIONAL GEOGRAPHIC
WASHINGTON, D.C.

TABLE OF CONTENTS

FOREWORD ★ 215

ABOUT THE FIRST LADIES: AN INTRODUCTION ★ 216–217

THE WASHINGTON ADMINISTRATION   218–219
    MARTHA WASHINGTON

THE JOHN ADAMS ADMINISTRATION   220
    ABIGAIL ADAMS

THE JEFFERSON ADMINISTRATION   221
    MARTHA JEFFERSON

THE MADISON ADMINISTRATION   222
    DOLLEY MADISON

THE MONROE ADMINISTRATION   223
    ELIZABETH MONROE

THE JOHN QUINCY ADAMS ADMINISTRATION   224
    LOUISA ADAMS

THE JACKSON ADMINISTRATION   225
    RACHEL JACKSON

THE VAN BUREN ADMINISTRATION   226
    HANNAH VAN BUREN

THE WILLIAM HENRY HARRISON ADMINISTRATION   227
    ANNA HARRISON

THE TYLER ADMINISTRATION   228–229
    LETITIA TYLER ★ JULIA GARDINER TYLER

THE POLK ADMINISTRATION   230
    SARAH POLK

THE TAYLOR ADMINISTRATION   231
    MARGARET TAYLOR

THE FILLMORE ADMINISTRATION   232
    ABIGAIL FILLMORE

THE PIERCE ADMINISTRATION   233
    JANE PIERCE

THE BUCHANAN ADMINISTRATION   234
    HARRIET LANE

THE LINCOLN ADMINISTRATION   235–237
    MARY TODD LINCOLN

THE ANDREW JOHNSON ADMINISTRATION   238
    ELIZA JOHNSON

THE GRANT ADMINISTRATION   239
    JULIA GRANT

THE HAYES ADMINISTRATION   240
    LUCY HAYES

THE GARFIELD ADMINISTRATION   241
    LUCRETIA GARFIELD

THE ARTHUR ADMINISTRATION   242
    ELLEN ARTHUR

THE CLEVELAND ADMINISTRATIONS   243
    FRANCES CLEVELAND

THE BENJAMIN HARRISON ADMINISTRATION   244
    CAROLINE HARRISON

THE MCKINLEY ADMINISTRATION   245
    IDA MCKINLEY

THE THEODORE ROOSEVELT ADMINISTRATION   246
    EDITH ROOSEVELT

THE TAFT ADMINISTRATION   247
    HELEN TAFT

THE WILSON ADMINISTRATION   248–249
    ELLEN WILSON ★ EDITH WILSON

THE HARDING ADMINISTRATION   250
    FLORENCE HARDING

THE COOLIDGE ADMINISTRATION   251
    GRACE COOLIDGE

THE HOOVER ADMINISTRATION   252
    LOU HOOVER

THE FRANKLIN D. ROOSEVELT ADMINISTRATION   253–255
    ELEANOR ROOSEVELT

THE TRUMAN ADMINISTRATION   256
    BESS TRUMAN

THE EISENHOWER ADMINISTRATION   257
    MAMIE EISENHOWER

THE KENNEDY ADMINISTRATION   258–259
    JACQUELINE KENNEDY

THE LYNDON B. JOHNSON ADMINISTRATION   260
    LADY BIRD JOHNSON

THE NIXON ADMINISTRATION   261
    PAT NIXON

THE FORD ADMINISTRATION   262
    BETTY FORD

THE CARTER ADMINISTRATION   263
    ROSALYNN CARTER

THE REAGAN ADMINISTRATION   264
    NANCY REAGAN

THE GEORGE BUSH ADMINISTRATION   265
    BARBARA BUSH

THE CLINTON ADMINISTRATION   266–267
    HILLARY RODHAM CLINTON

THE GEORGE W. BUSH ADMINISTRATION   268–269
    LAURA BUSH

RESOURCES/ILLUSTRATIONS CREDITS ★ 271

CREDITS ★ 272

As the nation's First Lady, Laura Bush performs many official duties and observes traditions established by the First Ladies who have served before her. Here she welcomes guests to the White House for a 2003 birthday celebration for opera legend Placido Domingo (at left).

Laura Bush

ONE OF MY FAVORITE FIRST LADIES, Lady Bird Johnson, said, "The Constitution of the United States does not mention the First Lady. The statute books assign her no duties; and yet, when she gets the job, a podium is there if she cares to use it." Over the last two hundred years, America's First Ladies have stepped up to the podium to help shape the Presidency and the nation.

Abigail Adams, wife of the first President to live in the White House, was one of her husband's greatest political advisors. President Polk also relied on the political astuteness of his wife, Sarah, who even edited her husband's speeches. As official hostess of the White House, Julia Tyler, who was dubbed "the Presidentress," arranged for a reporter to cover social gatherings there so all the world could read about them. This reporter was essentially the first press secretary of the White House. Caroline Harrison pursued her own causes as First Lady, including raising money for a local university, but only after the school agreed to accept women students.

Edith Roosevelt oversaw one of the most significant renovations of the White House. In 1902 the West Wing was built to separate the executive offices from the family's living quarters, where Edith and President Theodore Roosevelt lived with their six children. Edith Wilson was one of her husband's most trusted advisors. She was the first presidential wife to make an overseas trip with the President. Lou Hoover made the first radio broadcast by a First Lady from the White House. In 1931, she urged thousands of women to donate food and clothing to needy families. Another social activist, Eleanor Roosevelt, spent twelve years as First Lady fighting for civil rights while her husband, Franklin D. Roosevelt, was President.

Given their popularity with the public, many First Ladies have campaigned in support of their husbands. On campaign stops, Harry Truman would ask supporters if they wanted to meet the boss. His wife Bess would emerge to the delight and applause of the crowds. Lady Bird Johnson even had her own train, the Lady Bird Special, and made the first independent whistle-stop campaign by a candidate's wife. The First Lady who inspires me the most is, of course, my mother-in-law, Barbara Bush. I have relied on her advice and guidance for years, and especially since I came to the White House. A lover of books and reading, she used her podium to increase awareness for family literacy and continues to support programs to combat illiteracy today.

The stories of our First Ladies are a vivid reflection of American history, and they deserve to be shared and remembered. Abigail Adams once reminded her husband to "remember the ladies." Through *Our Country's First Ladies*, the history of America's First Ladies will continue to be told, one remarkable woman at a time.

Laura Bush

Laura Bush

FIRST LADY OF THE UNITED STATES

About the First Ladies

AN INTRODUCTION

WHEN GENERAL GEORGE WASHINGTON became the first President of the United States, he began setting the precedents, or customs, that would be followed by future chief executives. His wife Martha took on the same responsibility for the Presidents' spouses. Every presidential couple since has added new touches to the roles of President and First Lady, or discarded old ones when they became out of date. More than 200 years after Washington's time, the nation's First Family continues to follow examples set during his administration, as well as from those that have fallen in between.

Among the traditions that have evolved during the nation's 43 presidential administrations are some of its most famous terms. No one thought to call the President's wife the First Lady until the Hayes administration, for example. The suggestion of "Marquise" was considered and discarded. Early forms of address were "Presidentress," "Mrs. President," and "Lady." "First Lady" did not come into widespread use until the 20th century. It took more than a century for the official family residence to take on its classic name of the "White House," too. (Theodore Roosevelt gets credit for this term.) Earlier names were the "President's Palace" or, simply, the "President's House."

The 44 First Ladies profiled here hail from 19 states. New York State gave birth to nine. Ohio and Virginia were home to another six apiece. One First Lady (Louisa Adams) was even born abroad (in England). The First Ladies were the daughters of farmers (nine),

---

With the exception of the Washington administration, all U.S. Presidents have lived and worked at the White House (above). The building has become synonymous with the Presidency. It serves not only as the hub for the work of the chief executive, but as the base for the public and private moments of the President's family. Children have been born and married there—even died there. One woman became First Lady there by marrying the President. Other First Ladies have died there, or mourned the deaths of their husbands there. Wars and renovations have, at times, forced the First Family to relocate temporarily. Once the work is completed, however, and a fresh coat of paint is in place, the President and First Lady are at home in the White House again.

judges (another nine), ministers (five), and other men of diverse careers. Some were the daughters of slave owners. Others married them and helped supervise slave labor. First Ladies were all ages upon entering the White House—from 21 to 64. They lived anywhere from days (in the case of Abigail Fillmore) to decades after their husbands left office.

The earliest First Ladies, like all women from that time, had few educational opportunities. What schooling they had came at home. Many were in second marriages, because in that era death often ended marriages prematurely. Children were often lost for the same reason. Surviving children, other spouses, and formal education are all listed in the fact boxes that accompany the profiles. These essays offer a snapshot of the First Ladies. Basic background, the firsts they achieved, and notable stories help capture the personalities of these women.

During their service, First Ladies have established traditions: Caroline Harrison, for example, introduced the first Christmas tree to the White House. They have coped with inquisitive reporters: Frances Cleveland went so far as to establish a private residence near the White House to serve as a family retreat. They have set examples by their actions: Eleanor Roosevelt resigned from the Daughters of the American Revolution to protest the group's discrimination against Marian Anderson, an African-American vocalist. They have indulged personal habits in private: Dolley Madison used snuff, for example, and Grace Coolidge smoked cigarettes, but always off camera. Others have remained loyal to husbands distracted by romances with other women: Florence Harding tolerated and even helped conceal her husband's affairs, for example.

The responsibilities of First Lady come without the benefit of a job description or the rewards of a paycheck. It is a position gained through personal ties to the President. Most First Ladies earn this post through marriage. Some wives have withdrawn from the task, but the majority embraced the work, even if it was not of their choosing. Even today no salary is paid to these women despite the fact that the work of First Lady, like the Presidency itself, has grown into more than a full-time job.

Abigail Adams, the nation's second First Lady, summed up feelings about the role of political spouse that many of those who followed her would share. "I feel a pleasure in being able to sacrifice my selfish passions to the general good," she noted. Abigail explained that sharing a life of public service "has taught me to consider myself and family but as the small dust of the balance, when compared with the great community."

Martha Washington

THE WASHINGTON ADMINISTRATION ★ 1789 – 1797

WHEN GEORGE WASHINGTON BECAME THE FIRST PRESIDENT of the United States, Martha gave no thought to remaining at their Mount Vernon home while he served. Although some future First Ladies would think twice before moving to the nation's capital (Rachel Jackson may even have had a heart attack and died rather than leave home), Martha did not hesitate. She had, after all, followed her husband to various army outposts during the Revolutionary War, and she was not about to desert him now. Martha did not hesitate to serve as a visible partner during Washington's Presidency either, a show of boldness that would be absent in some of the First Ladies who followed her. Thus the nation's first Presidency began not only with the leadership of a strong chief executive, but with the confident presence of his spouse, too.

Martha had grown up years before the formation of the United States. During her childhood she and everyone around her was a subject of the royal crown of England. Her father was the planter John Dandridge. Her mother was named Frances Jones Dandridge. When she was 18 years old, she married Daniel Parke Custis, a wealth plantation owner. Martha bore him two children who lived beyond infancy. (Two others did not.) When Custis died eight years into their marriage, she became one of the wealthiest widows in Virginia. Two years later she married George Washington, by then a noted veteran of the French and Indian War. She was petite, a full foot shorter than the six-foot, two-inch-tall future President.

The earliest years of their marriage predate the turbulent Revolutionary War era. The couple raised Martha's children and managed their combined properties. During the Revolutionary War, Martha joined General Washington at his winter Army encampments. "Lady Washington," as she was called, darned soldiers' socks, organized relief efforts, and tended the sick. "Whilst our husbands and brothers are examples of patriotism, we must be patterns of industry," she explained.

Following the war, the couple returned to their plantation lifestyle at Mount Vernon. The evolving needs of the new nation brought the noted Revolutionary War hero out of this retirement, and by 1789 he had been named the country's first President. New York City hosted the earliest national capital.

When at home with George Washington she was known as "Dear Patsy," but to the new nation of the United States she became "Lady Washington." This miniature portrait dates from the early days of the American Revolution when Martha Washington was about 45 years old. Some dozen years later she would become the first woman to take on the role of First Lady. Washington kept the tiny painting with him in a locket.

Washington took the oath of office there on April 30, 1789. By the end of May, Martha had joined him at the rented homes that would serve as office and residence for the new chief executive. Later the pair would move with the government to another temporary home, this time in Philadelphia. She and Washington are the only presidential couple who did not live at the executive mansion now known as the White House. (It was still being built during Washington's Presidency.)

> "I have learned from experience that the greater part of our happiness or misery depends upon our dispositions, and not upon our circumstances."
>
> — Martha Washington

The new President and his wife worked to establish traditions and ceremony to suit their new roles. Various forms of address were considered for both of them, with "Lady Washington" becoming the preferred title for Martha. The chief executive was addressed simply as "Mr. President" in a tradition that continues to this day. The two collaborated on how best to dress, entertain, and behave. It was important to set a tone free from the haughty style of European royalty and yet dignified enough to suit the head of a new government and his wife. Crowns were out. Bowing was in. (Hand-shaking came later, during Thomas Jefferson's administration.) Politics was not to be discussed in social settings. Events ended after the President and his wife left the room.

The Washingtons settled on a social calendar that included a gentlemen-only gathering on Tuesday afternoons (hosted by Washington alone) and a co-ed reception on Friday evenings (Martha and George hosted these together). Sundays were a day of rest from official duties. The couple established the tradition of a New Year's Day open house the first time this date came up on the presidential calendar. In addition to such planned events, Martha kept busy with the time-consuming practice of "calling" on other important wives. Since these women did the same thing, too, they often failed to find one another at home. Then custom required the disappointed visitor to leave behind a "calling card." Etiquette required the recipient of such cards to return the calls. With no telephones, Internet, or wireless service at one's disposal (not to mention no better transportation than horse and carriage), such a circuit easily became an exercise in exasperation. Nonetheless Martha tried to return all calls before three days had elapsed.

When George Washington left the Presidency after his second term (another precedent, and eventually, a law), he and Martha were finally free to settle for good at Mount Vernon. They returned happily to the pastoral setting, and they welcomed frequent visitors. Although Martha's children had both died by that time, they had grandchildren to enjoy. The former President died suddenly during the administration of his successor. Martha lived not even three years more. The pair were buried beside one another, establishing one final tradition for future presidential couples to follow.

PRESIDENT	George Washington, 1st President (1732–1799)
MAIDEN NAME	Martha Dandridge
BORN	June 21, 1731, in New Kent County, Va.
WEDDING	Jan. 6, 1759
AGE AT MARRIAGE	27 years old
THEIR CHILDREN	None
AGE AS FIRST LADY	57 years old
PREVIOUS MARRIAGE	Daniel Parke Custis (1711–1757), June of 1749, John (1754), Martha (1756)
DIED	May 22, 1802, at Mount Vernon, Va.
AGE AT DEATH	70 years old
GRAVE	Mount Vernon, Va.

Abigail Adams

THE JOHN ADAMS ADMINISTRATION ★ *1797 – 1801*

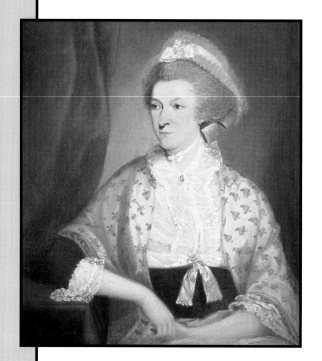

As First Lady, Abigail Adams stayed true to her character. Although she continued the social customs begun by her predecessor, she brought a more active and challenging mind to the job, too. That lively wit was one of the qualities that had first attracted John Adams to his future bride, then 17. Abigail, the daughter of Congregational minister William Smith and his wife, Elizabeth Quincy Smith, wed the future President two years later. Their respect for one another as intellectual equals sustained their marriage forever after, often through the letters they exchanged during the long absences caused by Adams's government service.

With rare exception Abigail stayed home in Massachusetts while her husband traveled. She managed the family farm, marketed their crops, raised the couple's four children, and kept herself and her husband (via their correspondence) informed about local politics. "In all she appears [to have done] equally well," observed a grandson years later. She did join her husband during one of his foreign service tours in Europe, however. From 1784 to 1788 she lived abroad with Adams, first in France and then in England. Such experiences aided her later when she became First Lady.

Abigail was the first First Lady to live in the White House. Her tenure there was brief, since she first resided with her husband at the temporary nation's capital in Philadelphia. When she joined her husband in Washington, D.C., the executive mansion was still under construction, as, indeed, was most of the capital city itself.

The volumes of correspondence she exchanged with her husband and other key figures of the era remain a valuable record, not only of her personal relationships but also of the times themselves. Often quoted is advice she sent to her husband during the drafting of the Declaration of Independence. She wrote in 1776: "Remember the ladies and be more generous and favorable to them than your ancestors!"

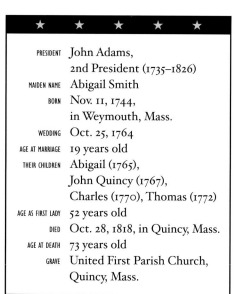

★	★	★	★	★

PRESIDENT	John Adams, 2nd President (1735–1826)
MAIDEN NAME	Abigail Smith
BORN	Nov. 11, 1744, in Weymouth, Mass.
WEDDING	Oct. 25, 1764
AGE AT MARRIAGE	19 years old
THEIR CHILDREN	Abigail (1765), John Quincy (1767), Charles (1770), Thomas (1772)
AGE AS FIRST LADY	52 years old
DIED	Oct. 28, 1818, in Quincy, Mass.
AGE AT DEATH	73 years old
GRAVE	United First Parish Church, Quincy, Mass.

In 1800 Abigail Adams moved into the still incomplete White House. She grumbled in private about its inconveniences, but carefully instructed others to "say that I wrote you the situation is beautiful." The dignified First Lady refused to pose for a portrait without a cap on her head.

Martha Jefferson

THE JEFFERSON ADMINISTRATION ★ *1801 – 1809*

As THE NATION'S THIRD PRESIDENT, THOMAS JEFFERSON brought a previously unknown problem with him to the job: He lacked a wife. Whereas the nation's first two Presidents had wives to partner with them during their administrations, Jefferson did not. His one and only marriage had ended more than 18 years earlier with the death of his wife, Martha. Few details survive about her, and no portrait exists of her likeness. Even though Martha Jefferson never actually served as First Lady, she is still accorded that honor in many history books in recognition of her standing as a President's wife.

Martha, like Jefferson, was born and raised in Virginia. She was the daughter of a planter and lawyer, John Wayles, and his wife Martha Eppes Wayles. Martha was a widow when she met the future President. Her first marriage had ended after two years with the death of her husband. Their son would not survive either. Martha and Jefferson were wed soon after this boy's death. The newlyweds made do with temporary quarters while their future home of Monticello took shape nearby. They shared a devotion to music throughout their marriage. Jefferson would play violin to Martha's harpsichord. She sang well, too.

Over the ten years of their marriage, Martha gave birth to six children, but few survived infancy. Only three were alive at the time of her death in 1782, and just two survived to adulthood. One of these, a daughter named for her mother but known as "Patsy," acted as hostess during her father's administration. (Jefferson's other daughter, Mary, died during his term.)

Dolley Madison, longtime friend of the President and wife of his Secretary of State, assisted as well. The social customs of the times required a woman to be present as hostess whenever women were among the invited guests. The aid of these women made it possible for President Jefferson to entertain properly.

★ ★ ★ ★ ★	
PRESIDENT	Thomas Jefferson, 3rd President (1743–1826)
MAIDEN NAME	Martha Wayles
BORN	Oct. 19, 1748, in Charles City County, Va.
WEDDING	Jan. 1, 1772
AGE AT MARRIAGE	23 years old
THEIR CHILDREN	Martha (1772), Mary (1778)
AGE AS FIRST LADY	Deceased
PREVIOUS MARRIAGE	Bathurst Skelton (1744–1768), Nov. 20, 1766
DIED	Sept. 6, 1782, at Monticello, Charlottesville, Va.
AGE AT DEATH	33 years old
GRAVE	Monticello, Charlottesville, Va.
ACTING FIRST LADIES	Dolley Madison (friend), Martha "Patsy" Jefferson Randolph (daughter)

The portrait shown is not of Thomas Jefferson's wife, Martha (of whom no likeness survives), but of his eldest daughter, also named Martha. The miniature painting was done when the girl was 17. Some dozen years later this young woman would substitute regularly for her deceased mother as her father's hostess. Martha "Patsy" Jefferson Randolph gave birth to the first child at the White House, too, a son named in honor of James Madison.

Dolley Madison

THE MADISON ADMINISTRATION ★ *1809 – 1817*

DOLLEY MADISON WAS NO NEWCOMER to the White House social scene when her husband became the nation's fourth President. Already she had served Thomas Jefferson as a hostess. Even after her husband's Presidency, she endured as the grand dame of Washington, D.C. society. Dolley set standards for entertaining, advised younger First Ladies, and even introduced a President's son (Abraham Van Buren) to his bride.

As the daughter of John and Mary Coles Payne, who were merchants and former planters, Dolley was raised with the simple lifestyle of the Quaker faith. Her first marriage ended after only three years with the death of husband John Todd from yellow fever. Their son, John Payne Todd, survived. James Madison, still a bachelor at age 43, began courting her the following year, and the couple were soon married. She was 17 years younger than her new husband and several inches taller. She referred to him playfully as the "great little Madison" and called him by his last name throughout their marriage.

Dolley was the first First Lady to attend a husband's Inauguration. During the War of 1812, she gained lasting fame for spiriting valuable documents and furnishings out of the White House even as the sounds of battle could be heard in the distance. She insisted that the portrait of George Washington be cut from its frame (which was screwed to the wall) rather than leave it behind. When she and her husband returned to the White House, they found it burned and in ruins.

For the rest of Madison's Presidency, the couple lived in the nearby Octagon House so the White House could be rebuilt.

Freed by her second marriage from the lifestyle of her childhood Quaker faith, Dolley Madison dressed and entertained lavishly. Gilbert Stuart painted this portrait of Dolley five years before James Madison became President. Dolley's political skills are credited with helping her husband win reelection during the War of 1812. After her husband's death in 1836, she relocated from their Virginia home to the nation's capital. Reckless spending by her adult son complicated the finances of her retirement years.

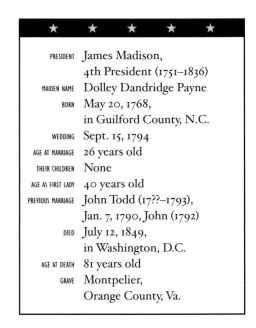

PRESIDENT	James Madison, 4th President (1751–1836)
MAIDEN NAME	Dolley Dandridge Payne
BORN	May 20, 1768, in Guilford County, N.C.
WEDDING	Sept. 15, 1794
AGE AT MARRIAGE	26 years old
THEIR CHILDREN	None
AGE AS FIRST LADY	40 years old
PREVIOUS MARRIAGE	John Todd (17??–1793), Jan. 7, 1790, John (1792)
DIED	July 12, 1849, in Washington, D.C.
AGE AT DEATH	81 years old
GRAVE	Montpelier, Orange County, Va.

Elizabeth Monroe

THE MONROE ADMINISTRATION ★ 1817 – 1825

★ ★ ★

"Mrs. Monroe is an elegant,
accomplished woman.
She possesses a charming mind
and dignity of manners."

— *newspaper commentary, 1817*

★

LIKE ALL OF THE EARLY FIRST LADIES, Elizabeth Monroe was born as a British subject. Her parents were Hannah Aspinwall Kortright and Lawrence Kortright, a British Army officer and successful New York City merchant. Her father remained neutral during the Revolutionary War. It appears that Elizabeth met her future husband while he was attending the 1785 session of the Continental Congress in New York. The two were married the next year.

Elizabeth is most remembered for the life she helped save during the French Revolution. She and James Monroe were stationed in Paris at the time, with her husband serving as foreign minister there for President George Washington. Marie-Adrienne Lafayette, the wife of Revolutionary War ally the Marquis de Lafayette, was imprisoned and at risk of being sent to the guillotine. Elizabeth made a dramatic visit to see her. Rather that risk offense to Elizabeth's husband (and, by extension, the U.S. government) revolutionary leaders ordered the release of their prisoner.

When Elizabeth reached the White House, she rejected one social custom. No longer would the First Lady return social calls. Although the move was received coolly at the time, other First Ladies were certainly happy to follow her precedent.

★	★	★	★	★

PRESIDENT	James Monroe, 5th President (1758–1831)
MAIDEN NAME	Elizabeth Kortright
BORN	June 30, 1768, in New York, N.Y.
WEDDING	Feb. 16, 1786
AGE AT MARRIAGE	17 years old
THEIR CHILDREN	Eliza (1787), Maria (1803)
AGE AS FIRST LADY	58 years old
DIED	Sept. 23, 1830, at Oak Hill, Leesburg, Va.
AGE AT DEATH	62 years old
GRAVE	Richmond, Va.

"Though no longer young, she is still a very handsome woman," noted one White House guest in 1825 about First Lady Elizabeth Monroe. Maria Monroe, the youngest of the Monroes' two daughters, was married during her father's first term of office. Although not the first White House wedding (that distinction falls to the Madison administration), hers was the first one for a President's child.

Louisa Adams

THE JOHN QUINCY ADAMS ADMINISTRATION ★ *1825 – 1829*

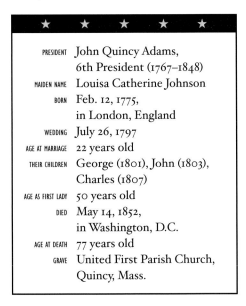

LOUISA ADAMS, THE NATION'S ONLY FOREIGN-BORN FIRST LADY, met her future husband for the first time when she was living with her parents in France. She was four years old; John Quincy Adams was 12. Louisa's father, Joshua Johnson, was an American businessman living overseas with his British wife, Catherine Nuth Johnson. Louisa had been born at their home in London, England, but soon after her family had moved to France for their safety during the American Revolution.

Some 15 years passed before the future President and First Lady crossed paths again. By then Louisa's family had returned to London, and her father was serving as a diplomat for the U.S. government. Louisa's first visit to the United States came in 1801 after she had married John Quincy Adams.

In 1809 her husband's own diplomatic career took them to Russia where he served as U.S. Foreign Minister during the Madison Administration. In 1814 national business called him to the west. Soon after he asked Louisa to join him. She traveled by carriage through winter weather for 40 days from St. Petersburg to meet him in Paris. Her chief traveling companion was their eight-year-old son, Charles. Two older sons, George and John, were already in school in the United States at the time. The Adams's infant daughter had died the previous year.

Louisa, who preferred the city of Washington, D.C., over country life at the family homestead in Massachusetts, was nonetheless apprehensive when John Quincy Adams became President in 1825. Their one term in the White House was marred by persistent sniping between members of political parties and pointed criticism of her husband. Her own health concerns, including depression, became a problem, too.

The couple's retirement from politics was brief. John Quincy Adams returned to the Washington scene as a U.S. Congressman in 1831. After his death in 1848, Louisa remained in Washington, D.C. She died four years later.

PRESIDENT	John Quincy Adams, 6th President (1767–1848)
MAIDEN NAME	Louisa Catherine Johnson
BORN	Feb. 12, 1775, in London, England
WEDDING	July 26, 1797
AGE AT MARRIAGE	22 years old
THEIR CHILDREN	George (1801), John (1803), Charles (1807)
AGE AS FIRST LADY	50 years old
DIED	May 14, 1852, in Washington, D.C.
AGE AT DEATH	77 years old
GRAVE	United First Parish Church, Quincy, Mass.

The noted portrait artist Gilbert Stuart painted this likeness of Louisa Adams in 1821 when she was 46 years old. Four years later she became First Lady. Louisa enjoyed playing the harp, composing music, and writing poetry.

Rachel Jackson

THE JACKSON ADMINISTRATION ★ *1829 – 1837*

ALTHOUGH RACHEL JACKSON LIVED TO HEAR OF HER HUSBAND'S election to the Presidency, she died from a heart attack before he could take office. Andrew Jackson blamed his political opponents for her death, knowing that she had been troubled by the slanderous remarks that fell on him—and on her—during his presidential campaign. Many critics focused on their distant past and the details of Rachel's two marriages. "Those vile wretches who have slandered her must look to God for mercy," Jackson is said to have remarked during her burial service.

Rachel's first marriage took place when she was 17, after she had grown up on the country's western frontier as the daughter of a surveyor. She was one of 11 children born to John and Rachel Stockley Donelson. Her marriage to Lewis Robards was troubled by his fits of jealousy, and twice she was separated from him. During the first interlude she met and fell in love with Andrew Jackson. When her husband filed for divorce in 1791, Rachel and Jackson were married. Not until 1794 did they learn that this divorce had never been granted, thus making their marriage illegal. Although the divorce later came through and they remarried, charges of adultery, or living with one person while being married to another, plagued them from then on.

The Jacksons never had children of their own, but they helped raise members of their extended family. Two relatives stood in for Rachel as First Lady. One niece, Emily Donelson, assumed the role of White House hostess when Jackson became President. She served until her death in 1836 at age 28. Another niece by marriage, Sarah Yorke Jackson, stepped in for the remainder of the Presidency.

★ ★ ★ ★ ★

PRESIDENT	Andrew Jackson, 7th President (1767–1845)
MAIDEN NAME	Rachel Donelson
BORN	June 15?, 1767, in Halifax County, Va.
WEDDING	Aug. 1791 and Jan 17, 1794
AGE AT MARRIAGE	24 years old
THEIR CHILDREN	None
AGE AS FIRST LADY	Deceased
PREVIOUS MARRIAGE	Lewis Robards (dates uncertain), March 1, 1785 (ended in divorce)
DIED	Dec. 22, 1828, at The Hermitage, Nashville, Tenn.
AGE AT DEATH	61 years old
GRAVE	The Hermitage, Nashville, Tenn.
ACTING FIRST LADIES	Emily Donelson (niece), Sarah Yorke Jackson (nephew's wife)

This miniature portrait of Rachel Jackson (in oval frame) is like one that Andrew Jackson carried with him after his wife's sudden death in 1828 on the eve of his Presidency. Had Rachel survived to become First Lady, she would likely have continued her habit of smoking a corncob pipe once in the White House. Instead Rachel's niece, Emily Donelson (above, left), took her aunt's place as First Lady. She gave birth to three of her four children at the White House before dying from tuberculosis near the end of Jackson's Presidency.

Hannah Van Buren

THE VAN BUREN ADMINISTRATION ★ *1837 – 1841*

MARTIN VAN BUREN, LIKE HIS PREDECESSOR and mentor Andrew Jackson, came to the White House as a widower. His wife Hannah had died nearly 18 years earlier when she was only 35 years of age.

Hannah, the daughter of Dutch-speaking John and Maria Quackenboss Hoes, grew up in the same New York State community as her future husband. The two were not only distant cousins but childhood sweethearts, as well. Martin fondly called his wife Jannetje, the Dutch version of Hannah, throughout their marriage. The two of them spoke Dutch at home, not English.

Little information was recorded about this early wife of a President. It is known that she was a faithful church member, first with the Dutch Reformed Church and later the Presbyterian denomination. She gave birth to five sons in ten years, four of whom lived into adulthood. Hannah became ill when her youngest son was still an infant and died soon after he turned two. Tuberculosis, at that time a fatal lung disease, is blamed with ending her life. Her gravestone pays tribute to her as "a sincere Christian, a dutiful child, tender mother, affectionate wife."

Hannah's death ended the Van Buren marriage after only 11 years. Even though Van Buren was only 36 years old, he never remarried. At the time of his election in 1836, none of his sons were married either. All five bachelors moved into the White House together.

His eldest son Abraham married some eighteen months later. Abraham served as secretary to his father, and his new wife, Angelica Singelton Van Buren, became the hostess of the White House.

A gold brooch bears this likeness of Hannah Hoes Van Buren (above, left) and was worn by one of her nieces. Angelica Singleton Van Buren (above, right), who married Hannah's eldest son during the second year of Martin Van Buren's administration, served as First Lady in the place of her deceased mother-in-law.

★ ★ ★ ★ ★	
PRESIDENT	Martin Van Buren, 8th President (1782–1862)
MAIDEN NAME	Hannah Hoes
BORN	Mar. 8, 1783, in Kinderhook, N.Y.
WEDDING	Feb. 21, 1807
AGE AT MARRIAGE	23 years old
THEIR CHILDREN	Abraham (1807), John (1810), Martin (1812), Smith (1817)
AGE AS FIRST LADY	Deceased
DIED	Feb. 5, 1819, in Albany, N.Y.
AGE AT DEATH	35 years old
GRAVE	Kinderhook, N.Y.
ACTING FIRST LADY	Angelica Singleton Van Buren (daughter-in-law)

Anna Harrison

THE WILLIAM HENRY HARRISON ADMINISTRATION ★ 1841

W HEN ANNA HARRISON AND HER HUSBAND parted in early 1841 so he could travel east for his Inauguration, the couple expected to be reunited later that year in Washington, D.C. Anna planned to make the difficult journey from their home in Ohio after winter weather ended. Instead William Henry Harrison died shortly after taking office, making his Presidency the shortest on record and preventing his wife from serving as First Lady. Had their plans worked out, the nation's second oldest President would have introduced the nation's oldest First Lady, at age 65, to the White House.

Anna was the daughter of John Cleves Symmes, a judge, and Anna Tuthill Symmes. She met her future husband while traveling as a young woman with her father to the western frontier. The pair were married secretly soon after. From then on she and William made their homes variously at frontier forts (where he served as an Army officer), in the nation's capital (during his service in Congress), and at the fledgling government seat for the Indiana Territory (where he was governor).

She bore nine children, making her the mother of more children than any other President's wife. In the end she would outlive all but one of them. Her surviving child, John Scott Harrison, was the father of future President Benjamin Harrison.

Knowing his wife's arrival in the nation's capital would be delayed, President-elect Harrison had recruited his daughter-in-law to serve temporarily in Anna's place. Jane Irwin Harrison, whose own husband had died three years earlier, thus served as First Lady for this briefest of presidential administrations.

PRESIDENT	William Henry Harrison, 9th President (1773–1841)
MAIDEN NAME	Anna Tuthill Symmes
BORN	July 25, 1775, in Morristown, N.J.
WEDDING	Nov. 25, 1795
AGE AT MARRIAGE	20 years old
THEIR CHILDREN	Elizabeth (1796), John Cleves (1798), Lucy (1800), William (1802), John Scott (1804) Benjamin (1806), Mary (1809), Carter (1811), Anna (1813)
AGE AS FIRST LADY	65 years old
DIED	Feb. 25, 1864, in North Bend, Ohio
AGE AT DEATH	88 years old
GRAVE	Harrison Tomb State Memorial, North Bend, Ohio
ACTING FIRST LADY	Jane Irwin Harrison (daughter-in-law)

This portrait of Anna Harrison (above, right) was painted when she was in her late 60s, two years after the death of her husband, President William Henry Harrison. She is still dressed in the traditional mourning color of black. Her daughter-in-law Jane Irwin Harrison (above, left), served in her place as First Lady during the nation's shortest Presidency. Soon after her husband's death, Congress awarded Anna the first presidential widow's pension, a stipend of $25,000 that equaled the Chief Executive's salary.

Letitia Tyler

THE TYLER ADMINISTRATION ★ *1841 – 1845*

LETITIA TYLER CAME TO THE WHITE HOUSE an invalid, having been partially paralyzed by a stroke two years before her husband became President. She was the first First Lady to die during a Presidency when a second stroke claimed her life early in John Tyler's administration. She was 51, making her the youngest presidential wife to die during or after a Presidency. (A few wives died at younger ages, but their deaths occurred long before their husbands became President.)

Letitia grew up on a Virginia plantation, the daughter of Robert and Mary Brown Christian. She and the future President, also a Virginian, courted for five years before marrying. Letitia gave birth to seven children in 15 years, all of whom survived to adulthood. An eighth child died young.

Tyler's Presidency began with the death in office of William Henry Harrison. He was the first Vice President to succeed a deceased President. First Lady Letitia Tyler confined herself to the upstairs family quarters at the White House and directed the affairs of the mansion from there. Her new daughter-in-law, Priscilla Cooper Tyler, took over as official White House hostess. She noted that "mother attends to and regulates all the household affairs and all so quietly that you can't tell when she does it."

Priscilla, a former actress, had married the Tylers' oldest son Robert the same year that Letitia suffered her first stroke. She continued to serve as White House hostess until she and her husband moved to Philadelphia in 1844. With Letitia now dead, a Tyler daughter, Letitia Tyler Semple, stood in briefly as First Lady. Her role ended when the surprise marriage of John Tyler and Julia Gardiner brought yet another First Lady to the Tyler administration.

This portrait of Letitia Tyler was painted before she suffered a crippling stroke in her late 40s. Upon arriving at the White House two years later, she passed along the hostess duties of the First Lady to her daughter-in-law, Priscilla Cooper Tyler. Letitia attended one official function at the White House, the wedding of daughter Elizabeth in January of 1842. A second stroke ended her life nine months later, making her the first First Lady to die during a Presidency.

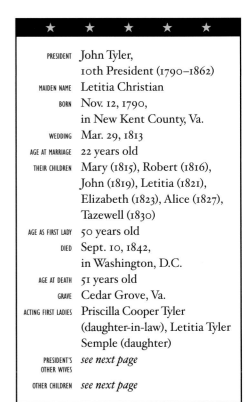

PRESIDENT	John Tyler, 10th President (1790–1862)
MAIDEN NAME	Letitia Christian
BORN	Nov. 12, 1790, in New Kent County, Va.
WEDDING	Mar. 29, 1813
AGE AT MARRIAGE	22 years old
THEIR CHILDREN	Mary (1815), Robert (1816), John (1819), Letitia (1821), Elizabeth (1823), Alice (1827), Tazewell (1830)
AGE AS FIRST LADY	50 years old
DIED	Sept. 10, 1842, in Washington, D.C.
AGE AT DEATH	51 years old
GRAVE	Cedar Grove, Va.
ACTING FIRST LADIES	Priscilla Cooper Tyler (daughter-in-law), Letitia Tyler Semple (daughter)
PRESIDENT'S OTHER WIVES	see next page
OTHER CHILDREN	see next page

Julia Gardiner Tyler

THE TYLER ADMINISTRATION ★ 1841 – 1845

THE SECRET COURTSHIP OF JULIA GARDINER and President John Tyler grew out of a period of personal loss for both individuals. Tyler's first wife, Letitia, had died during his Presidency 17 months earlier, and Julia's father, state senator David Gardiner, had just been killed in a gun explosion. John Tyler and Julia had first met some months before Letitia's death and had begun courting soon after it. Julia agreed to their secret engagement after her father's accidental death during a Potomac River cruise attended by both the President and his future First Lady.

The couple were married four months later at a private ceremony in New York City not far from the bride's Long Island birthplace. Two of Julia's siblings attended the wedding, as may have her mother, Juliana McLachlan Gardiner. Only one Tyler child knew in advance of the wedding and attended, a son who was within a year of the same age as his new stepmother.

At 24 Julia Tyler became the youngest First Lady to that point, and the second youngest ever. (Only Grover Cleveland's White House bride, Frances, would be younger.) With 30 years

separating their ages, Julia and John Tyler hold the record for the greatest age difference between a President and his First Lady.

Julia's brief tenure as First Lady lasted for the final eight months of her husband's Presidency. Then the pair retired to a Virginia plantation that became home to their five sons and two daughters. These offspring, combined with the seven surviving children of his first marriage, make John Tyler the father of more children than any other President.

Tyler's second marriage lasted 17 years, ending with his death in 1862. Julia lived another 27 years. During the Civil War she favored the Confederate cause over her Yankee origins even though she lived in New York during much of the war.

★	★	★	★	★

PRESIDENT	John Tyler, 10th President (1790–1862)
MAIDEN NAME	Julia Gardiner
BORN	May 4, 1820, in Gardiners Island, N.Y.
WEDDING	June 26, 1844
AGE AT MARRIAGE	24 years old
THEIR CHILDREN	David (1846), John Alexander (1848), Julia (1849), Lachlan (1851), Lyon (1853), Robert (1856), Pearl (1860)
AGE AS FIRST LADY	24 years old
DIED	July 10, 1889, in Richmond, Va.
AGE AT DEATH	69 years old
GRAVE	Hollywood Cemetery, Richmond, Va.
PRESIDENT'S OTHER WIVES	*see previous page*
OTHER CHILDREN	*see previous page*

Although painted three years after her service as First Lady, this portrait still captures the youthful beauty that Julia Tyler brought to the White House near the end of President John Tyler's administration. She was the first woman to marry a sitting President.

Sarah Polk

THE POLK ADMINISTRATION ★ *1845 – 1849*

Sᴀʀᴀʜ Pᴏʟᴋ's ᴛᴇɴᴜʀᴇ ᴀs Fɪʀsᴛ Lᴀᴅʏ followed a series of administrations where youthful stand-ins had shouldered most of the responsibilities of White House hostess. Sarah sought no such assistance and approached her job with an expanded view of its scope.

The daughter of successful planter Joel Childress and his wife, Elizabeth Whitsitt Childress, Sarah met her future husband through a common school instructor. Better educated than the average girl of that era, Sarah married James K. Polk some eight years later while he was serving in the Tennessee House of Representatives. Their 25-year marriage produced no children, leaving Sarah free to become more involved in her husband's career than most wives of the time.

Unlike many other political wives, Sarah lived with her husband in Washington, D.C., after he became a member of the U.S. Congress. She screened his professional reading, offered political advice, built networks of her own among Washington insiders, and even helped draft his speeches.

After her husband became President, Sarah continued such efforts. Yet she met the social responsibilities of First Lady, as well. Dancing was downplayed because of her religious beliefs. She preferred to entertain with gracious, informed conversation and fine dining. The first White House Thanksgiving dinner was held under her direction. She introduced gas lights, too. (Candles had sufficed before.)

The Polks enjoyed the briefest of any shared presidential retirement. James K. Polk died just 103 days after leaving office. Sarah went on to live 42 more years, outliving her husband by a greater span of time than any other First Lady. For the rest of her life she wore the mourning color of black.

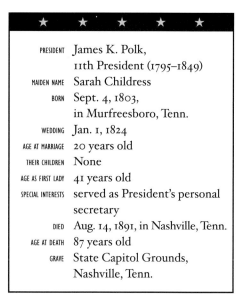

PRESIDENT	James K. Polk, 11th President (1795–1849)
MAIDEN NAME	Sarah Childress
BORN	Sept. 4, 1803, in Murfreesboro, Tenn.
WEDDING	Jan. 1, 1824
AGE AT MARRIAGE	20 years old
THEIR CHILDREN	None
AGE AS FIRST LADY	41 years old
SPECIAL INTERESTS	served as President's personal secretary
DIED	Aug. 14, 1891, in Nashville, Tenn.
AGE AT DEATH	87 years old
GRAVE	State Capitol Grounds, Nashville, Tenn.

This portrait copies one made of Sarah Polk during her husband's Presidency. Sarah came to the White House as one of the nation's youngest First Ladies, only 41 years of age. Her youth, combined with the couple's childless household, left her with the time and energy to maintain a close involvement in her husband's administration. Polk, whose own health was more frail than hers, relied on her for secretarial work as well as advice.

Margaret Taylor

THE TAYLOR ADMINISTRATION ★ *1849 – 1850*

MARGARET "PEGGY" TAYLOR RESUMED THE PATTERN interrupted by Sarah Polk of delegating the duties of First Lady to a younger family member. This trend may have been fueled by the popularity at that time of youth and beauty. It may also have allowed Presidents' wives to escape the risk of social criticism. Many of the First Ladies from the middle decades of the 19th century had not enjoyed the same experiences as the earliest wives of Presidents. Few had traveled abroad, for example, or been entertained at royal courts.

Prior to her husband's unexpected nomination for the Presidency, Peggy Taylor had anticipated retirement with her career-soldier husband on their Southern plantation. During the election campaign she is said to have prayed for Zachary Taylor's defeat. When her prayers went unanswered, she moved into the second floor of the White House and generally remained there. Excuses for her isolation included poor health and an earlier pledge to give up social gatherings if her husband came home safely from the Mexican War (which he did).

★	★	★	★	★

PRESIDENT	Zachary Taylor, 12th President (1784–1850)
MAIDEN NAME	Margaret Mackall Smith
BORN	Sept. 21, 1788, in Calvert County, Md.
WEDDING	June 21, 1810
AGE AT MARRIAGE	21 years old
THEIR CHILDREN	Ann (1811), Sarah (1814), Mary (1824), Richard (1826)
AGE AS FIRST LADY	60 years old
DIED	Aug. 18, 1852, in Pascagoula, Miss.
AGE AT DEATH	63 years old
GRAVE	Zachary Taylor National Cemetery, Louisville, Ky.
ACTING FIRST LADY	Mary Elizabeth Taylor Bliss (daughter)

Peggy had grown up on a Maryland plantation, the daughter of Walter and Ann Mackall Smith. She met Taylor during a visit to Kentucky, and they were married a year later. Peggy gave birth to five girls and one boy in the next 16 years, often shadowing the moves of her husband from one military outpost to the next. Two of their daughters died young.

Their youngest surviving daughter, Mary Elizabeth, took on the role of First Lady for her mother. Recently married, the young "Betty" Bliss hosted official functions with "the artlessness of a rustic belle and the grace of a duchess," according to one visitor. Peggy Taylor was content to mingle with family and friends in the private quarters of the Executive Mansion. Her daughter's reign as First Lady ended with the President's death.

No portrait survives to capture the likeness of Margaret "Peggy" Taylor, the wife for 40 years of Zachary Taylor. Her daughter, Mary Elizabeth "Betty" Taylor Bliss (above), took over official duties of First Lady for her mother, who declined the role.

Abigail Fillmore

THE FILLMORE ADMINISTRATION ★ *1850 – 1853*

Abigail Fillmore, the first First Lady to work outside of the home, met her future husband on the job. He was 19. She was 21 and a new schoolteacher. It was Millard Fillmore's first time in a classroom, and he gained not only an education but also a wife. After marrying, Abigail kept her job (another First Lady first) until she had children.

Abigail's father, a Baptist minister named Lemuel Powers, died soon after his daughter's birth. Her mother, Abigail Newland Powers, raised her daughter and a son on New York State's frontier. Abigail grew up with a love of reading. After they were married, Fillmore made a habit of returning home from business trips with a new book for his wife. The couple maintained a shared interest in politics, too. A mutual friend noted that Fillmore "never took any important step without [his wife's] counsel and advice."

When Fillmore's political career—and the death of Zachary Taylor—brought his family to the White House, Abigail continued the tradition of appointing a young First Lady assistant. Her teenage daughter, Mary Abigail, or "Abby," served as hostess on many occasions. Although she played that role herself at other times, the President's wife preferred to work on a project she had taken on with the aid of funds from the U.S. Congress: the creation of a White House library.

Abigail Fillmore earned the unfortunate distinction of having the shortest retirement of any First Lady. She caught a cold after attending the snowy Inauguration of her husband's successor. Her cold turned into pneumonia, and she died before the month was out. Millard Fillmore became the first former President to remarry when he was wed five years later to Caroline Carmichael McIntosh, herself a widow.

Abigail Fillmore, at 5 feet 6 inches in height, was tall for a 19th-century woman but still considerably shorter than her 6-foot-tall husband. Her likeness here was captured by an early photographic process known as a daguerreotype. The date of the photo is not recorded.

★ ★ ★ ★ ★

PRESIDENT	Millard Fillmore, 13th President (1800–1874)
MAIDEN NAME	Abigail Powers
BORN	Mar. 13, 1798, in Stillwater, N.Y.
WEDDING	Feb. 5, 1826
AGE AT MARRIAGE	27 years old
THEIR CHILDREN	Millard (1828), Mary (1832)
AGE AS FIRST LADY	62 years old
EARLIER CAREER	Schoolteacher
SPECIAL INTEREST	White House library
DIED	Mar. 30, 1853, in Washington, D.C.
AGE AT DEATH	55 years old
GRAVE	Forest Lawn Cemetery, Buffalo, N.Y.
ASSISTING FIRST LADY	Mary Abigail Fillmore (daughter)
PRESIDENT'S OTHER WIVES	Caroline Carmichael McIntosh (1813–1881), second wife (married Feb. 10, 1858)
OTHER CHILDREN	None

Jane Pierce

THE PIERCE ADMINISTRATION ★ *1853 – 1857*

UNHAPPINESS DOGGED THE STEPS OF Jane Pierce for much of her life. Her father Jesse Appleton, a Congregational minister and onetime president of Bowdoin College, died during her childhood. After Jane met Bowdoin graduate Franklin Pierce, her mother, Elizabeth Means Appleton, objected to their marriage. Pierce, after all, was a Democrat, and their family was not. (They married anyway.)

Although the couple began their marriage happily enough, Pierce's political career choice placed a growing strain on their union. Jane blamed the lifestyle of a politician with causing her husband to drink too much, and she disliked living in Washington, D.C. It is said that she fainted upon hearing the news of her husband's presidential nomination and later prayed regularly for his defeat.

Family tragedy struck between Pierce's victory and his Inauguration. Having already lost two of their three sons, their surviving son, Benjamin, died, too. He was killed in a train car derailment in January of 1853. His parents, who witnessed the accident, were devastated. Jane viewed the tragedy as a judgment from God against her husband's devotion to politics, and she declined to attend his Inauguration. Although she moved into the White House, she failed to participate in any social functions for most of the first two years of her husband's administration. Not until New Year's Day of 1855 did she make a formal appearance, and even after that her participation was irregular.

Abigail Kent Means, a childhood friend and aunt by marriage, stood in for her as White House hostess during these lapses. Varina Davis, another friend and the wife of Cabinet member Jefferson Davis (and future Confederacy president), assisted as well.

PRESIDENT	Franklin Pierce, 14th President (1804–1869)
MAIDEN NAME	Jane Means Appleton
BORN	Mar. 12, 1806, in Hampton, N.J.
WEDDING	Nov. 10, 1834
AGE AT MARRIAGE	28 years old
THEIR CHILDREN	Frank (1839), Benjamin (1841), one infant son, all died young
AGE AS FIRST LADY	46 years old
DIED	Dec. 2, 1863, in Andover, Mass.
AGE AT DEATH	57 years old
GRAVE	Old North Cemetery, Concord, N.H.
ASSISTING FIRST LADIES	Abigail Kent Means (friend and aunt of First Lady), Varina Davis (friend of First Lady)

Jane Pierce and her only surviving son, Benjamin, were captured in this photograph about 1850. Even the adored "Benny" had died by the time his parents entered the White House three years later. The tragedy was recalled in the opening words of his father's Inaugural Address, and it impaired his mother's ability to function as First Lady.

Harriet Lane

THE BUCHANAN ADMINISTRATION ★ *1857 – 1861*

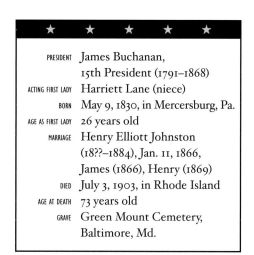

ONLY ONE PRESIDENT NEVER MARRIED—JAMES BUCHANAN. Although he brought no wife with him to the White House, he still needed someone to help plan and host the social events that came with his job. He delegated these tasks to his niece, Harriet Lane, a young woman whom he had helped raise following the deaths of her parents. (Her mother had been Buchanan's sister.) The 26-year-old Harriet, herself unmarried, moved into the White House with her uncle and went to work.

Harriet, who had traveled with Buchanan during his years of foreign service, brought royal court experience—and style— with her to the White House. (She had become acquainted with Queen Victoria, for example, during her uncle's diplomatic service in Great Britain.) As First Lady, Harriet restored a festive air to the executive mansion such as had not been seen in decades. She maintained a sense of civility in social gatherings that was particularly to her credit given the looming threat of civil war. She started fashion trends (necklines dropped) and inspired songwriters (one dedicated "Listen to the Mockingbird" to her).

A more serious side accompanied her air of graciousness, and she employed it to quiet effect during her uncle's administration. She did not hesitate to use her influence with the President when it might bring benefit to others. She planned seating arrangements so that artists might gain the ear of a helpful politician and so that political enemies were kept at a safe distance from each other.

Although her uncle never married, Harriet finally did marry when she was 35 years old. Her husband was a banker from Baltimore, Henry Elliott Johnston. Sadly both her husband and their sons died in the two following decades. Harriet left two legacies by which to be remembered. She donated her personal art collection to the federal government. The Smithsonian Institution established its National Collection of Fine Arts using this donation. Her bequest to Baltimore's Johns Hopkins Hospital funded what became the Harriet Lane Outpatient Clinics, a facility that cares for young people.

Harriet Lane served as First Lady for the nation's only bachelor President. She was no stranger to living in James Buchanan's household, having been raised under the care of this uncle after becoming an orphan when she was 11 years old. This portrait was painted 17 years after the end of her term as First Lady.

★ ★ ★ ★ ★	
PRESIDENT	James Buchanan, 15th President (1791–1868)
ACTING FIRST LADY	Harriett Lane (niece)
BORN	May 9, 1830, in Mercersburg, Pa.
AGE AS FIRST LADY	26 years old
MARRIAGE	Henry Elliott Johnston (18??–1884), Jan. 11, 1866, James (1866), Henry (1869)
DIED	July 3, 1903, in Rhode Island
AGE AT DEATH	73 years old
GRAVE	Green Mount Cemetery, Baltimore, Md.

Mary Todd Lincoln

FIRST LADIES ARE NO STRANGERS TO HARDSHIP, but few of them can match the personal tragedy and loss experienced by the wife of the nation's 16th President. Mary Todd Lincoln's husband died tragically, and all but one of her children did, too. At one point she was labeled insane and housed in an institution. By the end of her life she was nearly blind and partially paralyzed.

No one would have predicted such a sad ending would come for the bubbly daughter of a prosperous banker, Robert Smith Todd, and his wife Eliza Ann Parker Todd. Young Mary lived in comfort and received the best education then available to girls. Her training included French tutors, dance lessons, and boarding school. One tragedy befell her childhood— the death of her mother when she was six years old. Her father promptly remarried. Between his two wives he produced 15 children. Mary may have developed her outgoing, flamboyant style to gain parental attention in this large blended family. Her habit of spending money as a form of comfort probably dates to this period, too. Perhaps Mary felt buying new things helped make up for the loss of her mother.

When she was 21, Mary went to live with her older sister in Springfield, Illinois. Soon after she met her future husband at a dance party. Their courtship moved slowly, but eventually she and Abraham Lincoln were wed. The early years of their marriage were generally happy, marred only by the death of the second born of their four sons. Three-year-old "Eddie" died at a time when the absence of antibiotics and hospitals made such losses quite common.

Even before their marriage, Lincoln had begun to combine his legal experience with a career in politics. Mary was pleased, and she coveted the honor of President for her husband (and First Lady for herself) long before others might have considered such a goal to be reasonable. When her dream came true, she approached the role of White House hostess with an enthusiasm often missing from recent presidential spouses. Here, however, her story starts to go sour.

Mathew Brady, one of the nation's early professional photographers, took this picture of Mary Todd Lincoln during her years as First Lady. At five feet, two inches in height, she would have been dwarfed by her husband, Abraham Lincoln, the nation's tallest President at six feet, four inches.

Perhaps no one could have been expected to manage the social obligations for a nation engaged in civil war. This challenge hampered Mary's efforts from the get-go. For starters, she was suspect because she had grown up in a state bordering the Confederacy. The fact that several of her brothers were fighting for the Southern cause did not help either. These topics became part of an avalanche of bad press that dogged the First Lady almost from the moment she reached Washington, D.C. Such media attention grew out of the controversy of the Civil War and an expanding interest among readers in gossipy, social news.

It seemed that nothing Mary did was right. When she dressed in stylish clothes, she was attacked for spending more money than was appropriate during wartime. When she wore plainer attire, her appearance was criticized. She earned equal condemnation whether she entertained lavishly or modestly. Her reluctance to let

Suffering became a recurring theme in the life of Mary Todd Lincoln (above with her family, and on the facing page). She faced not only the sequential deaths of many loved ones but considerable public criticism. At one point she noted that she felt treated as "if I had committed murder in every state in this blessed Union." As First Lady she received so much hate mail that she had to have a staff member read incoming letters and remove inappropriate ones.

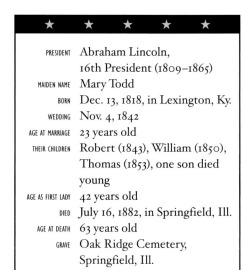

★ ★ ★ ★ ★	
PRESIDENT	Abraham Lincoln, 16th President (1809–1865)
MAIDEN NAME	Mary Todd
BORN	Dec. 13, 1818, in Lexington, Ky.
WEDDING	Nov. 4, 1842
AGE AT MARRIAGE	23 years old
THEIR CHILDREN	Robert (1843), William (1850), Thomas (1853), one son died young
AGE AS FIRST LADY	42 years old
DIED	July 16, 1882, in Springfield, Ill.
AGE AT DEATH	63 years old
GRAVE	Oak Ridge Cemetery, Springfield, Ill.

"Did ever woman have to suffer so much and experience so great a change?"

— Mary Todd Lincoln, *following the assassination of Abraham Lincoln*

★

her oldest son fight in the war drew criticism. So did her formula for curing the blues: shopping. Mary bought compulsively, buying more than she needed (hundreds of pairs of gloves, for example) and spending beyond her means. Her mounting debt became just one more stress.

One of Lincoln's three surviving sons—the middle boy, "Willie"—died suddenly in early 1862, probably from pneumonia. He was the only presidential child to die in the White House. The boy was just 11 years old, and both Lincolns were devastated. Mary grieved long and hard. This action, like just about everything else she did, drew criticism, too. How could her grief match the sorrow of families losing sons on the Civil War battlefields?

Mary's mental health was still fragile three years later when she faced the even greater shock of her husband's assassination. One moment Mary and Abraham were holding hands at a theater performance, the next minute he was mortally wounded. The timing of his death seemed especially cruel, coming just as the Civil War had ended and things were looking up for the nation and its First Family.

The bad fortune of Mary Todd Lincoln did not stop there. In debt and hounded by continuing negative press, she fled to Europe with her youngest son, "Tad." Although she found some peace there (and gained news of a Congressional pension that would relieve some of her financial woes), she returned home with an ill son. Tad soon died at just 18 years of age. Mary's mental health then deteriorated to the point where her only remaining son arranged to have her declared legally insane and placed in an institution (more to prevent her from spending his inheritance than because it was good for his mother). Such a pronouncement was like a death sentence for women of that era because it stripped them of all rights to property and made it difficult to seek the help of an attorney.

To her credit, Mary regained her equilibrium and engineered her release about four months later. She eventually was legally cleared of being insane, too. Both results were remarkable feats for that time. Her subsequent return to Europe brought the final tragedy, a bad fall that left her semi-paralyzed. Her sight was failing, too, partly the result of cataracts and partly from the irritation of extended periods of weeping.

Mary spent the final years of her life in seclusion at her sister's home in Springfield. Thus Mary Todd Lincoln came full circle, returning to the community where she first met her husband and the house where the two had been married so many years before. Her death followed his by 17 years. Her funeral included the minister's observation that the "bullet that sped its way and took her husband from earth took her too."

Eliza Johnson

THE ANDREW JOHNSON ADMINISTRATION ★ *1865 – 1869*

"WE ARE PLAIN PEOPLE, FROM THE MOUNTAINS of Tennessee," observed Martha Johnson Patterson after Abraham Lincoln's death made her father President. "I trust too much will not be expected of us."

Martha's mother Eliza was the daughter of a shoemaker, John McCardle, who died during her childhood, and his wife, Sarah Phillips McCardle. She became the youngest bride of a future President when, at 16, she married a newcomer to town. Andrew Johnson, just 18 years old, was the youngest groom to later become President. Eliza raised their five children amidst the challenges of an often-absent husband (because of his political career) and the unfolding tensions of Civil War. She lost both a son and a son-in-law during the conflict.

Eliza had only visited Washington, D.C., one time before her husband became President, and she had no interest in playing the role of White House hostess. She was so invisible (attending perhaps three events) that one newspaper suggested her existence was "almost a myth." Following earlier traditions, she entrusted her eldest daughter Martha with the social responsibilities of First Lady. Eliza preferred to manage the household from her private quarters, and she assisted her husband by screening important newspaper articles for him. The last of the reclusive First Ladies, Eliza added one more entry in the record books by dying just 168 days after her husband did, the narrowest gap between the deaths of any presidential spouses.

Eliza Johnson (top) did not pose for this portrait. Instead the artist based his painting on a photograph that had been taken of the First Lady during her years in the White House. Eliza's daughter, Martha Johnson Patterson (inset), handled hostess duties for her mother during her father's Presidency. The women persevered with their routines during the unprecedented impeachment trial of the President, confident he would be acquitted—and he was.

★ ★ ★ ★ ★	
PRESIDENT	Andrew Johnson, 17th President (1808–1875)
MAIDEN NAME	Eliza McCardle
BORN	Oct. 4, 1810, in Leesburg, Tenn.
WEDDING	May 17, 1827
AGE AT MARRIAGE	16 years old
THEIR CHILDREN	Martha (1828), Charles (1830), Mary (1832), Robert (1834), Andrew (1852)
AGE AS FIRST LADY	54 years old
DIED	Jan. 15, 1876, in Green County, Tenn.
AGE AT DEATH	65 years old
GRAVE	Andrew Johnson National Historical Site, Greenville, Tenn.
ASSISTING FIRST LADY	Martha Johnson Patterson (daughter)

Julia Grant

J ULIA AND ULYSSES S. GRANT, the first President to be elected following the Civil War, helped usher a new era and atmosphere into the recently united country. This period became known as the Gilded Age. It featured lavish spending (with an emphasis on quantity over quality) and widespread corruption (where behind-the-scenes influence helped one become rich). Both occurred during Grant's administration, with the spending drawing more admiration that criticism.

Julia had met her future husband and war hero when the West Point cadet visited her plantation home with her brother, Grant's fellow classmate. Neither her parents, Frederick and Ellen Wrenshall Dent, nor Grant's family approved of the match, but the pair eventually wed anyway. An almost nomadic life followed, with Julia accompanying her Army officer husband from post to post, even during parts of the Civil War.

Reaching the White House was a welcomed change. Julia embraced her role as executive hostess, an approach that her successors generally mirrored. She entertained with enthusiasm. One elaborate dinner featured 29 courses of food. She turned the first White House wedding since the Tyler administration into a celebrity affair. Some 500 guests were invited to their daughter's wedding breakfast. Such events made great newspaper copy for the growing market of women readers. Society columns developed, and early female journalists shared gossip and fashion reports about life in the nation's capital with their eager readers.

Julia Grant's autobiography, although not published until seven decades after her death, it is the earliest First Lady memoir to see print.

★	★	★	★	★

PRESIDENT	Ulysses S. Grant, 18th President (1822–1885)
MAIDEN NAME	Julia Boggs Dent
BORN	Jan. 26, 1826, in St. Louis, Mo.
WEDDING	Aug. 22, 1848
AGE AT MARRIAGE	22 years old
THEIR CHILDREN	Frederick (1850), Ulysses (1852), Ellen (1855), Jesse (1858)
AGE AS FIRST LADY	43 years old
DIED	Dec. 14, 1902, in Washington, D.C.
AGE AT DEATH	76 years old
GRAVE	General Grant National Memorial, New York, N.Y.

Because she had slightly crossed eyes, Julia Grant preferred to pose for photographs in profile rather than head on. Such a defect might have been "corrected" in portraits painted during an earlier era. Julia was the first presidential wife to be referred to as "first lady of the land." She called her years in the White House her life's "happiest period." During that time the use of the White House lawn was restricted for private use only.

Lucy Hayes

THE HAYES ADMINISTRATION ★ *1877 – 1881*

L<small>UCY</small> H<small>AYES WAS THE FIRST</small> F<small>IRST</small> L<small>ADY</small> to graduate from college. Her father, a physician named James Webb, died when she was two years old. Her mother, Maria Cook Webb, insisted that all three of her children, including her only daughter, receive a full education. At a time when many people debated the abilities of female students, Lucy was confident of their intelligence. "Woman's mind is as strong as man's—equal in all things and his superior in some," she observed.

Rutherford B. Hayes began calling on this bright, opinionated woman when her family moved to Cincinnati. The two were married after an 18-month-long engagement. Lucy bore eight children in the next 20 years, five of whom lived to adulthood. When the Civil War and, later politics, took Hayes away from home, Lucy often went with him, even if it meant leaving her children behind with relatives.

By the time Hayes became President, two of their children were still young enough to move into the executive mansion with their parents. Perhaps the presence of these youngsters helped inspire their mother to start the tradition of a public Easter egg roll on the White House lawn. Her style as First Lady was considerably more subdued than her predecessors. Most notable was the Hayes decision not to serve alcohol at White House events. This choice not only reflected their personal religious preferences but a growing national movement of temperance, or restraint in the use of alcohol. Later on she would earn the nickname "Lemonade Lucy" for this White House custom. Lucy's interests in education reform and women's rights, and her involvement in the advancement of her husband's political career, brought a new dimension to the role of First Lady.

The Woman's Christian Temperance Union, a national organization that discouraged the drinking of alcohol, applauded the example Lucy Hayes set by removing alcohol from the menu at White House social functions. In gratitude they commissioned a full-length portrait of her (shown partly above) that hangs today in the White House.

★	★	★	★	★

PRESIDENT	Rutherford B. Hayes, 19th President (1822–1893)
MAIDEN NAME	Lucy Ware Webb
BORN	Aug. 28, 1831, in Chillicothe, Ohio
EDUCATION	Wesleyan Female College
WEDDING	Dec. 30, 1852
AGE AT MARRIAGE	21 years old
THEIR CHILDREN	Sardis (1853), James (1856), Rutherford (1858), Frances (1867), Scott (1871)
AGE AS FIRST LADY	45 years old
SPECIAL INTERESTS	Temperance
DIED	June 25, 1889, in Fremont, Ohio
AGE AT DEATH	57 years old
GRAVE	Spiegel Grove National Historic Landmark, Fremont, Ohio

Lucretia Garfield

THE GARFIELD ADMINISTRATION ★ *1881*

★ ★ ★

"The wife of the President is the bravest woman in the universe."

— Newspaper commentary following the shooting of James A. Garfield in 1881

★

T HE PRESIDENCY OF JAMES A. GARFIELD lasted only 199 days. More than a third of that time was expended with the President's slow and agonizing death, the result of an assassination attempt. His illness became the focus of his wife Lucretia's time in the White House. Between that calamity and her own serious bout of malaria in earlier months, there was little time for her to establish herself as First Lady.

Lucretia grew up on a farm in northeastern Ohio. Her parents were named Zebulon and Arabella Green Mason Rudolph. Lucretia met her future husband through local schools and attended what later became known as Hiram College. Their relationship took years to gel, even after a lengthy courtship. Garfield's military service and early political career kept the newlyweds apart for all but five months of almost the first five years of marriage. Lucretia's natural independence did not help either. Over time "Crete" conformed to the customs of the era, slowly discarding her views on women's rights and equality.

Garfield's assassin is known to have stalked the President for weeks before firing what became a fatal shot. He claimed to have opted against shooting him when Garfield was escorting his ill wife out of Washington, D.C. "She clung so tenderly to the President's arm, that I did not have the heart to fire on him." After the President's death, Lucretia attended her husband's funeral—the first widow of a sitting President to do so.

PRESIDENT	James A. Garfield, 20th President (1831–1881)
MAIDEN NAME	Lucretia Rudolph
BORN	Apr. 19, 1832, in Hiram, Ohio
EDUCATION	Hiram College
WEDDING	Nov. 11, 1858
AGE AT MARRIAGE	26 years old
THEIR CHILDREN	Harry (1863), James (1865), Mary (1867), Irvin (1870), Abram (1872)
AGE AS FIRST LADY	48 years old
EARLIER CAREER	Schoolteacher
DIED	Mar. 14, 1918, in Pasadena, Calif.
AGE AT DEATH	85 years old
GRAVE	Lake View Cemetery, Cleveland, Ohio

Noted photographer Mathew Brady made this photograph of Lucretia Garfield some years before she became First Lady. In the early years of her marriage to James Garfield, she continued the career of schoolteacher that she had begun during their courtship.

Ellen Arthur

THE ARTHUR ADMINISTRATION ★ 1881 – 1885

CHESTER ARTHUR WAS STILL MOURNING THE SUDDEN LOSS of his wife, Ellen, when the death of James A. Garfield thrust him into the Presidency. Arthur's deceased wife Ellen was raised with the Southern traditions of a prominent, pre-Civil War family from Virginia. Slaves were part of their property. Her father, William Lewis Herndon, was a noted U.S. naval officer who had once led an expedition up the Amazon River. Her mother, Frances Elizabeth Hansbrough Herndon, was a well-connected society figure. During a visit to New York City, Ellen was introduced to her future husband by a cousin (and roommate to Arthur). They were married several years later.

The onset of the Civil War placed an early strain on their marriage, with Ellen favoring the cause of the South, unlike her northern-born husband. Such tensions eased later on.

Pneumonia felled Ellen unexpectedly when she was just 42 years of age. After attending a concert in New York City, Ellen got chilled while waiting for her carriage to take her home, and she developed a cold. Her illness progressed quickly, and Arthur, who was out of town at the time, raced home only to find her unconscious. She never revived and was dead within two days of becoming ill. Ellen left behind two children, the youngest of whom moved into the White House with her father when he became President.

Arthur recruited his youngest sister to assist in the upbringing of young "Nell" and to act as occasional hostess. The mother of four children herself, Mary Arthur McElroy left her own family a few months each year in order to perform these favors. During his Presidency, Arthur reintroduced alcohol to social occasions in the White House.

Ellen Arthur (above, left) died 20 months before her husband became President. Her grieving spouse is said to have had fresh flowers placed before this photo each day of his administration. He funded the installation of a stained glass window in Ellen's memory, too. The window was positioned in St. John's Episcopal Church, in whose choir his wife had previously sung, so that Arthur could see it from the White House at night. The President's sister, Mary Arthur McElroy (above, right), stepped in periodically to serve as White House hostess.

★ ★ ★ ★ ★

PRESIDENT	Chester A. Arthur, 21st President (1829–1886)
MAIDEN NAME	Ellen Lewis Herndon
BORN	Aug. 30, 1837, in Culpeper Court House, Va.
WEDDING	Oct. 25, 1859
AGE AT MARRIAGE	22 years old
THEIR CHILDREN	Chester (1864), Ellen (1871)
AGE AS FIRST LADY	Deceased
DIED	Jan. 12, 1880, in Albany, N.Y.
AGE AT DEATH	42 years old
GRAVE	Albany Rural Cemetery, Menands, N.Y.
ACTING FIRST LADY	Mary Arthur McElroy (President's sister)

Frances Cleveland

THE CLEVELAND ADMINISTRATIONS ★ 1885 – 1889 ★ 1893 – 1897

FRANCES CLEVELAND PACKED MANY FIRST LADY records into her life. At 21, she became the youngest one ever by marrying Grover Cleveland during his second year of office. She was the first (and only) First Lady to marry at the White House. During her husband's second term, she gave birth to the first (and only) presidential child born at the White House. Finally, she became the first widowed First Lady to remarry.

Her first marriage might have seemed unlikely to most who knew of Grover Cleveland and the fatherly role he had played almost since the birth of Frances to his law partner Oscar Folsom and Emma Cornelia Harmon Folsom. Cleveland had actually bought the child's first baby carriage. His commitment to the youth deepened after the death of Frances's father when she was eleven. Others who knew of Cleveland's closeness to the family speculated that the nation's second bachelor President might marry Frances's mother, not the daughter who was 27 years his junior.

But marry they did, in full White House style, 15 months into Cleveland's first term of office. Despite her youth, Frances stepped into her role of First Lady with an assured confidence.

The former President died in 1908 when Frances was only 43. About five years later she remarried, choosing an archaeology professor from Princeton University. Her grave lies beside Cleveland's.

PRESIDENT	Grover Cleveland, 22nd and 24th President (1837–1908)
MAIDEN NAME	Frances Folsom
BORN	July 21, 1864, in Folsomville, N.Y.
EDUCATION	Wells College
WEDDING	June 2, 1886
AGE AT MARRIAGE	21 years old
THEIR CHILDREN	Ruth (1891), Esther (1893), Marion (1895), Richard (1897), Francis (1903)
AGE AS FIRST LADY	21 years old
LATER MARRIAGE	Thomas Jex Preston, Jr. (1880–1955), Feb. 10, 1913
DIED	Oct. 29, 1947, in Baltimore, Md.
AGE AT DEATH	83 years old
GRAVE	Princeton Cemetery, Princeton, N.J.
ACTING FIRST LADY	Rose Elizabeth Cleveland (President's sister)

Before Frances Cleveland (top, painted in 1899) took over as First Lady for Grover Cleveland, the President's sister Rose Elizabeth Cleveland (inset photo) served as her brother's hostess. Rose, an accomplished college educator, left an academic post to assist Cleveland. She returned willingly to her former career when Frances appeared on the scene.

Caroline Harrison

THE BENJAMIN HARRISON ADMINISTRATION ★ *1889 – 1893*

CAROLINE HARRISON WAS THE DAUGHTER of John Witherspoon Scott and Mary Potts Neal Scott. Her father was a Presbyterian minister and college educator. He introduced his daughter to her future husband, having met him through school. Benjamin Harrison, grandson to President William Henry Harrison, married Caroline some five years later. They were the last presidential couple to have their marriage interrupted by Civil War service.

As First Lady, Caroline took on the task of overhauling the White House. She arranged for upgrades to the plumbing, ordered old floors replaced, had the first electric lights installed (which she was afraid to switch on and off), and waged war against the mansion's rodent and insect inhabitants. Her interest in art led her to design a custom set of dishes for use during the Harrison Presidency. She established the White House china collection with examples of patterns used in previous administrations, too.

Near the end of her husband's administration, Caroline became ill with tuberculosis, then a common and incurable disease. She died two weeks before the presidential election that left her husband defeated. The Harrison's daughter Mary Scott Harrison McKee stepped in as acting First Lady for the remaining months of the administration.

A few years later Harrison became the second former President to remarry. His new wife was a young widow named Mary Scott Lord Dimmick, a niece of his first wife. Their marriage lasted for the remaining four years of Harrison's life and produced one child. Mary outlived her husband by another 46 years.

During her White House years Caroline Harrison helped found the National Society of the Daughters of the American Revolution. She was its first president, too. After her death during Harrison's administration, the organization arranged for this portrait of Caroline to be painted and donated to the White House.

★ ★ ★ ★ ★

PRESIDENT	Benjamin Harrison, 23rd President (1833–1901)
MAIDEN NAME	Caroline Lavinia Scott
BORN	Oct. 1, 1832, in Oxford, Ohio
EDUCATION	Oxford Female Seminary
WEDDING	Oct. 20, 1853
AGE AT MARRIAGE	21 years old
THEIR CHILDREN	Russell (1854), Mary (1858)
AGE AS FIRST LADY	56 years old
DIED	Oct. 25, 1892, in Washington, D.C.
AGE AT DEATH	60 years old
GRAVE	Indianapolis, Ind.
ACTING FIRST LADY	Mary Scott Harrison McKee (daughter)
PRESIDENT'S OTHER WIVES	Mary Scott Lord Dimmick (1856–1948), second wife (married Apr. 6, 1896)
OTHER CHILDREN	Elizabeth (1897)

Ida McKinley

THE McKINLEY ADMINISTRATION ★ *1897 – 1901*

IDA MCKINLEY'S LIFE BEGAN WITH GREAT PROMISE. She was the eldest daughter of banker James Asbury Saxton and Catherine Dewalt Saxton. Her childhood included a privileged education and a tour of Europe. She was so full of energy that her father made her a teller in his bank, an unusual responsibility for a woman at that time. She met her future husband at a church picnic, and William McKinley made frequent visits to her teller's window (often with flowers in hand as well as bank business) as their friendship developed. Upon their marriage, Ida's father presented the couple with a house.

The rosy picture did not last much longer. Two years into her marriage Ida lost in rapid succession a favorite grandfather, her mother, and an infant daughter. Her other child "Katie" caught typhoid fever and died in 1876. Depression ruled the days of the formerly rosy Ida. Her physical health declined, and she began to have epileptic seizures. Ida's earlier mental and physical health never returned. She became an invalid, often sitting for hours occupied only by the task of crocheting endless pairs of slippers (literally thousands of them) that were given away to friends and charities.

William McKinley nursed and pampered his wife while managing to advance his political career, too. Ida struggled to meet the demands of First Lady after her husband became President. McKinley adjusted White House custom so that, instead of sitting at the opposite end of the table, he could sit next to his wife and cover her face with his handkerchief if she began to have a small seizure. At times Ida was snappish and rude in public, but McKinley always doted on his First Lady.

After being shot by an assassin early in his second term, McKinley's earliest thoughts were about his wife. "My wife—be careful...how you tell her—oh, be careful!" Ida handled the news and her husband's subsequent death with surprising strength. "He is gone," she later said, "and life to me is dark now." Her own death came some six years after the President's.

★ ★ ★ ★ ★	
PRESIDENT	William McKinley, 25th President (1843–1901)
MAIDEN NAME	Ida Saxton
BORN	June 8, 1847, in Canton, Ohio
EDUCATION	Brook Hall Seminary
WEDDING	Jan. 25, 1871
AGE AT MARRIAGE	23 years old
THEIR CHILDREN	Katherine (1872), Ida (1873), both died young
AGE AS FIRST LADY	49 years old
DIED	May 26, 1907, in Canton, Ohio
AGE AT DEATH	59 years old
GRAVE	McKinley National Memorial, Canton, Ohio

Emily Drayton Taylor painted this miniature likeness of Ida McKinley during her years in the White House. President McKinley and others were tight-lipped about the First Lady's health, describing her as prone to fainting spells and headaches. No mention was made of her actual condition, epilepsy, whose seizures were not well understood or controllable then.

Edith Roosevelt

★ ★ ★

"[Edith is] not only cultured but scholarly."

— President Theodore Roosevelt

★

THEODORE AND EDITH ROOSEVELT had been married 14 years before he became President following the assassination of William McKinley. But Edith was not the 26th President's first wife. Alice, his first wife, died within four years of their marriage. She left behind an infant girl of the same name whom her stepmother later helped raise.

Although not his first wife, Edith was one of Roosevelt's oldest acquaintances. The daughter of merchant Charles Carow and Gertrude Elizabeth Tyler Carow, Edith had grown up in New York City as Roosevelt's next-door neighbor. She had been best friends with one of his sisters, and Roosevelt had at one time even proposed to her. Edith declined then but accepted when he approached her again years later.

Over the next ten years, the Roosevelt family swelled to include another daughter and four sons. All of these children, as well as a zoo-like assortment of pets, settled into the White House when the youthful President took office with his young First Lady. Their stay in the executive mansion is filled with tales of family roughhousing, practical jokes, and general silliness. Edith often referred to her playful husband as her sixth child.

Although longevity graced Edith's life (she lived to be 87), it did not favor her husband (who died at 60) or their sons. Three of their sons died during the two World Wars. Only Archibald, although wounded in both, survived them. The Roosevelts are the only presidential couple to have children killed in combat.

Edith Roosevelt began the White House tradition of hanging portraits of the First Ladies along the ground-floor entryway to the Executive Mansion. Her portrait was painted in 1902.

★ ★ ★ ★ ★	
PRESIDENT	Theodore Roosevelt, 26th President (1858–1919)
MAIDEN NAME	Edith Kermit Carow
BORN	Aug. 6, 1861, in Norwich, Conn.
WEDDING	Dec. 2, 1886
AGE AT MARRIAGE	25 years old
THEIR CHILDREN	Theodore (1887), Kermit (1889), Ethel (1891), Archibald (1894), Quentin (1897)
AGE AS FIRST LADY	40 years old
SPECIAL INTERESTS	Clothing for the poor
DIED	Sept. 30, 1948, in Oyster Bay, N.Y.
AGE AT DEATH	87 years old
GRAVE	Young's Memorial Cemetery, Oyster Bay, N.Y.
PRESIDENT'S OTHER WIVES	Alice Hathaway Lee (1861–1884), first wife (married Oct. 27, 1880)
OTHER CHILDREN	Alice (1884)

Helen Taft

THE TAFT ADMINISTRATION ★ *1909 – 1913*

HELEN TAFT'S FATHER JOHN WILLIAMSON HERRON had been a law partner of Rutherford B. Hayes. When President Hayes and his wife celebrated their 25th wedding anniversary at the White House in 1877, the guests included 16-year-old Helen, her father, and Helen's mother Harriet Collins Herron. This visit prompted Helen's interest in someday becoming First Lady. She met William Howard Taft at a bobsledding party in Cincinnati two years later. It took seven years and at least three proposals before Helen agreed to marry. Helen encouraged her husband to pursue politics with his law degree instead of a courtroom career. This strategy eventually led the pair to the White House.

Helen's first act as First Lady established a shocking new precedent for executive spouses. Tradition had held that the outgoing President should escort the incoming one to the White House following Inauguration ceremonies. Knowing that Theodore Roosevelt planned to skip this formality, Helen maneuvered to seat herself in the place of honor beside her husband for his parade to the executive mansion.

A stroke put Helen at a disadvantage early in her husband's Presidency, robbing her of the power of speech for a time. She regained her health sufficiently to fulfill the traditional duties of First Lady and also to play an active role as an informal advisor and political partner to her husband. The Tafts celebrated their own 25th wedding anniversary with an elaborate White House party.

The former presidential couple returned to Washington, D.C., eight years after Taft's administration when he was appointed Chief Justice of the Supreme Court, a job the old lawyer had wished to hold for years. Taft and his wife were the first presidential couple to be buried in Arlington National Cemetery.

★ ★ ★ ★ ★	
PRESIDENT	William Howard Taft, 27th President (1857–1930)
MAIDEN NAME	Helen Herron
BORN	Jan. 2, 1861, in Cincinnati, Ohio
EDUCATION	Miami University (Ohio)
WEDDING	June 19, 1886
AGE AT MARRIAGE	25 years old
THEIR CHILDREN	Robert (1889), Helen (1891), Charles (1897)
AGE AS FIRST LADY	48 years old
DIED	May 22, 1943, in Washington, D.C.
AGE AT DEATH	82 years old
GRAVE	Arlington National Cemetery, Arlington, Va.

In 1910 Helen Taft posed wearing her inaugural gown for this portrait. Helen left behind a lasting reminder of her years as First Lady by arranging to have 3,000 Japanese cherry trees planted around the Tidal Basin near the Jefferson Memorial.

Ellen Wilson

THE WILSON ADMINISTRATION ★ 1913 – 1921

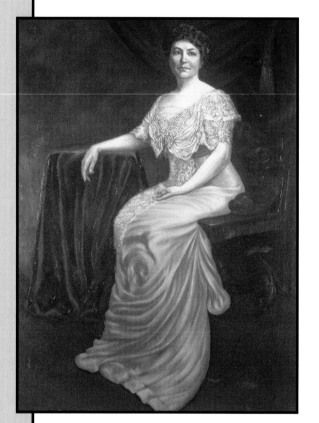

LIKE JOHN TYLER, WOODROW WILSON not only lost one wife during his Presidency but gained a new one, as well. He and his first wife Ellen had been married 27 years when they moved into the White House. Although the couple met as children, they did not begin courting until Ellen was 22 years old. By then Ellen's mother, Margaret Hoyt Axson, was dead, and Ellen was helping her father, Samuel Edward Axson, raise her younger siblings. Both her father and Wilson's were Presbyterian ministers.

Another two years passed before Ellen and Wilson were married. At that point he had become a professor at Bryn Mawr College, and she had studied art in New York City with an eye toward painting professionally. Although Ellen continued to paint throughout her life, the births of three daughters and her support of Wilson's academic and, then, political careers took precedence over her own. Ellen did establish an artist's studio for herself in the White House, however, and she even sold some of her work during her husband's Presidency. (Profits went to charities.)

As First Lady, Ellen set a precedent followed by many subsequent wives of Presidents. She not only identified a particular cause of special interest (as had Lucy Hayes, for example), she lobbied Congress to support her work, too. Ellen became the guiding hand in raising awareness about slum housing in the nation's capital.

Ellen became ill with Bright's Disease, a kidney ailment, in 1914. Congress rushed to pass the housing bill Ellen had sought. By the fall she was dead. The President was devastated, privately admitting he would welcome assassination. No such fate befell him. Instead, some seven months after his wife's death, he met the next Mrs. Wilson.

Ellen Wilson and her husband had three grown daughters when Woodrow Wilson became President. Ellen and the women set a precedent when Wilson addressed Congress early in his Presidency. The four took prominent seats in the chamber's balcony, an example that would become standard practice for future First Ladies and close family members. Ellen planned White House weddings for two of her three daughters during her 17 months as First Lady. The eldest one, Margaret, stepped in to assist as hostess when her mother's health began to fail.

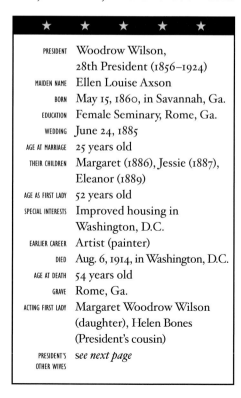

★ ★ ★ ★ ★	
PRESIDENT	Woodrow Wilson, 28th President (1856–1924)
MAIDEN NAME	Ellen Louise Axson
BORN	May 15, 1860, in Savannah, Ga.
EDUCATION	Female Seminary, Rome, Ga.
WEDDING	June 24, 1885
AGE AT MARRIAGE	25 years old
THEIR CHILDREN	Margaret (1886), Jessie (1887), Eleanor (1889)
AGE AS FIRST LADY	52 years old
SPECIAL INTERESTS	Improved housing in Washington, D.C.
EARLIER CAREER	Artist (painter)
DIED	Aug. 6, 1914, in Washington, D.C.
AGE AT DEATH	54 years old
GRAVE	Rome, Ga.
ACTING FIRST LADY	Margaret Woodrow Wilson (daughter), Helen Bones (President's cousin)
PRESIDENT'S OTHER WIVES	see next page

Edith Wilson

THE WILSON ADMINISTRATION ★ *1913 – 1921*

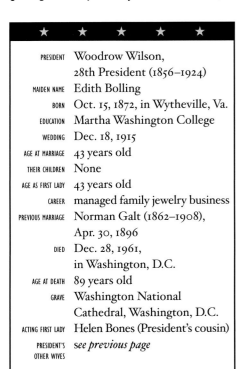

THE VERY WOMAN whom Woodrow Wilson asked to assist him after the death of his first wife in 1914 became the same person to introduce him to his future second wife the following year. Wilson's cousin, Helen Bones, was already familiar with the workings of the White House, having served as social secretary to the first Mrs. Wilson. One of her friends, a widow named Edith Bolling Galt, happened to be visiting Helen at the White House when bad weather brought the President home early from a golf game. The three sat down for tea in a chance encounter that quickly blossomed into romance. Edith and Wilson were married before the year was out.

The second Mrs. Wilson had grown up in a privileged home, the daughter of a judge named William Holcombe Bolling and his wife, Sallie White Bolling. Edith counted Pocahontas among her distant relatives, making her the only First Lady to claim Native American ancestry. She had been married 12 years to her first husband, a prosperous jewelry store owner, when he died suddenly. Their one child had died, too. Seven years later she met President Wilson. When he proposed Wilson told Edith, "...in this place time is not measured by weeks, or months, or years, but by deep human experiences."

As First Lady, Edith is most remembered for the role she played near the end of Wilson's administration. A stroke left the President gravely ill with 18 months left in his second term. Doctors instructed Edith to shelter him from as much strain as possible in order to aid his recovery. Edith did just that, setting herself up as an impenetrable wall that all people and paperwork had to face before possibly reaching the President. By limiting him to only the most essential tasks, she helped Wilson complete his Presidency. In so doing, however, she opened herself up to criticism of overreaching her place as a President's wife, a charge still leveled at times today.

★ ★ ★ ★ ★	
PRESIDENT	Woodrow Wilson, 28th President (1856–1924)
MAIDEN NAME	Edith Bolling
BORN	Oct. 15, 1872, in Wytheville, Va.
EDUCATION	Martha Washington College
WEDDING	Dec. 18, 1915
AGE AT MARRIAGE	43 years old
THEIR CHILDREN	None
AGE AS FIRST LADY	43 years old
CAREER	managed family jewelry business
PREVIOUS MARRIAGE	Norman Galt (1862–1908), Apr. 30, 1896
DIED	Dec. 28, 1961, in Washington, D.C.
AGE AT DEATH	89 years old
GRAVE	Washington National Cathedral, Washington, D.C.
ACTING FIRST LADY	Helen Bones (President's cousin)
PRESIDENT'S OTHER WIVES	see *previous page*

This portrait of Edith Wilson was painted soon after she became the President's second wife, and thus First Lady. Although her marriage to Wilson was cut short by his own death after eight years, and even though she outlived him by nearly four decades, Edith chose to be buried by this husband, not her earlier one.

Florence Harding

W HEN FLORENCE HARDING ENTERED the White House in 1921, she was the oldest woman yet (at age 60) to take on the duties of First Lady. She was also older than her husband was (by more than five years), a presidential seniority gap that has never been topped. Florence was the first divorcée to serve as First Lady, too.

Florence married both of her husbands despite the objections of her father, a prominent local banker. Her parents were named Amos and Louisa Bouton Kling. Her first marriage ended when her husband deserted her and their young son. They later divorced, he died young, and Florence's parents took over custody of her child (who died himself when he was a young man) while she restarted her life.

When Florence first spied Warren G. Harding, he was a relative newcomer in her small town, having just bought an ownership stake in the local newspaper. Before the next year was out, they had married. (Her father did not speak to her for seven years.) Soon after the wedding, Florence took on management responsibilities at her new husband's paper. When Harding turned to government service a few years later, she helped manage his political career, too. She encouraged him to make the White House his ultimate career goal and then helped him reach it.

As First Lady she brought a new level of openness to the White House. Visitors were welcome to stroll again on its grounds and to drop by the executive mansion for tours. On New Year's Days Florence willingly stood in receiving lines for hours until every visitor for the traditional open house had been greeted. At the same time, the President and his wife were tight-lipped about personal matters, including their own fragile healths. Citizens were stunned not only by Harding's sudden death during the third year of his administration, but by the death of Florence just over a year later. Only First Lady Eliza Johnson died more quickly after a presidential husband's death.

Florence Harding used makeup, one of the first First Ladies to do so. Cosmetics helped her conceal her age difference with the President (he was five years younger) and present a more youthful image as First Lady.

PRESIDENT	Warren G. Harding, 29th President (1865–1923)
MAIDEN NAME	Florence Mabel Kling
BORN	Aug. 15, 1860, in Marion, Ohio
WEDDING	July 8, 1891
AGE AT MARRIAGE	30 years old
THEIR CHILDREN	None
AGE AS FIRST LADY	60 years old
EARLIER CAREER	Journalism
PREVIOUS MARRIAGE	Henry DeWolfe (1859–1894), March, 1880 (ended in divorce), Marshall (1880)
DIED	Nov. 21, 1924, in Marion, Ohio
AGE AT DEATH	64 years old
GRAVE	Harding Memorial, Marion, Ohio

Grace Coolidge

THE COOLIDGE ADMINISTRATION ★ *1923 – 1929*

IT IS ONLY FITTING THAT THE FIRST MEETING of Grace and Calvin Coolidge was a funny one. The couple who became known for their playful wit caught their first glimpse of one another when Grace looked up from watering a garden to see Coolidge through an open window of a nearby building. He was shaving, wearing only his long underwear and a dress hat. She burst out laughing at the sight, he looked over and saw her, and the introduction that followed cemented their relationship.

Although the pair met in Massachusetts, they were both natives of Vermont. Grace's parents were Andrew Issachar Goodhue, an engineer and steamboat inspector, and Lemira Barrett Goodhue. Grace was the first First Lady to graduate from a coeducational college or university. Then she took further courses to prepare for a career in the education of the deaf, an interest that she pursued for the rest of her life. Her first job was teaching the deaf how to read lips.

Following the sudden death of Warren G. Harding, the Coolidges brought a New England style of natural simplicity to their years in the White House. The celebration of Charles Lindbergh's first transatlantic flight proved to be a high point. The bizarre death of their youngest son was a low. (The 16-year-old played tennis without wearing socks, gained a blister, developed blood poisoning, and died, all in a matter of a few days.)

After leaving the White House, Grace summed up her experience with words that might ring true to many First Ladies. "This was I and yet not I," she said of her role. "This was the wife of the President of the United States and she took precedence over me."

★	★	★	★	★

PRESIDENT	Calvin Coolidge, 30th President (1872–1933)
MAIDEN NAME	Grace Anna Goodhue
BORN	Jan. 3, 1879, in Burlington, Vt.
EDUCATION	University of Vermont
WEDDING	Oct. 4, 1905
AGE AT MARRIAGE	26 years old
THEIR CHILDREN	John (1906), Calvin (1908)
AGE AS FIRST LADY	44 years old
EARLIER CAREER	Schoolteacher for the deaf
DIED	July 8, 1957, in Northampton, Mass.
AGE AT DEATH	78 years old
GRAVE	Plymouth Notch Cemetery, Plymouth, Vt.

Calvin Coolidge loved to buy his wife clothes and sulked if she wore an evening gown more than once. She posed for her official portrait in a simple yet elegant full-length view. Her pet collie Rob Roy joined her. Grace had a pet raccoon at the White House, too.

Lou Hoover

THE HOOVER ADMINISTRATION ★ 1929 – 1933

THE ADVENTURESOME LIFESTYLE of Lou Hoover's youth became good preparation for her adult life. Midway through her childhood, she moved with her parents, banker Charles Delano Henry and Florence Ida Weed Henry, from Iowa to southern California. Her childhood featured camping expeditions, horseback riding, hunting trips, practice with taxidermy, and rock hunting. It's little wonder that one of her favorite organizations later on was the Girl Scouts, a group she headed for a time.

In 1894 she entered Stanford University as a geology student, the first woman ever to do so, and it was there that she met Herbert Hoover, a senior in the program. They married after her graduation and embarked on more than a decade of global travel through her husband's career as a mining geologist. Lou gave birth to two sons during this period, learning Chinese and several other foreign languages on the side. (She and her husband used Chinese as their private language during their White House years.) Although Lou never pursued paid work as a geologist, she did serve as equal partner with her husband in their five-year effort to translate an important historic text about metallurgy, the study of metals. Their translation of the 16th-century Latin work went on to win a prestigious award.

Lou brought many innovations to her years as First Lady. She developed a catalog of historic White House furnishings. She gave nationally broadcast radio addresses. She even reformed the custom that kept pregnant women out of White House receiving lines. One tradition fell by the wayside during the Hoover administration—the annual open house on New Year's Day. Perhaps Hoover's election loss in 1932, the nation's deepening economic crisis, and the event's long receiving lines led to the vacation the Hoovers took at the beginning of their last year at the White House.

Herbert Hoover was already working in China when his future wife graduated from Stanford University. Knowing that she would now be willing to marry him, he sent her a wedding proposal by telegram. (Global long-distance phoning was not an option then.) Lou cabled back with her acceptance. This portrait copies one made of First Lady Lou Hoover.

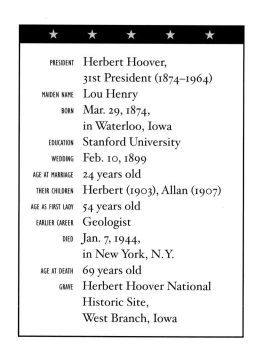

PRESIDENT	Herbert Hoover, 31st President (1874–1964)
MAIDEN NAME	Lou Henry
BORN	Mar. 29, 1874, in Waterloo, Iowa
EDUCATION	Stanford University
WEDDING	Feb. 10, 1899
AGE AT MARRIAGE	24 years old
THEIR CHILDREN	Herbert (1903), Allan (1907)
AGE AS FIRST LADY	54 years old
EARLIER CAREER	Geologist
DIED	Jan. 7, 1944, in New York, N.Y.
AGE AT DEATH	69 years old
GRAVE	Herbert Hoover National Historic Site, West Branch, Iowa

Eleanor Roosevelt

THE FRANKLIN D. ROOSEVELT ADMINISTRATION ★ *1933 – 1945*

★ ★ ★

> *"...no matter how plain*
> *a woman may be*
> *if truth and loyalty are*
> *stamped upon her face*
> *all will be*
> *attracted to her."*

— Eleanor Roosevelt, *age 14*

★

ELEANOR ROOSEVELT EXPANDED THE ROLE of First Lady into a rainbow of new dimensions. In the process she established yardsticks by which those who followed her to the White House would almost inevitably be measured. She is the nation's longest-serving First Lady because her husband was the longest-serving President. (He won four elections and held office just over 12 years in all.) Eleanor modeled a new level of activism for former First Ladies, too.

The role that Eleanor assumed during adulthood was light years away from her tentative, reserved childhood. Her parents were named Elliott Roosevelt and Anna Livingston Hall Roosevelt. Eleanor, always shy, forever feeling awkward, lost her mother when she was eight. Her father, whom she adored, was often absent because of alcoholism problems. By the time she was 10, he had died, too. Not until Eleanor was sent to an English boarding school in her mid-teens did she find an environment and role models that helped her begin to overcome her lack of self-confidence.

Eleanor had only recently returned to the United States when she bumped into a distant and rarely seen cousin during a train ride: Franklin D. Roosevelt. The chance encounter led to love and, within three years, marriage. Eleanor was given away at her wedding by her father's older brother, a

This multifaceted portrait was painted of Eleanor Roosevelt about five years after she left the White House. She was 65 years old and almost as active in her retirement years as she had been during her tenure as First Lady. The artist, Douglas Chandor, sought to capture Eleanor's energy and range of talents in the portrait.

man who just happened at that time to be President of the United States—Theodore Roosevelt. (Eleanor was his favorite niece.)

The early years of Eleanor's marriage to Franklin followed the usual conventions of the day. There were many pregnancies (six in 11 years), with five children surviving infancy. She quit her pre-marriage volunteer work. When it came to matters of household management, Eleanor deferred to her overbearing mother-in-law, who lived next door.

Then several experiences contributed to Eleanor's growing independence. One was World War I, an event that brought increased opportunities and responsibilities to many women. Another was the shock of learning that her husband was involved romantically with another woman. The affair ended, and their marriage survived, but Eleanor

Eleanor Roosevelt was the most on-the-go First Lady up to that time, actively representing her husband, Franklin D. Roosevelt. Her energy didn't flag in later years. She is shown above in Paris during her time as representative to the United Nations. As First Lady, she and her husband hosted the first visit to the United States of British monarchs. Eleanor and Queen Elizabeth, wife of King George VI (at left in oval photo), made an open-car appearance during the 1939 event.

began to think more about meeting her own needs, not just those of the people around her. An additional factor was the sudden onset in her husband during 1921 of polio, a disease that left him crippled for the rest of his life. Eleanor encouraged his recovery—and at the same time built her own confidence—by doing the political legwork that helped him gain elected office.

"The future is literally in our hands to mold as we like. But we cannot wait until tomorrow. Tomorrow is now."

— Eleanor Roosevelt, *Tomorrow is Now*, published after her death

This political partnership would last for the rest of their marriage, and it eventually landed them in the White House. Their lengthy stay there coincided with some of the most challenging years of the 20th century, including the Great Depression and World War II. Such events placed greater demands than ever on the Presidency. The combination of Eleanor's growing independence, her increased leadership as partner to a disabled husband, and the demands of the times set the stage for her to become the most active First Lady yet seen.

Precedents fell by the wayside, and new ones took their places. Gone was the limiting view of First Lady as little more than hostess. Eleanor, who had already served as "eyes and ears" for her wheelchair-bound husband, extended her habit of traveling in his place. She spoke on his behalf at the Democratic Party Convention (new), stood in for him at meetings with interest groups (new), and traveled abroad as his representative (also new). She supported her own causes more publicly and persistently than had any other First Lady—from labor rights for women to greater rights for children to civil rights for African Americans. She lobbied privately with her husband on other points—including the importance of bringing more women into the government. (Roosevelt agreed, appointing the first woman to a presidential Cabinet, among many other gains.)

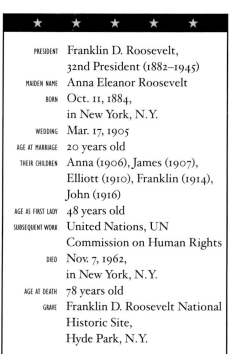

PRESIDENT	Franklin D. Roosevelt, 32nd President (1882–1945)
MAIDEN NAME	Anna Eleanor Roosevelt
BORN	Oct. 11, 1884, in New York, N.Y.
WEDDING	Mar. 17, 1905
AGE AT MARRIAGE	20 years old
THEIR CHILDREN	Anna (1906), James (1907), Elliott (1910), Franklin (1914), John (1916)
AGE AS FIRST LADY	48 years old
SUBSEQUENT WORK	United Nations, UN Commission on Human Rights
DIED	Nov. 7, 1962, in New York, N.Y.
AGE AT DEATH	78 years old
GRAVE	Franklin D. Roosevelt National Historic Site, Hyde Park, N.Y.

Eleanor established the First Lady tradition of meeting with reporters by holding weekly press conferences, some 348 sessions in all by the time her tenure had ended. Her insistence that these events be women-only created a demand for female reporters and brought scores of new women into journalism. Eleanor kept in touch with the reading public directly, too, through a weekly column, "My Day," that was carried across the country.

"The story is over," Eleanor stated following the sudden death of her husband just three months into his fourth term of office. In fact, though, the story of her own involvement in public service was not over. Two Presidents—Harry S. Truman and John F. Kennedy—appointed her to represent the United States as part of its delegation to the United Nations. In that capacity she helped draft the body's Universal Declaration of Human Rights. The same values of mutual respect that guided her own life helped frame this vision for the wider world.

Bess Truman

★ ★ ★

"I never make a report or deliver a speech without her editing it."

— Harry S. Truman, *commenting on the role Bess Truman played on his U.S. Senate staff*

BESS AND HARRY S. TRUMAN RACKED UP the longest courtship in presidential history, and that's without counting the fact that the couple first met during a Sunday School class when she was only five and he just six. Even after reaching adulthood, some 15 years passed before the pair were married. By then both of them were in their thirties.

When Bess was 18, her father, David Willock Wallace, a local government official, killed himself. Bess was left with her mother, Madge Gates Wallace, and her three younger siblings. Bess grew up as a talented athlete. She excelled at tennis, baseball, basketball, fencing, ice skating, even the shot put. Truman was so devoted in wooing Bess that he built her a tennis court.

The Trumans moved into the White House following the death of Franklin D. Roosevelt. As with every other First Lady, Bess established her own interpretation of the job, all the while trying not to be too intimidated by her predecessor's example. She canceled Eleanor Roosevelt's traditional press conferences (eventually Bess agreed to answer written questions for inquisitive reporters), took trains instead of planes (judging trains to be more dignified), and declined all public speaking opportunities (she preferred to be in the background).

By living to 97 years of age, Bess set one final presidential record. No other First Lady ever lived so long.

The official portrait of Bess Truman is actually a copy of one that remained in Bess's possession after leaving the White House. Extensive renovations of the executive mansion forced the First Family to live in nearby Blair House during the second term of Truman's administration.

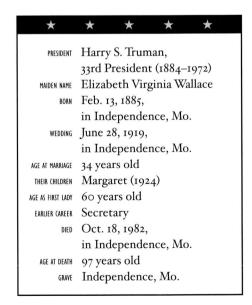

★ ★ ★ ★ ★	
PRESIDENT	Harry S. Truman, 33rd President (1884–1972)
MAIDEN NAME	Elizabeth Virginia Wallace
BORN	Feb. 13, 1885, in Independence, Mo.
WEDDING	June 28, 1919, in Independence, Mo.
AGE AT MARRIAGE	34 years old
THEIR CHILDREN	Margaret (1924)
AGE AS FIRST LADY	60 years old
EARLIER CAREER	Secretary
DIED	Oct. 18, 1982, in Independence, Mo.
AGE AT DEATH	97 years old
GRAVE	Independence, Mo.

Mamie Eisenhower

WHEN MAMIE AND DWIGHT D. EISENHOWER reached the White House after 36 years of marriage, they created their own personal record. The White House was the first home the couple ever moved into with any kind of permanency. Up until then, thanks to Eisenhower's previous military career, they had moved at least 27 times.

Mamie met her future husband when he was a 25-year-old Second Lieutenant in the U.S. Army. She was only 18 and was staying with her parents, John Sheldon Doud, a meat packer, and Elivera Carlson Doud, at the family's winter home in Texas. (The rest of the year they lived in Denver, Colorado.)

By the time Eisenhower became President, Mamie was a practiced hostess. At home in the White House, Mamie helped host a seemingly endless parade of foreign dignitaries for state visits. She shook hands with thousands of more ordinary visitors, often greeting hundreds of strangers a day. She added the first official staff member to the First Lady's office, the "acting secretary to the President's wife." The Eisenhowers relaxed at the executive mansion, too. "At last I've got a job where I can stay home nights, and, by golly, I'm going to stay home," observed the President.

During the Eisenhower administration the U.S. Congress finally replaced the rag-tag series of prior pension plans for presidential widows with a comprehensive program. Until then pensions had been granted of varying amounts to hit-or-miss lists of widows. The new law stated that any widow (present and future) of a former President was entitled to a pension, and it set a value for the stipend of $10,000 per year. That amount was later increased to $20,000 in 1971, but it has not been changed since.

★ ★ ★ ★ ★	
PRESIDENT	Dwight D. Eisenhower, 34th President (1890–1969)
MAIDEN NAME	Mamie Geneva Doud
BORN	Nov. 14, 1896, in Boone, Iowa
WEDDING	July 1, 1916
AGE AT MARRIAGE	19 years old
THEIR CHILDREN	John (1922)
AGE AS FIRST LADY	56 years old
DIED	Nov. 1, 1979, in Washington, D.C.
AGE AT DEATH	82 years old
GRAVE	Eisenhower Center, Abilene, Kans.

Mamie Eisenhower chose an Inaugural gown in her favorite color, a shade that became widely known as "Mamie pink." Her bangs became a fashion trademark, too. A trend follower as well as a trendsetter, the First Lady was content to wear costume jewelry (imitation versions of real pearls and jewels) and eat family suppers on TV trays, just like average Americans of the day.

Jacqueline Kennedy

THE KENNEDY ADMINISTRATION ★ *1961 – 1963*

J UST AS JOHN F. KENNEDY INTRODUCED A YOUTHFUL SPIRIT to the Presidency, Jacqueline Kennedy likewise did the same for the role of the First Lady. She was just 31 years old when she became First Lady. Only Frances Cleveland and Julia Tyler came to the post at a younger age than did the woman who became affectionately known to the nation as "Jackie." Her husband (whom many called "Jack") was, at age 43, the youngest man ever elected President. (Theodore Roosevelt became President at a younger age, but through succession, not election.)

Jackie was the first First Lady to be born in the 20th century. Her parents were the stockbroker John Vernou Bouvier III and Janet Norton Lee Bouvier. They divorced the year that Jackie turned 11. Her mother remarried two years later. Jackie's stepfather, Hugh Auchincloss, was quite wealthy, and Jackie enjoyed a privileged childhood with private schools, horseback riding, and multiple family homes. She attended Vassar College, studied abroad in Paris, and earned a bachelor's degree in art from George Washington University. Jackie had become a professional photographer in Washington, D.C., by the time she met her future husband, then a U.S. senator, at a dinner party in 1951. Their wedding was a society affair with 800 guests, extensive media coverage, and a blessing sent by the Pope. Two pregnancies failed before the birth of the first Kennedy child, a daughter named Caroline. John, Jr., followed in late 1960, arriving after his father had won the presidential election, but before his Inauguration. Caroline and John became the first small children of a President to move into the White House since Theodore Roosevelt's administration.

The new First Lady juggled the demands of motherhood with social duties and her commitment to several key interests. Her efforts were aided by a growing staff in the office of the First Lady. At times she recruited Lady Bird Johnson, the Vice President's wife, to fill in for her at social functions. She insisted that her children's lives remain a private matter, not an easy task to accomplish given the public's eagerness for any and all news about this youthful First Family. Even if news about the children was scarce, "Jack and Jackie" were themselves idolized and imitated. The "Jackie look" set fashion trends in everything from hairstyles, to dress lengths, to the wearing of hats.

Even before her husband's Inauguration, Jackie declared her intention to restore the historic style of the White House. Her announcement became a precedent for other First Ladies-to-be. Once in the

---

Jacqueline Kennedy posed for this portrait in 1970, a decade after her husband was elected President. The youthful First Lady had set new precedents for independence by traveling for fun without the President. Her adventures led her to such places as the Mediterranean, India, and Italy.

White House, Jackie used her interest in art history to direct the research, fundraising, and effort necessary for a full-scale redecoration of the executive mansion. The classic White House look that today's visitors take as a given was established under her leadership. Antiques, period wallpaper, and extensive use of art all brought a unified elegance to the home. The mansion's first guidebooks were developed at this time, both to explain the significance of the collection, and to help fund its preservation. When the project was completed in early 1962, Jackie led the nation on a televised one-hour tour of the White House. No First Lady had ever made such extensive use of this newest medium of communication. Jackie promoted the performing arts with equal enthusiasm during her tenure.

Although Jackie often stayed behind during her husband's frequent travels, circumstance placed them together on Kennedy's ill-fated trip to Texas in November of 1963. The two were seated side-by-side in a convertible—one of several vehicles in a presidential motorcade through the streets of Dallas—when shots rang out. The President was mortally wounded and never regained consciousness. In less than an hour he was dead. Soon after Lyndon B. Johnson was sworn in as President in a makeshift ceremony aboard the presidential plane. Jackie Kennedy stood beside Johnson, wearing the same outfit she had worn earlier in the day. Now it was stained with her dead husband's blood. She is the only presidential widow to attend the swearing in of her husband's successor.

In the days and years that followed, Jackie did much to assure her husband would be well remembered. She dictated details for his funeral that made it solemn and memorable—from the use of the horse-drawn caisson that carried the body to the presence of a riderless horse in the procession. Her own bearing and that of her young children during the public events won sympathy and admiration from around the world. As time passed, she devoted much energy to the development of Kennedy's presidential library.

But Jackie did not remain a widow. Only 34 years old when her husband died, she was remarried before she turned 40. Her second husband was a wealthy shipowner from Greece named Aristotle Onassis. He was 23 years older than Jackie. Their marriage lasted until his death in 1975. Then Jackie moved to New York City and developed a career in book publishing. No other former First Lady had worked full-time until then. She collaborated on historic preservation projects, too.

When she died of cancer some two decades later, her son recalled her commitment to a "love of words, the bonds of home and family, and her spirit of adventure."

★ ★ ★ ★ ★	
PRESIDENT	John F. Kennedy, 35th President (1917–1963)
MAIDEN NAME	Jacqueline Lee Bouvier
BORN	July 28, 1929, in Southampton, N.Y.
EDUCATION	Vassar College, George Washington University
WEDDING	Sept. 12, 1953
AGE AT MARRIAGE	24 years old
THEIR CHILDREN	Caroline (1957), John (1960)
AGE AS FIRST LADY	31 years old
SPECIAL INTERESTS	Historic preservation, the arts
EARLIER CAREER	Professional photographer
LATER CAREERS	Book editor, advocate for historic preservation
LATER MARRIAGE	Aristotle Socrates Onassis (1906–1975), Oct. 20, 1968
DIED	May 19, 1994, in New York, N.Y.
AGE AT DEATH	64 years old
GRAVE	Arlington National Cemetery, Arlington, Va.

★ ★ ★

"...if you bungle raising your children, I don't think whatever else you do well matters very much."

— Jacqueline Lee Bouvier Kennedy

★

Lady Bird Johnson

THE LYNDON B. JOHNSON ADMINISTRATION ★ 1963 – 1969

CLAUDIA ALTA TAYLOR EARNED HER NICKNAME AS A BABY when she was pronounced as "pretty as a ladybird" by a caregiver. She became known as "Lady Bird" forever after. Her mother, Minnie Lee Pattillo Taylor, died when Lady Bird was just five years old, and the girl was raised by an aunt and her father, a rancher and merchant named Thomas Jefferson Taylor. Lady Bird excelled at school. By the time she met her future husband at age 21, she had already earned not only an undergraduate degree from the University of Texas but had completed advanced training through its school of journalism, too.

Lyndon B. Johnson fell in love with Lady Bird at once. He was introduced to her by a mutual friend one night and proposed to her the next day. Johnson applied what would later become his legendary powers of persuasion, and the couple were wed before two months had passed. Over the years Lady Bird would help advance her husband's political career as his partner, his financial backer, and an unpaid office manager (taking charge of it entirely when war and illness twice took Johnson away from the U.S. Congress). She established her own professional life, too, as the owner of a growing radio broadcasting company.

Lady Bird expanded the definition of the First Lady's role through her tireless promotion of two causes: her husband and the beautification of America. In support of the first, she campaigned more extensively than had any other First Lady. As for beautification, she tirelessly promoted passage of the Highway Beautification Act that helped reduce the clutter of billboards and roadside junkyards along the nation's highways. Years later she encouraged the planting of wildflowers along highways, a successful effort that she supports to this day from her home in Texas.

The professionalism of the office of First Lady was completed during Lady Bird Johnson's tenure. More than a dozen staff members helped support what had become a full-time job. The former First Lady's leadership on beautification was recognized when the Redwood National Park established the Lady Bird Johnson Grove in her honor.

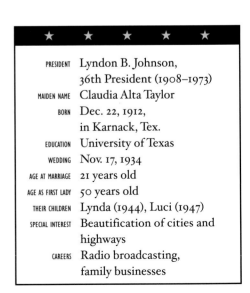

PRESIDENT	Lyndon B. Johnson, 36th President (1908–1973)
MAIDEN NAME	Claudia Alta Taylor
BORN	Dec. 22, 1912, in Karnack, Tex.
EDUCATION	University of Texas
WEDDING	Nov. 17, 1934
AGE AT MARRIAGE	21 years old
AGE AS FIRST LADY	50 years old
THEIR CHILDREN	Lynda (1944), Luci (1947)
SPECIAL INTEREST	Beautification of cities and highways
CAREERS	Radio broadcasting, family businesses

Pat Nixon

> "It takes heart
> to be in political life."
>
> — Patricia Ryan Nixon

PARALLELS ECHO BETWEEN THE LIVES of Pat Nixon and her First Lady predecessor. Thelma Catherine Ryan earned an early nickname, too. She became "Pat" for having been born on the eve of St. Patrick's Day. Like Lady Bird Johnson, Pat's mother died during her youth. (Katharine Halberstadt Bender Ryan died when Pat was 13.) By 17 Pat had become an orphan following the death of her father, William Ryan, a coal miner and farmer. A hardscrabble existence followed, and only after great effort and economizing was she able to put herself through college.

The future First Lady met her husband-to-be when the two of them were cast in the same community theater production. Like Lyndon B. Johnson, Richard M. Nixon proposed to his wife upon meeting her. Their courtship lasted longer (two years), but it eventually led to marriage, and a similar career track put this couple into the White House, too.

Pat strengthened the tradition of recent First Ladies to support a national cause. Her efforts went toward several, most notably the promotion of community volunteer work. When scandals began to cloud Nixon's administration, she stood by her husband. "I believe in him, and I am proud of his accomplishments," she said. When the President eventually went on television to announce that he would resign from office, Pat was at his side, albeit almost in tears, with other supportive family members.

PRESIDENT	Richard M. Nixon, 37th President (1913–1994)
MAIDEN NAME	Thelma Catherine Ryan
BORN	Mar. 16, 1912, in Ely, Nev.
EDUCATION	University of Southern California
WEDDING	June 21, 1940
AGE AT MARRIAGE	28 years old
THEIR CHILDREN	Patricia (1946), Julie (1948)
AGE AS FIRST LADY	56 years old
SPECIAL INTEREST	Volunteering
EARLIER CAREERS	Schoolteacher, price analyst
DIED	June 23, 1993, in Park Ridge, N.J.
AGE AT DEATH	81 years old
GRAVE	Yorba Linda, Calif.

Pat Nixon traveled more extensively than any other First Lady up to that time, visiting some 83 nations in all. She joined her husband for his historic trips to China and the Soviet Union, and she made solo appearances elsewhere, including in South America and Africa.

Betty Ford

THE FORD ADMINISTRATION ★ *1974 – 1977*

BETTY FORD HAD BARELY ADJUSTED to becoming the wife of a Vice President when her husband was elevated to the office of President. Although Ford had never sought the Presidency, the job was his anyway. His wife, by association, became First Lady, like it or not.

The daughter of William Stephenson Bloomer, a salesman, and Hortense Neahr Bloomer, Betty developed an early interest in modern dance. At one point she trained in New York with the noted choreographer Martha Graham and danced in one of her troupes. When Betty met her husband, she was newly divorced and living back in Michigan. Ford was a 35-year-old bachelor on the brink of his political career. He was actually late for their wedding, showing up with muddy shoes after attending a political rally for himself.

Helping handicapped children became one of the themes of Betty's activism during her years as First Lady. She had explored this need earlier in life by teaching dance to children with disabilities. She drew on other personal experiences and convictions, too. When breast cancer led to radical surgery soon after her husband became President, Betty used her own example to educate others about an illness that was rarely discussed publicly before then. She hoped her openness would help save lives by promoting the basics of early detection.

That same desire to help others prompted her years later to come forward and publicly discuss her addiction to alcohol and painkillers. Once again she sought to help others face concerns that were not regularly discussed at the time. She established the Betty Ford Clinic to help patients deal with similar addictions.

Betty Ford advocated for increased women's rights during her husband's Presidency. She encouraged Gerald R. Ford to name the first woman to the U.S. Supreme Court (he named a man instead). She lobbied states to ratify the Equal Rights Amendment (some did, but not enough to make it law). She spoke out in favor of reproductive choice, too, a freedom only recently granted by the Supreme Court.

PRESIDENT	Gerald R. Ford, 38th President (1913–present)
MAIDEN NAME	Elizabeth Anne Bloomer
BORN	Apr. 18, 1918, in Chicago, Ill.
WEDDING	Oct. 15, 1948
AGE AT MARRIAGE	30 years old
THEIR CHILDREN	Michael (1950), John (1952), Steven (1956), Susan (1957)
AGE AS FIRST LADY	53 years old
SPECIAL INTEREST	Handicapped children
EARLIER CAREERS	Model, professional dancer, dance teacher
PREVIOUS MARRIAGE	William C. Warren, 1942 (ended in divorce)

Rosalynn Carter

THE CARTER ADMINISTRATION ★ *1977 – 1981*

Rosalynn Carter helped her husband Jimmy Carter overcome his relative obscurity and win election to the White House. Their divide-and-conquer strategy, with each person campaigning separately, helped them double their exposure. It also expanded the trend of increased involvement in campaigns by political spouses, especially those married to presidential hopefuls.

Rosalynn was the third of the past four First Ladies to grow up in a single-parent home. Her father, a mechanic and school bus driver named Wilburn Edgar Smith, died when she was 13. Her mother, Allethea Murray Smith, supported her family as a seamstress and depended heavily on Rosalynn, as the eldest of four children, for help. Although Rosalynn and her future husband had grown up as neighbors in the same small town (Rosalynn had even been best friends with Carter's sister), the two did not become sweethearts until years later. Carter, at home on leave from the U.S. Naval Academy, told his mother after their first date: "She's the girl I want to marry." By the next year he had.

Like her predecessor, Rosalynn worked for passage of the Equal Rights Amendment. She chose mental health as her advocacy issue, serving as honorary chair of a Commission on Mental Health established by the President.

A youthful 53 when she left the White House, Rosalynn joined her husband in one of the most active and influential retirements of a former chief executive and First Lady. Her account of their White House years was a bestseller. Through the Carter Center she and her husband advocate for democratic elections, human rights, international health care, mental health programs, and other social causes. She works with Habitat for Humanity, too.

★ ★ ★ ★ ★	
PRESIDENT	Jimmy Carter, 39th President (1924–present)
MAIDEN NAME	Rosalynn Smith
BORN	Aug. 18, 1927, in Botsford, Ga.
EDUCATION	Georgia Southwestern College
WEDDING	July 7, 1946
AGE AT MARRIAGE	18 years old
THEIR CHILDREN	John (1947), James (1950), Jeffrey (1952), Amy (1968)
AGE AS FIRST LADY	49 years old
SPECIAL INTEREST	Mental illness
EARLIER CAREER	Bookkeeper for family peanut business

Rosalynn Carter played a more active role than any previous First Lady in the policy of her husband's administration. She represented the government as an official spokesperson to foreign governments (a First Lady first) and sat in on cabinet meetings at times (another first). "There is very seldom a decision that I make that I don't discuss with her, tell her my opinion and seek her advice," said President Jimmy Carter.

Nancy Reagan

THE REAGAN ADMINISTRATION ★ *1981 – 1989*

★ ★ ★

"My life really began
when I married my husband."

— Nancy Reagan

★

THE WOMAN WHO BECAME KNOWN AS NANCY REAGAN started life with a completely different name—Anne Frances Robbins—a name she rarely used. Her family quickly nicknamed her "Nancy," effectively changing her first name. Her last name changed some years after her parents were divorced. Her biological father was an auto salesman named Kenneth Robbins. Her mother, an actress named Edith Luckett Robbins, eventually remarried. Edith's second husband, a neurosurgeon named Loyal Davis, went on to adopt Nancy during her teen years.

Nancy pursued acting as a career, too, majoring in it at Smith College. She acted on Broadway and made 11 films in Hollywood. She met Ronald Reagan during their years in the movie business after consulting with him on a union matter. They were married a few years later. Reagan's acting career led him to politics and, at an older age than any of his predecessors, to the White House. His tenure was marred in its early months by an assassination attempt. Nancy turned to an astrologer for advice on the safety of the President's travel plans. This dependence as well as her attempts to influence policy were criticized when they became publicly known later on. As First Lady she encouraged young people to "just say no" to using illegal drugs.

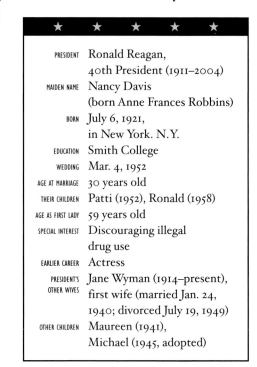

PRESIDENT	Ronald Reagan, 40th President (1911–2004)
MAIDEN NAME	Nancy Davis (born Anne Frances Robbins)
BORN	July 6, 1921, in New York. N.Y.
EDUCATION	Smith College
WEDDING	Mar. 4, 1952
AGE AT MARRIAGE	30 years old
THEIR CHILDREN	Patti (1952), Ronald (1958)
AGE AS FIRST LADY	59 years old
SPECIAL INTEREST	Discouraging illegal drug use
EARLIER CAREER	Actress
PRESIDENT'S OTHER WIVES	Jane Wyman (1914–present), first wife (married Jan. 24, 1940; divorced July 19, 1949)
OTHER CHILDREN	Maureen (1941), Michael (1945, adopted)

During their retirement years Nancy Reagan became caregiver to her husband when he developed Alzheimer's disease (which causes memory loss). When Ronald Reagan died in 2004 she headed a week-long program of memorials for her husband in spite her own age of 82.

Barbara Bush

THE GEORGE BUSH ADMINISTRATION ★ *1989 – 1993*

HISTORY REPEATED ITSELF when Barbara Bush became First Lady. Just like Abigail Adams, she was the wife of a two-term Vice President, turned one-term President. And like Abigail, her eldest son would eventually become President, too. This wife of one President and mother of another grew up outside New York City in the suburban community of Rye, New York. Her parents were a magazine publisher named Marvin Pierce and his wife Pauline Robinson Pierce.

Barbara met her future husband at a holiday dance when she was 16 and he was 17. It was love at first sight for both of them. Barbara later observed that she ended up marrying the first man she kissed. The pair have had a longer marriage than any other presidential couple. The newlyweds lived together in Connecticut while George Bush attended Yale University. Then they began a string of more than two dozen moves as Bush's careers took them first to Texas and, after he entered politics, to Washington, D.C., New York City, and points abroad.

By the time they reached the White House, Barbara was 64 years old, making her the oldest woman to take on the duties of First Lady. (Anna Harrison was a year older when her husband became President, but she did not accompany him to the White House.) Barbara threw her support behind a number of causes, most notably literacy, or the ability of people to be able to read. She donated the sizeable profits from the bestseller *Millie's Book* (which she wrote while First Lady from the point of view of the family dog) to the cause. She promoted AIDS awareness, Head Start, and the needs of senior citizens and the homeless, too. "If it worries you, then you've got to do something about it," she said.

PRESIDENT	George Bush, 41st President (1924–present)
MAIDEN NAME	Barbara Pierce
BORN	June 8, 1925, in Bronx, N.Y.
EDUCATION	Smith College
WEDDING	Jan. 6, 1945
AGE AT MARRIAGE	19 years old
THEIR CHILDREN	George W. (1946), Robin (1949), John (1953), Neil (1955), Marvin (1956), Dorothy (1959)
AGE AS FIRST LADY	64 years old
SPECIAL INTEREST	Promoting literacy

Barbara Bush earned the nickname "the silver fox" from her children after her hair turned prematurely white. As First Lady she rarely commented on policy matters, particularly when her opinions differed from the President's. Therefore she made news when she twice disagreed with him in public, once by supporting women's reproductive freedom and, on another occasion, by objecting to laws that permitted the sale of military assault weapons.

Hillary Rodham Clinton

THE CLINTON ADMINISTRATION ★ 1993 – 2001

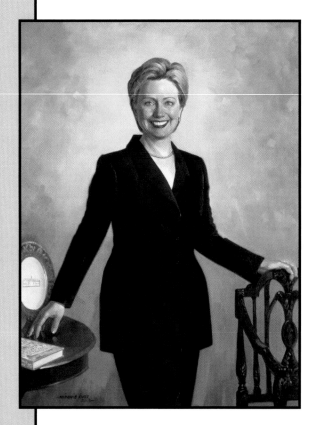

HILLARY CLINTON WAS THE FIRST BABY BOOMER First Lady, that is the first to have been born following World War II. During her eight years as First Lady, she combined the commitment of Eleanor Roosevelt with the style of Jacqueline Kennedy—two predecessors whom she greatly admired. She set new precedents for combining career, marriage, and family.

Hugh Rodham and Dorothy Howell Rodham encouraged their oldest child and only daughter to study hard and imagine any career for herself. This daughter of a drapery business owner and a homemaker followed her parents' advice. She was president of her senior high school class and a member of the National Honor Society. She chose to attend prestigious Wellesley College, majored in political science, and graduated with high honors. Classmates chose her to represent them as the first senior speaker at their commencement ceremonies. Hillary progressed from Wellesley to Yale Law School, making her the first First Lady to earn an advanced degree.

It was at Yale that Hillary met her future husband. She introduced herself to William Jefferson "Bill" Clinton after they kept eying one another at the law library. "If you're going to keep looking at me, and I'm going to keep looking back, we at least ought to know each other," she suggested. So began their romantic and political partnership. In her studies, Hillary took a particular interest in family law and the rights of children. As a law student she interned with the Children's Defense Fund. After her graduation she served as one of only three women (on a 41-member team) who advised the House Judiciary Committee about the possible impeachment of President Richard M. Nixon.

A continuing interest in Bill Clinton led Hillary to take a teaching post at the law school of the University of Arkansas where her future husband taught, too. By the next year she and Clinton had married. Soon after her husband became first the Attorney General and then the Governor of Arkansas. Even then Hillary continued to work, moving from the law school to become partner in a major law firm. She was so well regarded in her work there that she was twice named to a prestigious list of the "100 Most

---

For the first seven years of her marriage, Hillary continued to use her maiden name rather than adopt her husband's. Not everyone sympathized with this show of independence (although the practice was gaining popularity at the time). Later, in a concession to political pressure, she adopted the name Hillary Rodham Clinton. Hillary set precedents on entering the White House (when she set up her own office in the President's West Wing headquarters) and after she left it (by wearing pants while posing for her official portrait, shown above).

Influential Lawyers in America." She regularly made more money each year than her husband. When the Clinton's only daughter was born, Hillary managed to juggle her career, her duties as wife of a public official, and the role of mother. Her efforts coincided with a growing trend among young women to combine multiple roles into one lifestyle.

"Our lives are a mixture of different roles. Most of us are doing the best we can to find whatever the right balance is.... For me, that balance is family, work, and service."

— Hillary Clinton, *1992 presidential campaign*

When the Clintons moved to the White House, Hillary left behind her post at the law firm. She did not abandon her professional interests, however, and she became a more active participant in the government than any First Lady to date. She offered her expertise and counsel to the President and other staff members. At the President's request she chaired a task force that studied ways to reform the nation's health care system. The effort tested the limits of a First Lady's role in setting policy, and in the end the group's recommendations failed to gain approval in Congress. Although Hillary tempered her style along the way (eventually she moved out of the West Wing office she had established as a new First Lady, for example), she continued to be a central figure in her husband's administration. She traveled widely on his behalf, at times bringing along their teenage daughter, Chelsea. She became an international champion for the rights of women and children. Taking a cue from Eleanor Roosevelt, she established her own weekly newspaper column, "Talking it Over." Hillary weathered charges of political misconduct (they proved to be false), defended her husband during his own charges of misconduct (also declared false), and stood by him when deceit over a romantic affair contributed to Bill Clinton's Congressional impeachment and trial (he was acquitted). She persevered on her own course, setting precedents small (like declaring the White House a smoke-free zone) and large (such as testifying on Capitol Hill in support of legislation).

Then Hillary broke the greatest precedent of all. In February of 2000 she made official an idea that she had considered for months: She would run for elected office. No other First Lady had ever attempted such a step, either before or after serving. Hillary's objective was to become a U.S. senator, and she spent much of the rest of her husband's Presidency working toward that goal. Chelsea even stepped in occasionally for her mother as hostess when the demands of campaigning competed with Hillary's social duties as First Lady.

On Election Day 2000, Hillary was able to proclaim that after "62 counties, 16 months, three debates, two opponents, and six black pantsuits" she had succeeded at her quest. First Lady Hillary Rodham Clinton completed her months in the White House as a senator-elect for the state of New York. Bill Clinton's retirement marked the beginning of a new career for his wife. Senator Clinton splits time between Washington, D.C., and her home in New York State.

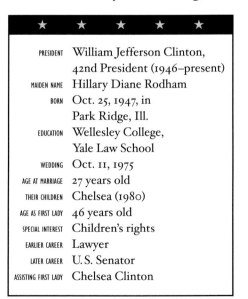

PRESIDENT	William Jefferson Clinton, 42nd President (1946–present)
MAIDEN NAME	Hillary Diane Rodham
BORN	Oct. 25, 1947, in Park Ridge, Ill.
EDUCATION	Wellesley College, Yale Law School
WEDDING	Oct. 11, 1975
AGE AT MARRIAGE	27 years old
THEIR CHILDREN	Chelsea (1980)
AGE AS FIRST LADY	46 years old
SPECIAL INTEREST	Children's rights
EARLIER CAREER	Lawyer
LATER CAREER	U.S. Senator
ASSISTING FIRST LADY	Chelsea Clinton

Laura Bush

★ ★ ★

"I think I temper
[George's boisterous] personality,
but I also think that he makes
life much more exciting for me."

— Laura Bush

★

HAD LAURA WELCH NOT ATTENDED the outdoor barbecue where she met her future husband, she might still be a school librarian. Instead she became the First Lady of Texas when George W. Bush won the governor's seat there. Then, some two decades later, she became First Lady of the Land in the nation's capital.

During her childhood, all Laura had wanted to do was become a schoolteacher. She grew up as the only child of Harold Bruce Welch, a home builder, and Jenna Louise Hawkins Welch, his bookkeeper. Laura made good on her childhood ambition after she graduated from Southern Methodist University in 1968. Her first job was teaching reading in an integrated public school in Dallas. Laura's love of books prompted her to return to school and gain a master's degree in library science in Austin from the University of Texas in 1973. She worked briefly at a public library in Houston, then returned to Austin as school librarian for a local elementary school.

Then Laura visited her hometown and attended the barbecue party where she met George W. Bush. The two had almost crossed paths before, having attended the same junior high school at one point. They lived in the same apartment complex during her Houston stay, too, but never met there. This time they connected. By the next evening they were on their first date together (playing miniature golf), and within three months they were married. Four years later they added twins to their family. Their daughters are fraternal, not identical twins, and are named for their grandmothers, one of whom was First Lady Barbara Bush.

Laura Bush (above, and, next page, seated at right) has turned her life-long love of reading into a career of activism. As First Lady she makes the promotion of literacy programs one of her most prominent activities.

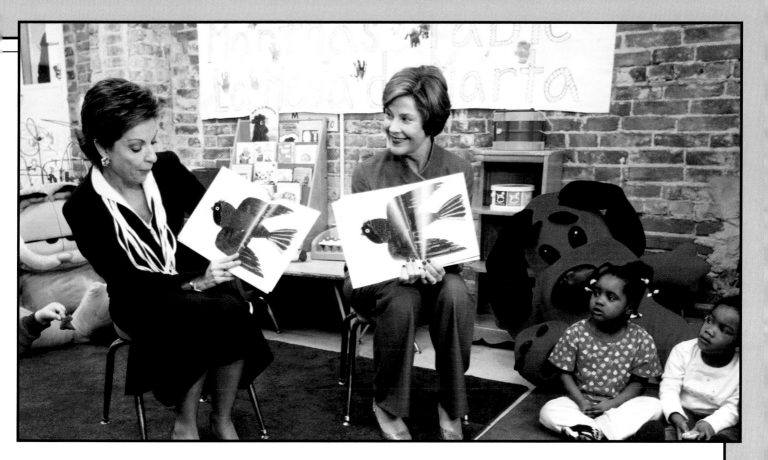

Laura and George W. Bush like to laugh about how she agreed to marry him only if she would never have to give political speeches for her future husband. Yet within a short while Laura had stepped from the quiet career of librarian onto a path that eventually led to the White House. "So much for political promises," Laura joked years later in one of the countless speeches she has given during her husband's political career.

Even though she may not sit behind a librarian's desk any longer, Laura remains committed to her love of books. As a governor's wife, and now as First Lady, she has championed the importance of books and literacy. In Texas she established a Texas Book Festival that raised some $1 million in funding for state libraries. Now her National Book Festival promotes the importance of reading, too.

Other causes have gained Laura's attention over the years, as well. They include women's health issues (such as breast cancer detection), the arts, early childhood education, Alzheimer's disease, historic preservation, and volunteerism. Although Laura has not played a visible role in policy-making, her husband counts on her for advice and feedback. Throughout their marriage she has blended attention to her favorite issues with support for her husband's career and devotion to her family. From her premarriage desire to avoid public speaking, she went on to become the first First Lady to speak in the President's place during his weekly scheduled radio address. Laura chose to talk about life for women in Afghanistan.

Barbara Bush has commended her daughter-in-law for having "a great philosophy in life—you can either like it or not, so you might as well like it." In addition she shares a belief held by many other First Ladies: If you work to make a difference, you will have done well with your life.

★	★	★	★	★

PRESIDENT	George W. Bush, 43rd President (1946–present)
MAIDEN NAME	Laura Welch
BORN	Nov. 4, 1946, in Midland, Tex.
EDUCATION	Southern Methodist University; University of Texas, Austin
WEDDING	Nov. 5, 1977
AGE AT MARRIAGE	31 years old
THEIR CHILDREN	Jenna and Barbara, twins (1981)
AGE AS FIRST LADY	54 years old
SPECIAL INTEREST	Promoting literacy
EARLIER CAREERS	Schoolteacher, librarian

First Lady Mary Todd Lincoln (left) and Julia Grant (shaking hands with Abraham Lincoln in this view of "Lincoln's Last Reception") juggled the challenges shared by other presidential wives of entertaining graciously even in the face of wars, economic hardships, and political fights.

Resources & Credits

REFERENCES AND RELATED RESOURCES

Anthony, Carl Sferrazza. *America's First Families*. New York: Simon & Schuster, 2000.

_____. *First Ladies, Vol. 1*. New York: Perennial, HarperCollins Publishers, 1990.

Baker, Jean H. *Mary Todd Lincoln: A Biography*. New York: W.W. Norton & Company, 1987.

Boller, Jr., Paul F. *Presidential Wives*. New York: Oxford University Press, 1998 (second edition).

Caroli, Betty Boyd. *The First Ladies*. Garden City, New York: Guild America Books (by arrangement with Oxford University Press), 2001 (third edition).

DeGregorio, William A. *The Complete Book of U.S. Presidents*. New York: Gramercy Books, 2002 (fifth edition).

Gould, Lewis L. *American First Ladies: Their Lives and Their Legacy*. London: Routledge, 2001 (second edition).

Kane, Joseph Nathan, Janet Podell, and Steven Anzovin. *Facts About the Presidents*. New York: H.W. Wilson Company, 2001 (seventh edition).

Klapthor, Margaret Brown. *The First Ladies*. Washington, D.C.: White House Historical Association and National Geographic Society, 1999 (ninth edition).

Pearce, Lorraine. *The White House: An Historic Guide*. Washington, D.C.: White House Historical Association and National Geographic Society, 1999 (twentieth edition).

Wead, Douglas. *All the Presidents' Children*. New York: Atria Books, 2003.

BOOKS FOR YOUNG READERS

Bausum, Ann. *Our Country's Presidents*. Washington, D.C.: National Geographic Society, 2005 (second edition).

Bausum, Ann. *With Courage and Cloth: Winning the Fight for a Woman's Right to Vote*. Washington, D.C.: National Geographic Society, 2004.

Mayo, Edith P., general editor. *The Smithsonian Book of the First Ladies*. New York: Henry Holt and Company, 1996.

PLACES TO VISIT

"First Ladies: Political Role and Public Image" permanent exhibit at the National Museum of American History, Smithsonian Institution, Washington, D.C.

First Ladies National Historic Site
Canton, Ohio

The White House, Washington, D.C.

WEB SITES

Library of Congress: American Memory— Portraits of the Presidents and First Ladies
http://www.memory.loc.gov/ammem/odmdhtml/preshome.html

Life in the White House
http://www.whitehouse.gov/history/firstladies/

National First Ladies' Library Education and Research Center
http://www.firstladies.org

Smithsonian National Museum of American History: First Ladies
http://americanhistory.si.edu/youmus/ex12ladi.htm

The White House: First Ladies' Gallery
http://whitehouse.gov/history/firstladies/

ILLUSTRATIONS CREDITS

Abbreviations:
LC — Library of Congress
WHC — White House Collection

214, Eliphalet F. Andrews; WHC; 216, WHC; Charles Willson Peale, The Mount Vernon Ladies' Association of the Union; 220, New York State Historical Association, Copperstown, New York; 221, Joseph Boze, Diplomatic Reception Rooms, Department of State; 222, Gilbert Stuart, WHC; 223, Attributed to John Vanderlyn, courtesy of Thomas J. Edwards and William K. Edwards; 224, Gilbert Stuart, WHC; 225 (left), Attributed to Ralph E. W. Earl, WHC; 225 (right), Louisa Catherine Strobel, Ladies Hermitage Association, Hermitage, Tennessee; 226 (left), National Park Service; 226 (right), Henry Inman, WHC; 227 (left), Artist unknown, William Henry Harrison Home, Courtesy of Francis Vigo Chapter, Daughters of the American Revolution, Vincennes, Indiana; 227 (right), Cornelia Stuart Cassady, courtesy of President Benjamin Harrison Memorial Home, Indianapolis, Indiana; 228, Artist unknown, reproduced by permission of John Tyler Griffin, great-great-grandson of Letitia and President Tyler; 229, Francesco Anelli, WHC, acquired in 1869, presented to the Executive Mansion by Mrs. Tyler; 230; George P. A. Healy, James K. Polk Ancestral Home, Columbia, Tennessee; 231, Daguerreotype by J. E. McClees, Smithsonian Institution; 232, Daguerreotype by an unknown artist, WHC; 233, Photographer unknown, daguerreotype owned by the Pierce Brigade, Concord, New Hampshire; 234, John Henry Brown, National Museum of American Art, Smithsonian Institution; 235, Mathew Brady, Lloyd Ostendorf Collection, Dayton, Ohio; 236, LC; 238 (upper), Byrd Venable Farioletti, after a photograph, Smithsonian Institution, 238 (lower), Charcoal drawing (possibly by Henry N. Barlow), Andrew Johnson National Historic Site, Greeneville, Tennessee; 239, Photograph by Mathew Brady, LC; 240, David Huntington, WHC; 241, Photograph by Mathew Brady, LC; 242 (left), Photographer unknown, LC; 242 (right), Steel engraving by John Sartain, WHC; 243 (upper), Anders L. Zorn, National Portrait Gallery, Smithsonian Institution; 243 (lower), Photographer unknown, Smithsonian Institution; 244, David Huntington, WHC; 245, Emily Drayton Taylor, WHC; 246, Theobald Chartran, WHC; 247, Bror Kronstrand, WHC; 248, Artist unknown, courtesy of Carnegie Library, Rome, Georgia. Photograph by Leviton-Atlanta; 249, Adolpho Muller-Ury, WHC; 250, Philip de László, WHC; 251, Howard Chandler Christy, WHC; 252, Richard M. Brown, after Philip de László, WHC; 253, Douglas Chandor, WHC, 254 (upper), courtesy Franklin D. Roosevelt Library; 254 (lower), Getty Images; 256, M. Greta Kempton, WHC; Thomas E. Stephens, WHC; 258, Aaron Shikler, WHC; 260, Elizabeth Shoumatoff, WHC; 261, Henriette Wyeth, WHC; 262, Feliz de Cossio, WHC, 263, George Augusta, WHC, 264, Aaron Shikler, WHC; 265, Herbert E. Abrams, WHC; 266, WHC; 268, Susan Sterner, White House; 269, Susan Sterner, White House; 270, (detail) Anton Hohenstein, lithograph by John Smith, LC

National Geographic Society

John M. Fahey, Jr.
PRESIDENT AND CHIEF EXECUTIVE OFFICER

Gilbert M. Grosvenor
CHAIRMAN OF THE BOARD

Nina D. Hoffman
EXECUTIVE VICE PRESIDENT, PRESIDENT OF
BOOKS AND EDUCATION PUBLISHING GROUP

Ericka Markman
SENIOR VICE PRESIDENT, PRESIDENT OF
CHILDREN'S BOOKS AND EDUCATION
PUBLISHING GROUP

Staff for this publication:

Nancy Laties Feresten
VICE PRESIDENT,
EDITOR-IN-CHIEF OF CHILDREN'S BOOKS

Jennifer Emmett
PROJECT EDITOR

Bea Jackson
ART DIRECTOR OF CHILDREN'S BOOKS

David M. Seager
ART DIRECTOR

Ruth Thompson
DESIGNER

Janet A. Dustin, Verónica E. Betancourt
ILLUSTRATIONS COORDINATORS

Virginia Koeth, Suzanne Patrick Fonda
EDITORS

Susan Kehnemui Donnelly
ASSOCIATE EDITOR

Margo Browning
COPY EDITOR

Rebecca E. Hinds
MANAGING EDITOR

Heidi Vincent
DIRECTOR OF
DIRECT RESPONSE SALES AND MARKETING

Daneen Goodwin
MARKETING DIRECTOR,
DIRECT RESPONSE SALES AND MARKETING

R. Gary Colbert
PRODUCTION DIRECTOR

Lewis R. Bassford
PRODUCTION MANAGER

Vincent P. Ryan
MANUFACTURING MANAGER

For my own first family:
Dolores, Henry, and David
— AB

★ ★ ★

Acknowledgments:
The publisher gratefully acknowledges the kind assistance
of the White House Historical Association, especially
Harmony Haskins, and the Office of the First Lady,
especially Gordon Johndroe, Rachael Sunbarger,
and Elizabeth Liptock,
for their generous support of the project.
Special thanks go to Robert D. Johnston, Ph.D. of the
University of Illinois at Chicago for reviewing and
commenting on *Our Country's First Ladies.*

★ ★ ★

The type for this supplement is set in Hoefler Text.
Design by Ruth Thompson

Printed in the United States of America

Direct Mail Regular Edition (2nd ed.) ISBN 0-7922-4169-X
Direct Mail Deluxe Edition ISBN 0-7922-4170-3

The world's largest nonprofit scientific and educational organization, the National Geographic Society was founded in 1888 "for the increase and diffusion of geographic knowledge." Since then it has supported scientific exploration and spread information to its more than nine million members worldwide.

The National Geographic Society educates and inspires millions every day through magazines, books, television programs, videos, maps and atlases, research grants, the National Geographic Bee, teacher workshops, and innovative classroom materials.

The Society is supported through membership dues and income from the sale of its educational products. Members receive NATIONAL GEOGRAPHIC magazine—the Society's official journal—discounts on Society products, and other benefits.

For more information about the National Geographic Society and its educational programs and publications, please call 1-800-NGS-LINE (647-5463), or write to the following address:

National Geographic Society
1145 17th Street N.W.
Washington, D.C. 20036-4688 U.S.A.

Visit the Society's Web site: www.nationalgeographic.com